Key Concepts in
Hospitality
Management

The SAGE Key Concepts series provides students with accessible and authoritative knowledge of the essential topics in a variety of disciplines. Cross-referenced throughout, the format encourages critical evaluation through understanding. Written by experienced and respected academics, the books are indispensable study aids and guides to comprehension.

Key Concepts in
Hospitality
Management

Edited by
ROY C. WOOD

Los Angeles | London | New Delhi
Singapore | Washington DC

Los Angeles | London | New Delhi
Singapore | Washington DC

SAGE Publications Ltd
1 Oliver's Yard
55 City Road
London EC1Y 1SP

SAGE Publications Inc.
2455 Teller Road
Thousand Oaks, California 91320

SAGE Publications India Pvt Ltd
B 1/I 1 Mohan Cooperative Industrial Area
Mathura Road
New Delhi 110 044

SAGE Publications Asia-Pacific Pte Ltd
3 Church Street
#10-04 Samsung Hub
Singapore 049483

Editor: Chris Rojek
Editorial assistant: Martine Jonsrud
Production editor: Katherine Haw
Copyeditor: Elaine Leek
Marketing manager: Michael Ainsley
Cover design: Wendy Scott
Typeset by: C&M Digitals (P) Ltd, Chennai, India
Printed by MPG Printgroup, UK

Editorial Material © Dr Roy C. Wood 2013
Chapter 1 © Dr Roy C. Wood 2013
Chapter 2 © Mr Gareth Currie 2013
Chapter 3 © Mr Bert Smit 2013
Chapter 4 © Mr Olaf W. Hermans 2013
Chapter 5 © Mr Geoff Marée 2013
Chapter 6 © Professor Stephen Ball 2013
Chapter 7 © Mr Gareth Currie 2013
Chapter 8 © Dr Roy C. Wood 2013
Chapter 9 © Professor Udo A. Schlentrich and
    Dr E. Hachemi Aliouche 2013
Chapter 10 © Mr Simen Kooi 2013
Chapter 11 © Dr Marc B. Stierand 2013
Chapter 12 © Mr John Mackillop 2013
Chapter 13 © Dr Bob Brotherton 2013
Chapter 14 © Dr Roy C. Wood 2013
Chapter 15 © Dr Frans Melissen 2013
Chapter 16 © Professor Peter O'Connor 2013
Chapter 17 © Mr Protyush Banerjee 2013
Chapter 18 © Ms Marina Brinkman-Staneva 2013
Chapter 19 © Professor Yvonne Guerrier 2013
Chapter 20 © Mr Rob van Ginneken 2013
Chapter 21 © Mr Michael Schwarz 2013
Chapter 22 © Professor Peter O'Connor 2013
Chapter 23 © Dr Marc B. Stierand 2013
Chapter 24 © Dr Constantinos Verginis 2013
Chapter 25 © Dr Susan Horner and Professor John Swarbrook 2013
Chapter 26 © Dr Roy C. Wood 2013
Chapter 27 © Professor Udo A. Schlentrich 2013
Chapter 28 © Professor G. Barry O'Mahony 2013
Chapter 29 © Professor Yvonne Guerrier 2013
Chapter 30 © Ms Jane F. Eastham and Dr Alisha Ali 2013
Chapter 31 © Mr Stan Josephi 2013
Chapter 32 © Professor G. Barry O'Mahony 2013
Chapter 33 © Dr Roy C. Wood 2013
Chapter 34 © Mr Theodore Benetatos 2013
Chapter 35 © Professor Judi Brownell 2013

First published 2013

Library of Congress Control Number: 2012944073

British Library Cataloguing in Publication data

A catalogue record for this book is available from
the British Library

ISBN 978-1-4462-0068-1
ISBN 978-1-4462-0069-8 (pbk)

For Sandra Miller, at last, and with gratitude

contents

key concepts in
hospitality management

contents

ix

acknowledgements

I would like to thank Professor Chris Rojek at Sage for commissioning this book and also Jai Seaman and Martine Jonsrud for their support and enthusiasm in seeing it through to production. Thanks are also due to, first, Sage Publishers for permission to include in this volume a shortened and updated version of Udo Schlentrich's entry *Meetings, Incentives, Conventions and Exhibitions (MICE)* (the original and longer piece having first appeared in B. Brotherton and R.C. Wood (eds) (2008) *The Sage Handbook of Hospitality Management*, London: Sage); and, second, to the Rosenberg International Centre of Franchising of the University of New Hampshire, USA, for permission to include a modified version of an earlier article by Dr Schlentrich on franchising, the original of which can be viewed at http://wsbe.unh.edu/Centers_WRCIF/FAQs.cfm.

Many people contributed to my sense of well-being during the production of this book, and Heather Robinson, Gareth Currie and Ashish Sachdeva deserve special mention for the laughter we have shared. Dr Nicos Vakis, a true gentleman as well as former founding Director of Administration at the University of Cyprus, lent moral and psychological support at a critical time. Gratitude also goes to the wonderful Karan Berry, who created a peaceful haven for me during two critical periods in this book's production, and to his wife, Shivali Berry, who never complained when I picked her husband's brains late into the evening. As I wrote some of my own entries for this book I found myself recalling many things I had learned from colleagues with whom I worked, all too briefly, at Oberoi Hotels and Resorts: thanks then to Nishant Bhatia, Major Rajesh Chauhan, Rohit Dar, David Mathews, Suzanne Reitz and Shailja Singh.

I am indebted to all those colleagues who contributed to the text with enthusiasm, and not least to those from the Academy of Hotel and Facility Management at NHTV Breda University of Applied Sciences, who embraced the project with great dedication and interest. Mention must also be made of the support given at NHTV by Joint Deans Gienke Osinga and Daphne Heeroma. Although many people have contributed to this book, the responsibility for any errors naturally falls to me as Editor.

Roy C. Wood
Breda, March 2012

about the editor

Dr Roy C. Wood FHEA, FIH has enjoyed a varied career in hospitality education and training. Amongst the positions he has held are: Professor of Hospitality Management at The Scottish Hotel School, University of Strathclyde, Glasgow (1996–2003); Principal and Managing Director of IMI Institute of Hotel and Tourism Management in Lucerne, Switzerland, a private university college; Dean of the Oberoi Hotels Centre of Learning and Development (responsible for both the corporate management training centre and the corporate apprenticeship programme); and Chief Operating Officer of the Gulf Hospitality and Tourism Education Company in Bahrain. Since February 2010 Roy Wood has been Lector (Associate Professor) in International Hospitality Management at NHTV Breda University of Applied Sciences, The Netherlands, during which time NHTV's hotel and facilities management academy has established itself as the leading research establishment of its kind in The Netherlands.

Dr Wood is the author, co-author, editor or co-editor of 15 books and more than 60 research papers in refereed journals as well as numerous other publications. His first book, *Working in Hotels and Catering* (Routledge, 1992; second edition 1997) remains a major reference point for the study of employment in the hospitality industry. *Strategic Questions in Food and Beverage Management* (Butterworth-Heinemann, 2000), which he both edited and contributed to, has sold several thousand copies around the world. He has most recently contributed to, and co-edited with Dr Robert Brotherton, *The Sage Handbook of Hospitality Management* (2008), the current definitive reference work in the hospitality field.

notes on contributors

Dr Alisha Ali is a Lecturer in Hospitality Business Management at Sheffield Hallam University, UK, where she is responsible for teaching, research and industry engagement.

Dr E. Hachemi Aliouche is Associate Professor in The Whittemore School of Business and Economics, University of New Hampshire, USA, and Associate Director of the Rosenberg International Centre of Franchising.

Professor Stephen Ball is Emeritus Professor of Hospitality Management at Sheffield Hallam University and an expert on operations management and entrepreneurship in hospitality organizations. He researches, publishes and delivers conference presentations about entrepreneurship.

Protyush Banerjee CHE is a graduate of IHM Pusa, New Delhi. He has worked as a manager in The Oberoi Hotel Group and as a lecturer at the Bahrain Institute of Hospitality and Retail.

Theodore Benetatos is Senior Lecturer and leader of postgraduate programmes at IMI University Centre, Lucerne, Switzerland.

Marina Brinkman-Staneva is a Lecturer in Hospitality Management in the Academy of Hotel and Facility Management at NHTV Breda University of Applied Sciences, The Netherlands.

Dr Bob Brotherton was formerly Principal Lecturer in Hospitality Management at Manchester Metropolitan University, UK, and is Visiting Professor at the Emirates Academy of Hospitality Management, Dubai, United Arab Emirates.

Professor Judi Brownell is a pioneering researcher on the role of women managers in the hospitality industry. She is Professor and Dean of Students in the School of Hotel Administration, Cornell University, USA.

Gareth Currie is currently Undergraduate Programme Leader at IMI University Centre, Lucerne, Switzerland. Prior to this he held several hotel management positions, latterly specialising in new openings for international hospitality companies.

Jane F. Eastham is Senior Lecturer in Supply Chain Management and Strategic Purchasing with a particular focus on the food and hospitality sectors at Sheffield Hallam University, UK.

Rob van Ginneken is Senior Lecturer in the Academy of Hotel and Facility Management at NHTV Breda University of Applied Sciences, The Netherlands, where he teaches and researches finance, accounting and wine studies.

Professor Yvonne Guerrier is Professor of Organization Studies at the University of Roehampton, London, UK, and a former Dean of the University's School of Business and Social Sciences. She is a noted authority on organizational and human resource issues in the hospitality industry.

Olaf W. Hermans is Senior Lecturer in Customer Relationship Management in the Academy of Hotel and Facility Management at NHTV Breda University of Applied Sciences, The Netherlands. He researches customer and service organization perspectives on intimacy and loyalty.

Dr Susan Horner is Senior Lecturer in Hospitality Management at Bournemouth University in the UK, where she is responsible for teaching and research in hospitality and tourism.

Stan Josephi pursued a managerial career in both the hotel industry and MIS sector. He is Senior Lecturer in Hotel Management in the Academy of Hotel and Facility Management at NHTV Breda University of Applied Sciences, The Netherlands.

Simen Kooi is Senior Lecturer in Hotel Management in the Academy of Hotel and Facility Management at NHTV Breda University of Applied Sciences, The Netherlands which he joined subsequent to a career in hotel management.

John Mackillop is Lecturer in Management Finance in the Academy of Hotel and Facility Management at NHTV Breda University of Applied Sciences, The Netherlands. He has taught in management schools in Scotland, Canada and Switzerland.

Geoff Marée enjoyed a long career as a designer until becoming Senior Lecturer in Innovation in the Academy of Hotel and Facility Management at NHTV Breda University of Applied Sciences, The Netherlands.

Dr Frans Melissen is Senior Lecturer in Management in the Academy of Hotel and Facility Management at NHTV Breda University of Applied Sciences, The Netherlands, where he specializes in researching sustainability issues in the hospitality and facilities industries.

Professor Peter O'Connor is Professor of Information Systems and Director of Hospitality Management Programmes at Essec Business School, France.

Professor Barry O'Mahony is Director of Research Development and Professor of Services Management in the Faculty of Business and Enterprise at Swinburne University of Technology, Melbourne, Australia.

Dr Udo A. Schlentrich is William Rosenberg Professor and Director of the Rosenberg International Centre of Franchising, University of New Hampshire, USA. Before entering education, he had a distinguished career in the hotel industry, including spells as a corporate executive with Hilton, Managing Director of The Dorchester Hotel, London and Vice-President of Omni International Hotels.

Michael Schwarz was formerly Associate Director at HVS Beijing where he oversaw the firm's day-to-day operation in North China. He is currently an MSc Real Estate Candidate at the National University of Singapore.

Bert Smit worked for many years in the events industry specializing in the management and marketing of zoological gardens. He is currently Senior Lecturer in Service Marketing and Branding in the Academy of Hotel and Facility Management at NHTV Breda University of Applied Sciences, The Netherlands

Professor John Swarbrooke is Professor of Tourism and Hospitality at Manchester Metropolitan University in the UK, where he is responsible for research in tourism, hospitality and events.

Dr Marc B. Stierand is Senior Lecturer in the Academy of Hotel and Facility Management at NHTV Breda University of Applied Sciences, The Netherlands. He researches and publishes on strategy, creativity and innovation.

Dr Constantinos Verginis is a Director with Deloitte and Touche based in Dubai, United Arab Emirates. He is the Travel Hospitality and Leisure Industry leader for the Middle East region.

Dr Roy C. Wood is Associate Professor of International Hospitality Management in the Academy of Hotel and Facility Management at NHTV Breda University of Applied Sciences, The Netherlands.

editor's introduction

Roy C. Wood

This book is intended for use by students seeking a concise and accessible review of key concepts that they are likely to encounter during the course of their studies in hospitality management. It is, in essence, an *introductory* work of reference. This means that, unlike a specialist dictionary, the entries are fewer and longer, and assume little or no prior knowledge of the concepts discussed. Thus, the text is also of potential value to the general academic reader seeking some insight into various aspects of management processes, procedures and practices in what is one of the world's most important – and growing – service industries.

The problem for the editor of a book such as this is deciding which concepts are 'key' and therefore what to include and what to leave out. It is probable that some readers will feel that certain concepts are absent that should not be. Other readers will, perhaps, feel that some concepts have been included which might better have been omitted. Four criteria have been employed in guiding the concept selection process. *First*, and universally, consideration has been given to the general subject fields and topics that are found in the curricula of undergraduate hospitality management diplomas and degrees. This involved comparing curricula from a considerable number and variety of educational establishments across the globe via published information on these institution's websites – not a perfect method but one that at least captures both continuities and variations in emphasis within different curricula.

The *second* criterion employed in determining which entries to include is to focus upon certain types of 'practical knowledge' that, if not unique to the management of hospitality, then are undoubtedly core to the business. A competent hospitality manager requires multiple skill sets that include, but go beyond, 'general' management knowledge, and an effort has been made to reflect this in the text. The concepts included that go under this broad heading are as follows:

- Accommodation, lodging and facilities management
- Beverages and beverage management
- Design for hotels
- Food, beverage and restaurant management
- Food production and service systems
- Front office management
- Gastronomy and haute cuisine
- Hotels and security
- Housekeeping management
- The meal experience
- Meetings, incentives, conferences/conventions and events/exhibitions (MICE)
- Revenue management

The *third* criterion employed in concept selection is, in effect, a mirror of the second. There are general management disciplines and concepts that, through research, have a known application in the hospitality sector. Here, a general concept or theoretical approach when applied to a particular industry or sector produces its own sub-set of knowledge reflecting the circumstances of that industry or sector. These concepts include those in the following list:

- Consumer behaviour in hospitality
- Customer relationship management in hospitality
- The hospitality finance environment
- Human resource management in hospitality
- Income statements in hospitality finance
- Information technology in hospitality
- Marketing in hospitality
- Operations management in hospitality
- Organizational behaviour in hospitality
- Procurement in hospitality
- Service quality in hospitality
- Strategy and strategic management in hospitality

The *fourth* and final criterion employed in selecting the entries for this book is best described as a contextual one. The hospitality industry does not function in a vacuum, nor for that matter does hospitality education and research. In recent years the increasing complexity and variety of the industry has generated much debate – some of it quite heated – over the importance or otherwise of certain topics and their underlying concepts. Some of these topics and concepts have emerged as part of general societal concern over the role of business in general – for example ecological and sustainability issues. Others have been particular to the hospitality industry, for example growing debates about how 'hospitality', 'hospitality management' and the 'hospitality industry' are defined and/or circumscribed. For someone new to the hospitality industry, all of these concepts provide a necessary context for understanding the sector and, again, increasingly feature in the curricula of degree and diploma programmes. They include the following:

- Entrepreneurship in hospitality
- Franchising
- Hospitality and hospitality management
- Hospitality management education
- Hotels, hospitality and sustainability
- Hotels and the internet
- Industry structure and sectors in hospitality
- Innovation in hospitality
- Investing in hotels
- Service, service industries and the hospitality sector
- Women, gender and hospitality employment

HOW TO USE THIS BOOK

The application of the above criteria to classify the concepts included in this book is necessarily somewhat artificial but has the advantage of transparency. For ease of use, the entries in this volume as with other reference works are in *alphabetical order*. However, for the user who wishes to treat the book holistically, as an introduction to the field of hospitality management (as opposed to, or in addition to, 'dipping' into the text as need demands), then the concept classification listings above offer alternative reading structures. For example, for someone wishing to first understand contextual issues in hospitality management then the list of concepts included under this heading are an obvious starting point, which may be followed by a reading of either the concepts core to the business of hospitality or equally by a study of those concepts that entail the application of generic management concepts to the sector.

Readers may also wish to note other features of this book's organization. *First*, following the heading for each entry, there is a short list of cross references to other immediately related concepts included within the book. *Secondly*, in each of the entries, the early paragraphs immediately after this list of cross-references contain a definition or statement of scope of the topic being considered. *Thirdly*, following this definition or statement of scope, each contributor has been asked to give a state-of-the-art summary and overview of the concept, including comment on its current status, where relevant, in terms of both academic debate and industry application. Also where relevant, consideration is given to strengths, weaknesses and controversies attendant on the concept and its applications. *Fourthly*, at the end of each entry are two sections – 'Further Reading' and 'References'. The Further Reading section contains additional references that the book's users may find particularly useful in adding to their depth of understanding. The References section gathers together all those sources cited in the entry. To add to the utility of the text, all these references together with citations in the Further Reading sections throughout the book are gathered into a single bibliography at the end of the volume. *Finally* here, each entry ends with the name of its contributor. A complete list of contributors and their affiliations is to be found at the beginning of the book.

BEYOND THIS BOOK

Although this book is an individual contribution within a series examining key concepts in a variety of subjects and disciplines, it can usefully be read alongside the companion volume *Key Concepts in Tourist Studies* (Smith, MacLeod and Hart Robertson, 2010). Further, for the student seeking a wider perspective on many of the topics in the text, a valuable additional resource is *The Sage Handbook of Hospitality Management* (Brotherton and Wood, 2008). *Key Concepts in Hospitality Management* is intended as an introductory guide to the 'anatomy' of its subject, hospitality management. The book is emphatically not a substitute for further reading. The volume is also unique in taking the 'conceptual approach' that it does. Past and many present introductions to hospitality management, though usually worthy, tend to an overly descriptive approach of the sectoral structure of the industry, although some also incorporate more advanced conceptual, analytical and, indeed, controversial topics (fair examples of the latter with an American bias include Barrows and Powers, 2008a, 2008b; for a somewhat more UK and international bias see Brotherton, 2000 and 2003 respectively).

For those who wish to discover more beyond this book or the references cited immediately above, an internet search will reveal other titles available. There are also, of course, a great many websites that merit frequent checking, including news and analysis sites, for example: *e hotelier* (http://ehotelier.com); *4 Hoteliers* (www.4hoteliers.com/index.php); *Hospitality Net*™ (www.hospitalitynet.org/index.html); *hotelmarketing.com* (www.hotelmarketing.com/); and *iworkinhotels.com* (www.iworkinhotels.com/). Also of use are industry and other organizational sites such as that of the *World Travel and Tourism Council* (see www.wttc.org) and the *World Economic Forum* (www.weforum.org/). Professional associations, for example the UK *Institute of Hospitality* (www.instituteofhospitality.org), also provide valuable resources, as do specialized consultancy companies such as *HVS International* (www.hvs.com).

CONCLUDING REMARKS

The hospitality industry is both exciting and challenging to work in, and to study. At its heart is a creative tension between upholding values of tradition appreciated by guests and customers, and the desire and need to innovate. Working in the industry can be hard for all categories of employee – hours may be long and unsocial, it can be difficult to achieve so-called work–life balance, and there can be frequent exposure to stressful situations. At the same time, in the best-run hospitality organizations there is genuine variety and interest in work, the satisfaction to be derived from contributing to the comfort and happiness of others, and extensive opportunities for those who are committed to advance quickly to senior positions and the rewards associated with them. Successful hospitality managers require a range of technical knowledge and skills, a versatility that is rarely required in other industries, at least at the start of a management career. Responsibility can come quickly in many parts of the world – it is not entirely unusual in some cases to find people in their mid- to late twenties acquiring their first general managership.

This book hopes to capture some of the excitement, challenge and above all diversity of a fascinating industry. The majority of contributors to this volume either hold, or have held positions in the hospitality sector and have sought, in their entries to the book, to share their knowledge and experience, to stimulate curiosity and to encourage engagement with the hospitality industry's many facets.

REFERENCES

Barrows, C and Powers, T (2008a) *Introduction to the Hospitality Industry*, 7th edn, New York: Wiley.
Barrows, C and Powers, T (2008b) *Introduction to Management in the Hospitality Industry*, 9th edn, New York: Wiley.
Brotherton, B (2000) *Introduction to the UK Hospitality Industry: A Comparative Approach*, Oxford: Butterworth–Heinemann.
Brotherton, B (2003) *The International Hospitality Industry: Structures, Characteristics, and Issues*, Oxford: Butterworth–Heinemann.
Brotherton, B and Wood, R C (2008) *The Sage Handbook of Hospitality Management*, London: Sage.
Smith, M, MacLeod, N and Hart Robinson, M (2010) *Key Concepts in Tourist Studies*, London: Sage.

Accommodation, Lodging and Facilities Management

See also: Design for hotels; Franchising; Front office management; Hotels, hospitality and sustainability; Hotels and security; Housekeeping management; Investing in hotels

Accommodation (in North America more typically 'lodging') management is regarded as one of the two core activities that lend the hospitality industry its distinctiveness as a sector, the other being food and beverage management. Facilities (or sometimes 'facility') management is an emergent discipline comprising a set of generic skills applicable to the management of the widest possible range of accommodation types, including such diverse facilities as offices, factories and retail outlets as well as various kinds of residential accommodation (Frapin-Beaugé et al., 2008). The term facilities management is useful in reminding us that even though the majority of businesses within the hospitality industry utilize some form of accommodation, the notion of accommodation management is typically associated with the hotel and related sectors, where some form of semi-private space is effectively rented from a vendor, by a guest/customer for a defined period.

ACCOMMODATION MANAGEMENT IN HOTELS: SCOPE AND ISSUES

Most of the skills required for effective accommodation management in hospitality organizations will also be required by any hotel of modest or greater size. These include:

- front office management (comprising reservations, night audit and, in high-end establishments, the bell captain's office and the concierge);
- housekeeping management (including the cleaning of all public and private spaces, although often an establishment's kitchens are excluded from the sphere of responsibility of the housekeeping department and are the sole responsibility of the head or executive head chef);
- engineering and maintenance (although in some instances this may be a separate department);
- revenue management (which may be a function of front office or, alternately, of a separate sales and marketing department); and
- safety and security management.

A number of enduring issues face the hotel accommodation sector. A *first* area of concern for even moderately sized hotels is that of the integration of the functions noted above, each of which may be discharged by a separate department or, in larger establishments, constitute sub-units of the room (or rooms) division whose head will be a senior member of the hotel's management team. Even where functions are embodied in sub-units that are nominally part of an integrated rooms division department, there is a danger that each sub-unit will act more or less autonomously and with its own agenda often, though not always, inconsistent with the stated objectives of the wider rooms division department. There are four principal reasons why such a situation can arise, as follows.

a   Although all the functions described above share in the status of being accommodation-related, the tasks and skills associated with each are distinct. This can lead to the development of strong sub-unit/functional work cultures which are inwardly focused and resistant to integration and change – in plain English: creating a 'them and us' culture (Shamir, 1981).
b   The nature of work in functional sub-units of the rooms division is, as elsewhere in hospitality organizations, often highly pressured, creating tension between sub-units. One example is the case of the relationship between front office and housekeeping, where the latter have both limited staff and time each day to prepare rooms to the required standard and are placed under pressure to 'release' rooms to the front office for allocation to incoming guests (Verginis, 1999).
c   Variations in perception as to the value of particular types of work can also be a source of tension between sub-units of the rooms division. For example, work in housekeeping is physically demanding and dirty, and often contrasted with the perceived easiness of working in other functional sub-units, such as front office or security.
d   Finally, most hotel chains rely on standard operating procedures (SOPs) for the definition of required performance in establishing standards and performing work tasks. When SOPs are created and revised, the need for integration of processes and procedures is sometimes neglected and the requirement to meet such standards is often invoked by the managers of functional sub-units as an imperative even where they create conflict situations with other sub-units whose managers are attempting to meet the demands of *their* SOPs.

A *second* enduring issue for the hotel accommodation sector that arises at least partly from the various tensions attendant on functional integration is high labour turnover. There is substantial evidence to suggest that in certain countries and cultures, high labour turnover afflicts all sectors of the hospitality industry and all departments of a hotel (Wood, 1997). One potential consequence of this instability is the difficulty faced by management in maintaining coherent and high-performing work teams in the various functional sub-units, as well as the likelihood of increased costs resulting from recruitment and training.

Thirdly, an issue more relatively recent in origin concerns the extent to which certain hotel services, especially in the rooms division, can be outsourced – that is, performed by external companies ('contractors') in return for a fee (Rawstron, 1999). In many countries, hotels' laundry services are normally outsourced and there are numerous examples of other services being treated similarly, for example security, grounds and garden maintenance, pest control and guest room cleaning.

Theoretically, outsourcing can be beneficial because it: (a) allows organizations to focus on their core competencies by employing supposedly better equipped and experienced specialists to perform certain tasks deemed to be 'non-core'; and (b) reduces organizations' administrative costs. Potential disadvantages of outsourcing include: (a) difficulties in ensuring contractors deliver the required standard; (b) more complex supervision and monitoring needs to ensure standards; and (c) relative absence of control over human resource deployment.

Fourth, as with the hospitality industry more generally, there is great diversity in the global hotel sector and many international companies operate a number of brands in often different market segments. If there is not quite yet a hotel to suit the budget of every potential traveller then this is not far from the truth. Confusion can arise among customers as to both brand difference and comparability and can be complicated by variations 'within brand' between countries. For example, in some countries certain international hotel brands offer a full range of facilities and services that are not offered in hotels of the same brand in their countries of origin or elsewhere. The scope for guest confusion should, theoretically, be reduced, if not eliminated, by hotel grading schemes, historically presented in the form of 'star' ratings (see Wood, 2010). Unfortunately, most national (government sponsored) and independent (motoring and other transport related) schemes vary considerably in what and how they assess and classify hotels and there is, further, no international classification standard for hotels to aspire to. Increasingly, and not without contro-versy, internet-based travel sites such as TripAdvisor®, which carry hotel reviews contributed by travellers, are coming to serve as a preferred substitute for official or pseudo-official grading schemes. Hoteliers have complained both about the partial-ity of such internet-based review systems and the potential for abuse (for example 'false' negative reviews being posted on such sites by rivals seeking to damage the reputation of other establishments).

Finally here, the relationship between real estate and hospitality and the role of franchising and management contracts in the international hospitality industry is of growing importance, not least in the hotel sector, where a key means for a company to expand its brand overseas is via a management contract. Typically here, costs of construction are borne by the hotel/building owner and a hotel company 'sells' its brand standards and manages a hotel for a defined period according to mutually agreed legal and operational standards and a share of the financial returns. These methods of growth and development can reduce strategic and operational risk for a company but also generate tensions between owners and operators, not least in respect of the maintenance of brand standards. Knowledge and study of these arrangements is a growing requirement for managers in the industry.

HOSPITALITY ORGANIZATIONS WITHOUT ACCOMMODATION: THE CASE FOR A FACILITIES MANAGEMENT APPROACH?

Hospitality organizations without guest room accommodation still need to make provision for truncated services in housekeeping ('cleaning'), certain front office functions (notably reservations), maintenance and security. Again, one or more of these functions may be outsourced – especially, in relatively small operations, maintenance and security. There is a danger that in hospitality organizations not offering guest room accommodation (notably food and beverage businesses), less importance is attached to these functions to the detriment of health and hygiene, customer experience and satisfaction, and operational efficiency. It is thus sensible for management to have both an overview of all housekeeping and cleaning-related functions and clear standard operating procedures for ensuring consistency of approach throughout the organization. The requirements of hospitality organizations (or organizations in which hospitality plays a major but not core role) without guest accommodation suggests the value of considering a 'facilities management' (FM) approach to the accommodation function. As noted earlier, FM is an emergent discipline embodying the idea that there exists a set of generic skills applicable to the management of all types of accommodation.

The FM concept has had only limited impact on the more traditional sectors of the hospitality industry (Jones, 2002; Ransley and Ingram, 2004) because for many large hospitality organizations, especially hotels, 'facilities management' has become overly-associated with the negative aspects of 'outsourcing', for example loss of control over core processes such as housekeeping and difficulties in maintaining brand standards when using external contractors. Also, while outsourcing can, cost-wise, be an attractive option, the negotiation and monitoring of contracts and contract compliance is a detailed process and many hospitality organizations have yet to develop the internal competencies required for the effective management of such relationships. Away from larger organizations, many hospitality companies are small and medium-sized businesses, often owner-operated, and this makes outsourcing uneconomic.

FM is not, however, only about outsourcing. It is concerned with generating models for the effective and integrated management of various types of accommodation: a developing subject but one where evident applications and benefits to the hospitality industry are yet to be fully developed and demonstrated. For this reason at least, hospitality managers should maintain an awareness of developments in the FM field.

FURTHER READING

Bardi, J A (2010) *Hotel Front Office Management*, 5th edn, New York: Wiley.
Schneider, M, Tucker, G and Scoviak, M (1998) *The Professional Housekeeper*, 4th edn, New York: Wiley.
Stipanuk, D M (2006) *Hospitality Facilities Management and Design*, East Lansing: EIAHLA.
Verginis, C S and Wood, R C (eds) (1999) *Accommodation Management: Perspectives for the International Hotel Industry*, London: Thomson.

REFERENCES

Frapin-Beaugé, A J M, Verginis, C S and Wood, R C (2008) 'Accommodation and facilities management', in Brotherton, B and Wood, R C (eds) *The Sage Handbook of Hospitality Management*, London: Sage. pp. 383–99.

key concepts in
hospitality management

Jones, C (2002) 'Facilities management in medium-sized UK hotels', *International Journal of Contemporary Hospitality Management*, 14, 2: 72–80.

Ransley, J and Ingram, H (2004) *Developing Hospitality Properties and Facilities*, 2nd edn, Oxford: Butterworth–Heinemann.

Rawstron, C (1999) 'Housekeeping management in the contemporary hotel industry', in Verginis, C S and Wood, R C (eds) *Accommodation Management: Perspectives for the International Hotel Industry*, London: Thomson. pp. 114–27.

Shamir, B (1981) 'The workplace as a community: the case of British hotels', *Industrial Relations Journal*, 12, 6: 45–56.

Verginis, C (1999) 'Front office management', in Verginis, C S and Wood, R C (eds) *Accommodation Management: Perspectives for the International Hotel Industry*, London: Thomson. pp. 97–113.

Wood, R C (1997) *Working in Hotels and Catering*, 2nd edn, London: Thomson.

Wood, R C (2010) 'Let's make hotels get "five star" right', *The Hospitality Review*, 12, 4: 35–7.

Roy C. Wood

Beverages and Beverage Management

See also: Food, beverage and restaurant management; Food production and service systems; Gastronomy and haute cuisine; The meal experience; Procurement in hospitality

Beverages have long been an important focal point for both consumers and managers within the majority of hospitality businesses. The term 'beverage' is an umbrella term to include all liquids conventionally regarded as 'drinks', whether hot or cold or containing/not containing alcohol. 'Beverage management' normally denotes the activities of selection, procurement, storage and sale of beverages to achieve profit. In the past the term 'beverage' primarily referred in the hospitality context to alcoholic drinks wherein wine garnered most of the attention. Similarly, beverage and beverage management education in hospitality was largely product-oriented (Fattorini, 2000). However, across the industry in the last twenty years non-alcoholic drinks in the form of coffee and sparkling water have arguably seen the largest growth in popularity. This has been as much due to changes in economics and fashion as to the massive marketing efforts of global beverage companies. Research suggests that coffee shops are the fastest-growing segment of the restaurant business, with a 7% yearly growth rate. Les Montgomery, chief executive of Highland Spring, states that the sparkling water market is growing by 9% per year (Weston, 2010).

Thus, the beverage manager in the modern hospitality industry is not concerned with alcoholic beverages alone, but operates in an increasingly diverse sector with a greater range of products than ever before. The beverage manager's performance will ultimately be judged on an ability to meet budgets and maximize profit, so s/he must be in possession of a number of key skills. Riley (2005: 93) observes that for a food and beverage manager this means 'having a deep understanding of food and wine and other beverages ... being able to cost and control ... [.] On top of this would come the skills of hospitality and the commercial skills of marketing'. For the purposes of this discussion we can categorize these into three requirements: product knowledge; sales and marketing knowledge; and knowledge of the financial management of beverages.

PRODUCT KNOWLEDGE

In a short essay such as this it is clearly not possible to focus on individual beverage types and products. There are plentiful sources on such products (Edwards and Edwards, 2007; Katsigris and Thomas, 2011). Nevertheless, sound product knowledge is critical to a beverage manager's success not least because of the range of beverages available, the complex production processes that influence their quality and the service customs associated with different kinds and instances of beverages. Of equal importance is the extent to which in-depth product knowledge may be employed to positively influence future beverage sales as well as both complementing and acting as a counterweight to the knowledge of well-informed consumers. The industry sector will generally determine the knowledge base required. Essentially, the luxury hotel and fine dining restaurant segments will require the most comprehensive knowledge due to the sheer variety of beverages on offer, whereas bars and independent restaurants are likely to have much less choice and therefore more limited knowledge requirements.

A basic knowledge of products is generally acquired through a formal education where beginners study factors associated with the growth of raw ingredients (seasonality, climate variables and quality indicators); their subsequent processing, production and storage (fermentation, brewing, distilling, preparation); and the ways and means by which products arrive at the market place (distribution systems); and are finally marketed and served to the customer (merchandising). Of importance is awareness of what is required to ensure quality of the finished product at each of these key stages.

A major difficulty for those engaged in beverage management is keeping up to date on both products and processes, indicating a permanent need for continuing professional development. One obvious source of such knowledge and development is the supply chain through which beverages are purchased. Beverage company sales representatives can be of great help in facilitating free training courses to develop and augment basic knowledge, often held at the place of business. The need for extensive knowledge of all beverages offered for sale cannot be underestimated.

Today's beverage manager is ever more likely to come face-to-face with customers who have better knowledge of core products than the manager's own service team. Consumer culture is such that food and beverage is the subject of many popular TV series, book releases and internet websites and has spawned innumerable amateur enthusiasts. Such exposure can influence for better or for worse the subsequent forming of consumers' expectations, and emphasizes the importance of basic training for all staff prior to being placed in a customer service role.

SALES AND MARKETING

Beverage personnel possessing a sound product knowledge is the initial requirement if sales potential is to be maximized. For the most part, the majority of beverage marketing is external to the hospitality organization, the hard work of convincing the customer of the quality and desirability of particular brands being performed by the beverage companies rather than beverage managers or beverage personnel. Therefore the beverage manager's challenge is in maximising sales by being creative in terms of the selling techniques employed. Some popular sales techniques are shown in Table 1.

Table 1 Sales and marketing techniques by beverage type

Beverage type	Sales and marketing techniques
Wine	Food/menu pairing (recommending suitable beverages when food menu items are ordered); wine by the glass (smaller portioning to encourage consumption); wine displays
Beer	Font advertising (branding of beer pumps); merchandised produce (glassware, drink mats, bar towels; T-Shirts); gantry fridge display (bottled beer display using glass-fronted fridges); salty bar snacks; time-limited discounting (e.g. happy hours)
Spirits	Gantry display (spirits attractively arranged on shelves behind the bar); time-limited discounting
Liquors	Post-meal suggestive selling; liquor trolley
Cocktails	Weekly specials; preparation process (theatrical production methods that attract consumer attention); time-limited discounting
Soft drinks	Merchandised produce (e.g. glassware)
Coffee and tea	Suggestive selling; aromas, coffee-making process (e.g. using barista, professionally trained employees)

In a full-service hotel the bar staff provide perhaps the first opportunity to maximize a guest's average spend, encouraging expenditure via such means as attentive service and the upselling (recommending and promoting) of premium brands. The bar is often the meeting point where guests will convene prior to taking their seats in the restaurant. These pre-dinner drinks are the prelude to the meal and often set the service tone for the evening. If pre-dinner bar service leaves a positive impression, it may help to sell the bar as an after-meal venue for a digestif or 'nightcap'. Customer confidence in the bar will be stimulated if bar personnel have a positive approach, demeanour and outlook, and when required can demonstrate sound knowledge of the beverages being sold. Bar work can often be open-ended in terms of working hours and it is important to remember that no less profit is recorded from a drink sale at 1 a.m. than at 7 p.m. Sales of beverages at different styles of bars are no different: in all cases drinks should be served efficiently and with as little delay as possible in order to maximize customer satisfaction and profit.

A number of beverages, such as wine, mineral water and a variety of spirits, are generally associated with the meal experience, which can lead to strategies of selling food at much lower margins in the hope of attracting a critical mass of customers whose beverage choices will generate the majority of the profit. This 'loss leader' approach is commonplace in the industry as a competitive strategy and means of marketing, especially within saturated markets such as city centre lunch trade. Beverages typically represent around 30% of the overall restaurant bill and a general rule of thumb is that the more expensive the food then the greater is the selection of beverages offered. The drinks menu in an upscale restaurant will generally consist predominantly of wines of different styles, popular aperitifs, digestifs, and sparkling and still water. Apposite product knowledge is arguably more challenging for restaurant personnel than for those of the bar as guests in a restaurant are much more likely to ask for a recommendation from the server. This is particularly so in respect of recommendations as to appropriate wines to accompany the food selected, and this makes sound knowledge of the food menu a co-requisite foundation for beverage service personnel. The employment of a sommelier (a professionally trained wine expert) in more exclusive restaurants tempers the need for other front of house employees to be as well informed. In the huge corporate restaurant/hotel market, however, such employees are a luxury seldom afforded and front line operatives require at least basic knowledge of beverage products.

FINANCIAL MANAGEMENT OF BEVERAGES

Perusing the beverage menus across a variety of establishments will clearly show price differentials for the same products offered; for instance, a five-star hotel bar will charge significantly more for a Jack Daniels and Coca-Cola than a public house in a small town. This difference in selling price can be attributed to the additional service elements (table service, cocktail napkin, snacks, entertainment and so on); the ambience and exclusiveness of the outlet; the higher staff-to-guest ratio and the higher operating costs in general. Current industry benchmarks for beverage cost price are around the 12–20% level for alcoholic drinks, with non-alcoholic beverages achieving usually lower cost percentages. Compared with an average 25–35% cost percentage for food and higher associated labour and energy costs to facilitate food sales, this demonstrates the profit opportunities that a vendor can achieve through beverage sales.

Cost percentages only determine gross profit available from sales; the more important net profit will be determined by the beverage manager's ability to keep other costs in check. Fattorini (2000: 174) maintains that 'Drinks are generally simpler to control than food, but the systems that are used to ensure adequate control are much the same.' Arguably technological developments in more recent times have increased the ease with which beverages can be controlled. Developments in electronic point of sale (EPOS) and beverage dispense systems have all given the beverage manager more opportunities to better control sales and therefore maximize profits. Simple weekly and monthly stocktakes are required to compare actual sales against purchased produce to ensure no shortfall and identify any aspects of malpractice that may be occurring within or across outlets. Alcohol especially is an attractive commodity and along with other beverages requires to be held in a secure storage area with access granted only to necessary personnel. It is also good practice to maintain stock levels in beverage outlets at the minimum required to facilitate daily business demand. Replenishment can then be done by the personnel responsible for the storeroom prior to the next day's business commencing. It is then easier to identify stock shortages in the outlets themselves.

CONCLUDING REMARKS

Successful beverage management requires that practitioners and their teams are suitably versed in the products they are selling. Within operations that also sell food, further opportunities exist to upsell a range of beverages as suitable partners to the cuisine offered. With knowledgeable staff in place, the management of this domain then relies on operational competencies to ensure appropriate staffing levels to cope with customer demand and that appropriate monitoring and controlling of stock takes place. Today's beverage manager needs to be aware of changing consumer culture and proffer a range of contemporary alcoholic and non-alcoholic beverages through appropriate promotional and merchandising techniques.

FURTHER READING

Fattorini, J (1997) *Managing Wine and Beverage Sales*, London: Thomson.
Ninemeier, J D (2010) *Management of Food and Beverage Operations*, East Lansing: EIAHLA.
Plotkin, R (2011) *Successful Beverage Management*, Tucson: Barmedia.

REFERENCES

Edwards, G and Edwards, S (2007) *The Dictionary of Drink: A Guide to Every Type of Beverage*, Phoenix Mill: Sutton Publishing.
Fattorini, J E (2000) 'Is there such a thing as beverage management? Drink and the food and beverage consumer', in Wood R C (ed.) *Strategic Questions in Food and Beverage Management*, Oxford: Butterworth–Heinemann. pp. 172–86.
Katsigris, C and Thomas, C (2011) *The Bar and Beverage Book*, Hoboken: Wiley.
Riley, M (2005) 'Food and beverage management: a review of change', *International Journal of Contemporary Hospitality Management*, 17, 1: 88–93.
Weston, S (2010) 'Sparkling sales soar at Highland Spring', www.foodbev.com/news/sparkling-sales-soar-at-highland-spring, last accessed 15 January 2011.

Gareth Currie

Consumer Behaviour in Hospitality

See also: Customer relationship management in hospitality; Marketing in hospitality; Service quality in hospitality

Consumer behaviour is the study of why, where, when and how consumers buy, or do not buy a product or service (Jobber, 2001; Neal, 2004). Put another way, one can say that consumer behaviour is the *culmination* of reasons as to why people choose or do not choose to buy something. Research on consumer behaviour combines insights from the disciplines of psychology, sociology, cultural anthropology and economics and, in the hospitality context, focuses on understanding guests and customers and their dispositions and choices. Generally, consumer behaviour research focuses on any or all of the five different stages the consumer goes through when buying something: (1) awareness of a certain need; (2) information search; (3) evaluation of alternatives; (4) decision making; and (5) post-purchase evaluation (Solomon et al., 2006). These five stages of consumer behaviour form the basis of the discussion here.

AWARENESS OF NEEDS

A need is aroused when a consumer feels tension between the current state they are in and the state they want to be in, usually termed the ideal state. The magnitude of this tension determines the urgency or motivation a person feels to act to eliminate or reduce the tension (Solomon et al., 2006). Marketers try to create products and services that will arouse needs and thus generate such tensions between the current and desired states felt by consumers.

In consumer behaviour, it is usual to distinguish two types of needs: expressive and utilitarian. Expressive needs involve desires by consumers to fulfil social and/ or aesthetic requirements, and are mostly learned. Utilitarian needs involve desires by consumers to solve basic problems and are mostly related to innate needs such as the need for food or shelter (Mowen and Minor, 1998). Needs may therefore be classified according to whether they are learned or innate. There is also a measure of agreement among psychologists that needs are (a) rarely or never fully satisfied; and (b) accompanied by feelings and emotions.

INFORMATION SEARCH

Information search is the second step in consumer decision making and is defined as the process by which consumers survey their environment for appropriate data to make a decision or decisions to satisfy an aroused need (Solomon et al., 2006). In short, consumers start to look for information on products that might get them near to the ideal state generated by need arousal. For many products consumers only do an *internal search*. Based on previous experiences with the product, or based on the ongoing search for the best alternative, a decision is taken. 'Ongoing search' in this case is the continuous information processing consumers engage in when shopping, talking to (relevant) others and evaluating advertisements. For most products an internal search is combined with an *external search* in which consumers actively look for advertisements, offers, opinions of friends and other consumers to help them come to a decision.

In marketing campaigns both types of information search can be addressed, but details differ. When brands or companies want to create or maintain a 'top of mind position' in the internal and ongoing search, they want to be seen continuously. They focus on brand recognition rather than specific products on offer in their campaigns, so their product comes up in the internal search. When a company aims for new consumers or a higher than average consumption, they aim for the external part of information search making, for instance, special offers or discounts.

EVALUATION OF ALTERNATIVES

Evaluation of alternatives is the phase in which all the information acquired by potential buyers on different options is subject to analysis. By the end of this phase consumers reach a conclusion on which of the available alternatives can help them reach their ideal or desired state. During this process, consumers assess two things at the same time: what *they* think about available alternatives and what (relevant) others think of those alternatives. The second of these incorporates consideration of the extent to which consumers feel the desire to comply with the opinions of others. Combined evaluation of the two elements leads to a certain intention towards buying or not buying each of the available products.

After intentions are formed consumers mentally divide all alternatives into three sets of options: the evoked set, the inert set and the inept set. The *evoked set* comprises the alternatives the consumer is actually considering, the short list. It is made up from alternatives that were positively evaluated based on the internal information search (already known and/or experienced) and the external information search, alternatives that are new to the consumer. The *inert set* consists of those brands in the product category for which the consumer has neither a positive nor negative evaluation. The consumer is aware of them but does not have sufficient information to evaluate them. The *inept set* consists of those products the consumer has rejected from his or her purchase consideration, either because s/he has had an unpleasant experience or because s/he has received negative feedback from other sources (Narayana and Markin, 1975). Of course, all marketers want their product to be in the first of these sets, but in practice the average consumer may have relatively few products in their evoked set.

Going from needs to wants: getting into the evoked set

It was noted earlier that there are two basic types of needs, utilitarian and expressive. For the hospitality industry it is important to understand that competition is focused mostly on the latter. Utilitarian needs are similar to the first two need levels of Maslow's (1946) famous hierarchy of needs, covering food, shelter and security. Of course, the way utilitarian needs are met can differ in terms of quality. For example, when a consumer has the means to do so, s/he will add expressive needs to his or her utilitarian needs, perhaps having dinner in a nice restaurant rather than a simple piece of bread and butter at home.

To get a product or service into the evoked set, it is necessary in product/service quality, branding and promotion to create forms of symbolism likely to generate in potential consumers a positive intention towards that product or service. This is the point where perceived consumer needs translate into desires or wants. That is, if a product/service can be created that, in the perception of a consumer, stands to close the gap between actual and ideal state, then that consumer will become more favourably disposed towards it. The role of symbolism in the product/service offer is to persuade the consumer that a purchase will help create and sustain their personal identity, their self image. Together with economic circumstances, motivation and purpose, 'symbolic consumption' is at the very heart of understanding, for example consumer choice of hotels. Because all hotels must, by definition, offer similar basic products, it is important that consumers have the possibility for symbolic consumption, so that by staying at 'X' hotel or by regularly staying at the properties of 'Y' hotel chain, their self-image and desires are rooted in and perhaps even intensified by the ethos of the product.

DECISION MAKING

How does a consumer evaluate the alternatives at hand subsequent to their information search and what leads to the final decision to purchase one product or service rather than another? Psychological research suggests that three factors combine to create such decisions: opportunity, capacity and motivation (Poiesz, 1999). *Opportunity* is the extent to which time and circumstances stimulate or obstruct behaviour associated with the decision. *Capacity* is the extent to which a person has the traits, power, skills and instruments to act or behave in a certain way. *Motivation* is the extent to which a person is interested in (the expected result of) the decisional behaviour.

When a consumer compares different products s/he will choose the one with the highest (potential) product of the three factors. Products that score low on one or more of the three factors are unlikely to be chosen. Some products score better on opportunity, others on capacity. The choice between products/services that score equally on capacity and opportunity will be determined by the power of the symbolic attributes of those products and services. One purpose of the branding of products and services is to encourage consumer loyalty by associating the brand with their self-image and identity. One demonstrates the kind of person one is by one's consumption behaviour – choosing a Rolls-Royce rather than a mass produced car; or eating in a Michelin-starred restaurant rather than a fast food chain; or staying in a Four Seasons hotel rather than a budget hotel chain (assuming in all cases that the consumer has the economic power to make such choices).

POST-PURCHASE EVALUATION

Previous experiences of products and services have a large influence on consumer behaviour and post-purchase evaluation is thus important to future consumer behaviour. Post-purchase evaluation brings us into the world of customer satisfaction. Understanding how customer satisfaction is constructed helps to predict whether a consumer will buy a product again.

Mowen and Minor (1998) define consumer satisfaction as the overall attitude consumers have toward a good or service after they have acquired and used it. Consumer satisfaction is the balance between perceived quality and expected quality. This involves not only the product itself but also the effort put into acquiring it, the interaction with sales staff and other elements that make up the purchasing process. The buying process generates expectations of the quality of alternatives. Post-purchase evaluation is the set of sentiments the consumer generates when reflecting on how accurate the assessment was that led to the purchase of a particular product or service. In crude terms three outcomes are possible – expectations were not met, expectations were met, and expectations were exceeded. It is important to understand that consumer satisfaction is largely dependent of the perception of the delivered quality. This does not necessarily mean the actual quality.

Keller et al. (2008) identify five basic dimensions of perceived quality that are at the core of post-purchase evaluation: (a) product or service performance; (b) service effectiveness, efficiency and empathy; (c) reliability, durability and serviceability; (d) style and design; and (e) price. The importance of each of these five dimensions may vary from product to product or service to service. The result of post-purchase evaluation feeds back into stages 2 (information search) and 3 (evaluation of alternatives) of the decision making process and thus partly determines whether the product or service stays in the evoked set.

CONCLUDING REMARKS

Consumer behaviour is an increasingly complex and frequently underrated field of study compared to marketing (of which it is usually considered a part). The hospitality industry is characterized by increasing market complexity. This suggests a growing need for greater understanding of the multiplicity of behavioural factors involved in consumer purchase decisions of hospitality products and services. The interdisciplinary study of consumer behaviour is one route to such understanding.

FURTHER READING

Cahill, D J (2006) *Lifestyle Market Segmentation*, New York: Haworth Press.

REFERENCES

Jobber, D (2001) *Principles and Practice of Marketing*, 3rd edn, North Ryde: McGraw-Hill Irwin.
Keller, K L, Apéria, T and Georgson, M (2008) *Strategic Brand Management: A European Perspective*, Harlow: Pearson Education.

Maslow, A H (1946) 'A theory of human motivation', in Harriman, P L (ed.) *Twentieth Century Psychology: Recent Developments in Psychology*, New York: Philosophical Library. pp. 22–48.

Mowen J and Minor M (1998) *Consumer Behaviour: A Framework*, 5th edn, Harlow: Prentice Hall.

Narayana, C L and Markin, R J (1975) 'Consumer behaviour and product performance: an alternative conceptualization', *Journal of Marketing*, 39, 4: 1–6.

Neal, C M (2004) *Consumer Behaviour*, North Ryde: McGraw-Hill Irwin.

Poiesz, Th B C (1999) *Gedragsmanagement: Waarom Mensen zich (niet) Gedragen*, Wormer: Immerc.

Solomon, M R, Bamossy, G, Askegaard S and Hogg, M K (2006) *Consumer Behaviour: A European Perspective*, 3rd edn, Harlow: Prentice Hall.

Bert Smit

Customer Relationship Management in Hospitality

See also: Consumer behaviour in hospitality; Marketing in hospitality; Service quality in hospitality

key concepts in
hospitality management

18

Customer relationship management (CRM) is 'a strategy with integrated cross-functional processes facilitated by information technology, leveraging knowledge to enhance long-term customer and shareholder value' (Hermans and Mount, 2010: 12). At the heart of any customer relationship management strategy is the central tenet of relationship marketing, namely that marketers should shift their focus away from acquiring new customers to 'attracting, maintaining and enhancing customer relationships' (Berry, 1995: 236). However, many CRM implementations, not least in the hospitality sector, have turned into exercises of knowledge management and system integration, neglecting the dynamics of customers' relations and encounters with service companies (Mitussis et al., 2006). Service organizations continue to find a challenge in moving from discrete service exchanges (which typically provide service for money, ignore the identity of the customer and come with narrow content and limited communication) to relational service exchanges (which are viewed in terms of their history and anticipated future and provide partners with complex personal satisfactions that stem from who and how we exchange rather than what we exchange) (Dwyer et al., 1987). This leads many writers (e.g. Gronroos, 1995) to conclude that frontline service employees in 'high involvement work systems' remain the primary relationship builders, that these employees should engage in relatively discrete relational behaviours and have access to rich information on individual customers, a process labelled as *informational empowerment* (Hermans and Van Ravesteijn, 2011). This approach raises major issues for organizations that rely too heavily on standardized quality and process controls or implement total quality management too rigidly (Hales and Klidas, 1998).

UNDERSTANDING LOYAL CUSTOMERS' NEEDS

Of importance to understanding the nature and importance of CRM is the observation that 'basic' service satisfaction experienced by a customer is a necessary yet insufficient prerequisite of their propensity to repeat purchase (Storbacka et al., 1994). The trust and commitment required to evoke loyal customer behaviour is driven by absence of opportunism, shared values, individualized communication and relational benefits (Hennig-Thurau and Klee, 1997).

In their study of the behavioural aspects of loyal customers in hospitality, Shoemaker and Lewis (1999) found that loyal customers/guests are subject to less outspoken emotions (which helps to develop stable relationships) although they are highly likely to disapprove of aggressive variable pricing practices. They are also less likely to ask about price when making reservations; purchase more services from the hotel; act as a great source of word of mouth referrals; and are likely to be more open in sharing their service quality concerns with management. In return they ask 'favours' such as personal recognition upon arrival, the transfer and use of information from previous stays (for example information related to their preferences) and relevant information about the hotel which may influence their stay experience (for example future dates when the hotel is sold out). They tend to take previously received benefits for granted (that is, they have a high sense of entitlement).

Shoemaker and Lewis (1999) observed that hotels often fail to collect relevant customer information to develop a meaningful dialogue. Three types of such information can be distinguished: the service preference profile, which drives customization; the personal information profile, which drives personalization; and finally the relationship expectations, which drive the relationship as a dedicated object in the mind of customers. The last category of information makes us aware that loyalty is not based on benefits *per se* but on desirable mental and emotional states such as closeness, rapport and friendship (e.g. Gremler and Gwinner, 2000). Related to the degree of depth of mutual knowing and understanding, are (a) the desired degree of relationship formality and (b) the extent of the sharing/updating of information across organizational units and members. Privacy (O'Connor, 2008a) and affect (Mattila, 2006) have proven to be key drivers of relationship success, but overly formal management of both may actually jeopardize loyal guests' perceived levels of privacy and positive affect as relationship-conducive emotional processes.

DIFFERENT PERSPECTIVES AND MANAGEMENT APPROACHES TO CRM

Zablah (2004) describes five possible perspectives or approaches to CRM: CRM as a process, a strategy, a philosophy, a capability or a technological system.

Process approaches to CRM focus on the processes required in getting to know loyal customers and to serve and interact with them based on that information to achieve loyalty (e.g. Kumar and Shah, 2004). *Strategic* perspectives are concerned with how different parts of organizations deal with different tiers of loyalty (equity) in the customer database (e.g. Payne and Frow, 2005). In their article on customer equity management Bell et al. (2002) state that 9% of all Hilton guests make 56% of the group's profit, which calculates down to the low cost of advertising, the low cost of sales (for example use of direct booking channels) and service (for example few complaints), and remarkably to the low cost of real estate since loyal customers allow for better franchise and leasing deals. *Philosophical* frameworks demonstrate the importance of companies building strategies around networks of stakeholders, including customers, instead of only applying simplistic marketing approaches that consider customers as targets of 4P marketing strategies (Gummesson, 1994). Jarrat's (2004) CRM *capability* framework focuses on the infrastructure and learning and behavioural skills required to face and serve large amounts of loyal customers over time. Minghetti (2003) describes a customer-centric *information system* in hospitality, but the exponentially growing range of customer technologies adopted by service companies (for example online loyalty card systems, concierge systems, complaint handling systems, call centres, content and campaign management systems and systems to track customer comments in social media) have made CRM technology integration extremely complex, even problematic for the quality of service relationships if organizations fail to maintain 'a holistic vision on the customer that is at the core of relationship marketing' (Mitussis et al., 2006: 576).

CONCLUDING REMARKS: PRINCIPLES OF A SUCCESSFUL LOYALTY PROGRAMME

On a strategic marketing level, McCall et al. (2010) argue that a successful loyalty programme fosters customer engagement, establishes a two-way value proposition, capitalizes on customer data, properly segments customers in profitability tiers, develops strategic partnerships, caters for consumers' desire for choice, avoids commoditization and wild discounting, and embraces new technologies. Hermans and Melissen (2008) believe that loyalty is primarily built through smart sequences of enhanced interpersonal encounters between customers and service employees. They distinguish seven critical relationship dimensions that continuously guide the *relationship shaping dialogue* between the service organization and the loyal customer, seeking and maintaining common ground between them.

The *strategy* dimension is concerned with how a mutually desirable model for a service relationship can be revealed when customers and organizations share their relational motivations and orientation (e.g. Bendapudi and Berry, 1997). The *relationship dimension* focuses on the importance of a service relationship to the customer and organization and translates into mutual prioritizing and commitment (Johnson and Selnes, 2004), for example by increasing the share of spending by the customer and a higher VIP status granted by the organization to the customer. The *change* dimension focuses on the employees with whom the customer wishes to build rapport (Gutek et al., 1999), and on the competencies and freedom of action these employees should be granted, their level of accountability, development and the extent to which their empowerment is managed (Batt, 2000). The *knowledge (or system) dimension* concerns what partners know about each other. This is reflected in the effort by the customer to become knowledgeable about the company, its services and the employees (Alba and Hutchinson, 1987) and by the organization to brief and debrief its employees before, during and after each encounter with the loyal customer (Shanks and Tay, 2001). The *content dimension* is concerned with which part of service and communication makes repeat purchases and the encounters actually relational in the eyes of the customer and the organization. This perception of 'special status' (Czepiel, 1990: 13) emerges from dedicated value-generating processes like recognition, surprise, education, activation and rewarding of loyal customers. The *privacy dimension* concerns how far customer and organization allow each other into each other's life (customer perspective) and systems (organizational perspective). This translates into a negotiated relationship trajectory in which ever-more sensitive information is shared (e.g. Henderson and Snyder, 1999). Finally, the *performance dimension* focuses on what *fruits* do customer and service organization believe they are *entitled* to in their service relationship? This translates into mutual understanding of the psychological contract both are pursuing (e.g. Mason et al., 2006).

FURTHER READING

Dyché, J (2004) *The CRM Handbook*, Boston: Addison-Wesley.
Payne, A (2005) *Handbook of CRM: Achieving Excellence Through Customer Management*, Oxford: Butterworth–Heinemann.

REFERENCES

Alba, J W and Hutchinson, J W (1987) 'Dimensions of consumer expertise', *Journal of Consumer Research*, 13, 4: 411–54.
Batt, R (2000) 'Strategic segmentation in front-line services: matching customers, employees and human resource systems', *International Journal of Human Resource Management*, 11, 3: 540–61.
Bell, D, Deighton, J, Reinartz, W J, Rust, R T and Swartz, G (2002) 'Seven barriers to customer equity management', *Journal of Service Research*, 5, 1: 77–85.
Bendapudi, N and Berry, L L (1997) 'Customers' motivations for maintaining relationships with service providers', *Journal of Retailing*, 73, 1: 15–37.
Berry, L (1995) 'Relationship marketing of services – growing interest, emerging perspectives', *Journal of the Academy of Marketing Science*, 23, 4: 236–45.
Czepiel, J (1990) 'Service encounters and service relationships: implications for research', *Journal of Business Research*, 20, 1: 13–21.
Dwyer, F R, Schurr, P H and Oh, S (1987) 'Developing buyer–seller relationships', *Journal of Marketing*, 51, 2: 11–27.
Gremler, D D and Gwinner, K P (2000) 'Customer–employee rapport in service relationships', *Journal of Service Research*, 3, 1: 82–104.
Gronroos, C (1995) 'Relationship marketing: the strategy continuum', *Journal of the Academy of Marketing Science*, 23, 4: 252–4.
Gummesson, E (1994) 'Making relationship marketing operational', *International Journal of Service Industry Management*, 5, 5: 5–20.

Gutek, B A, Bhappu, A D, Liao-Troth, M A and Cherry, B (1999) 'Distinguishing between service relationships and encounters', *Journal of Applied Psychology*, 84, 2: 218–33.

Hales, C and Klidas, A (1998) 'Empowerment in five-star hotels: choice, voice or rhetoric?', *International Journal of Contemporary Hospitality Management*, 10, 3: 88–95.

Henderson, S C and Snyder, C A (1999) 'Personal information privacy: implications for MIS managers', *Information and Management*, 36, 4: 213–20.

Hennig-Thurau, T and Klee, A (1997) 'The impact of customer satisfaction and relationship quality on customer retention: a critical reassessment and model development', *Psychology and Marketing*, 14, 8: 737–64.

Hermans, O and Melissen, F (2008) 'Introducing the CRM-7–18 model: analysing the need for and introducing a framework for phased design and implementation of guest relationship programs', *Proceedings of the 26th EuroChrie Conference, Dubai, 11–14 October.*

Hermans, O and Mount, D (2010) *Customer Relationship Management in Hospitality: A Theoretical Introduction and Guidelines for Applying the CRM-7–18 Model*, Breda: University of Applied Science.

Hermans, O and Van Ravesteijn, C (2011) 'Informational empowerment: customer dialogue technology and service employees', *Proceedings of the 12th International Research Symposium on Service Excellence in Management (QUIS12), Ithaca, NY, 2–5 June.*

Jarratt, D (2004) 'Conceptualizing a relationship management capability', *Marketing Theory*, 4, 4: 287–309.

Johnson, M D and Selnes, F (2004) 'Customer portfolio management: toward a dynamic theory of exchange relationships', *Journal of Marketing*, 68, 2: 1–17.

Kumar, V and Shah, D (2004) 'Building and sustaining customer loyalty for the 21st century', *Journal of Retailing*, 80, 4: 317–29.

Mason, D D M, Tideswell, C and Roberts, E (2006) 'Guest perceptions of hotel loyalty', *Journal of Hospitality and Tourism Research*, 30, 2: 191–206.

Mattila, A S (2006) 'How affective commitment boosts guest loyalty (and promotes frequent-guest programs)', *Cornell Hotel and Restaurant Administration Quarterly*, 47, 2: 174–81.

McCall, M, Voorhees, C and Calantone, R (2010) 'Building customer loyalty: ten principles for designing an effective customer reward program', *Cornell Hospitality Report* 10, 9.

Minghetti, V (2003) 'Building customer value in the hospitality industry: towards the definition of a customer-centric information system', *Information Technology and Tourism*, 6: 141–52.

Mitussis, D, O'Malley, L and Patterson, M (2006) 'Mapping the re-engagement of CRM with relationship marketing', *European Journal of Marketing*, 40, 5–6: 572–89.

O'Connor, P (2008a) 'E-mail marketing by international hotel chains', *Cornell Hospitality Quarterly*, 49, 1: 42–52.

Payne, A and Frow, P (2005) 'A strategic framework for customer relationship management', *Journal of Marketing*, 69, 4: 167–78.

Shanks, G and Tay, E (2001) 'The role of knowledge management in moving to a customer-focused organization', *Proceedings of the 9th European Conference on Information Systems, Bled, Slovenia, June 27–29.*

Shoemaker, S and Lewis, R C (1999) 'Customer loyalty: the future of hospitality marketing', *International Journal of Hospitality Management*, 18, 4: 345–70.

Storbacka, K, Strandvik, T and Gronroos, C (1994) 'Managing customer relationships for profit: the dynamics of relationship quality', *International Journal of Service Industry Management*, 5, 5: 21–38.

Zablah, A (2004) 'An evaluation of divergent perspectives on customer relationship management: towards a common understanding of an emerging phenomenon', *Industrial Marketing Management*, 33, 6: 475–89.

Olaf W. Hermans

Design for Hotels

See also: Accommodation, lodging and facilities management; Front office management; Hotels and security; Housekeeping management; Innovation in hospitality

Design of hotels is a structural activity, closely related to the hotel concept, its strategy and any questions of corporate identity. It supports hotel branding and marketing which in turn supports and moulds design choices. Design is used to create and develop new environments and products and plays an important role in the success of a hotel, influencing the atmosphere that guests will experience during their stay and supporting or, in too many cases of bad design, constraining, a hotel's operational processes. Ideally, any hotel design process is holistic and integrative (encompassing, for example, everything from design of guest rooms and public areas to the choice of cutlery and crockery) involving a complex set of choices and decisions directed towards supporting people and processes.

THE NATURE OF HOTEL DESIGN

Hotel design as a specialist form of building design evolved rapidly in the last quarter of the twentieth century after arguably lagging behind that of many other industries (West and Purvis, 1992). In the 1980s, the hotel developer Ian Schrager introduced the concept of the 'boutique hotel', one example of which, Morgans Hotel in New York, opened in 1984, heralding a global boom of boutique hotel developments and promoting the notion of hotel design as distinct and specialized. In 1993 Claus Sendlinger initiated the marketing brand 'Design Hotels', which in 2010 had membership of over 190 independent hotels worldwide. Many hotels, especially since the late 1980s, have profited from the magnetic power of designers' names. Philippe Starck (France) and Toshi Juki Kyta (Japan) have created so-called signature hotels in cities like Miami, Paris, New York and Tokyo. Fashion brands such as Armani (Milan and Dubai), Bulgari (Milan and Bali), Versace (Dubai and the Gold Coast) and Diesel (The Pelican Hotel, Miami Beach) have co-operated on design with hotel brands. Although design is a generic requirement for all hotels, 'designer hotels' have in themselves become a market segment attractive to design- and fashion-conscious guests. They have arguably contributed to a widening general interest in hotel design questions, as is reflected in such magazines as *Hotel Design* (USA) and *Sleeper* (UK) and websites like www.hoteldesigns.net and hotel.worldinteriordesign network.com.

Design is, of course, an increasingly specialized profession and design companies have emerged that specialize in, or support specialization in, hotel design – for example Gettys Hotel Design and Development (www.gettys.com) and HBA/ Hirsch Bedner Associates Design Consultants (www.hbadesign.com). Many of these firms offer 'turnkey services' whereby they take responsibility for, and care of, the complete design process, from first ideas to the final execution of those ideas via a series of stages that include planning, design concept, design development, documentation, bidding and design implementation. This ensures the holistic and integrative approach to design referred to earlier.

THE IMPORTANCE OF THE CLIENT BRIEF

When commissioning a hotel design, redesign or refurbishment, it is important that a hotel's corporate and/or unit management prepares a clear brief, is conscious of the implications of their design requirements, and can intelligently assess what is ultimately presented to them by the designer. A clear brief will contain specifications to be used when briefing the designer and will cover such matters as budgets, deadlines, timing and scheduling, size, functionality, style, partners, sustainability and responsibilities. Subsumed within this innocent-looking list must be awareness of the implications for sustaining the chosen design over its defined lifespan (until the next redesign or refurbishment) in terms of operational factors such as the cleaning, maintenance and replacement of items and materials relative to their availability and cost. There is little point in installing expensive designer furniture in a guest room if that furniture, damaged as a result of normal wear and tear, cannot be replaced at a budgeted, affordable price (because, for example, it is no longer manufactured) over the defined period of existence of the design concept.

A good commissioner of design is aware of these issues and knows how to communicate them to the designer, making clear what the organization's wishes and demands are, what is expected, and what contextual constrains have to be taken into consideration. Those who commission design should also know when to take a step back and leave developments to the professionals. Because design is an iterative process, with new insights evolving regularly at various points in the design process, organizations should ensure that from start to finish of the design process they field a responsible, and preferably the same, representative or representatives available for discussion on all aspects of design decision making.

In the case of both new and existing hotels (undergoing a redesign or refurbishment), a hotel general manager could be just such a person. A hotel manager is a versatile manager but few have any training in design and, of course, have other wide-ranging responsibilities. Whoever the organization appoints to interface with the provider of design services (and several large international hotel corporations appoint an experienced and specialist furnishings, fittings and effects manager to such a role in both new-build and refurbishment projects), they must be properly briefed on the organization's requirements and have the authority to act for the organization in dealings with the designer.

A core issue with all aspects of hotel design or redesign/refurbishment is the continuing involvement, if any, of the designers after all project work has been completed. This may be part of the client brief and subsequent contractual arrangement between the hotel (company) and designer, or may simply be an informal arrangement. As one might imagine, original reasons for certain furniture settings, colour schemes and the use of products in certain processes can fade away. While solving daily problems, staff members come up with solutions that deviate from the design concept. Such activities need to be carefully monitored and, given the operational pressures facing most hotels, maintaining a relationship with the original designer or design team offers several advantages, not least the maintenance of a hotel's original design integrity.

CHAINS VERSUS INDIVIDUAL HOTELS

When a hotel belongs to a chain, it is likely that the design of a new hotel or the redesign or refurbishment of an existing one is regulated through corporate standards, often expressed through the medium of a house-style manual which embodies the corporate identity and branding of the chain.

When the Starwood hotel chain decided to develop a new brand, the 'Aloft' chain, it celebrated the opening of the first hotel in 2007 in *Second Life*, an internet-based 'virtual world' environment. Visitors from around the globe were invited to a virtual stay in the hotel and asked to communicate their experiences and ideas to Starwood. About a year later the first real-life Aloft hotel was opened. The comments of its virtual visitors had been used for refining the design of many different aspects of the concept (www.virtualaloft.com/). A process like the Aloft example can be executed by a large well-resourced chain such as Starwood. For a single new, non-chain, hotel, other rules apply. One of the advantages of designing a single hotel is the fact that contextual demands and opportunities can be made very clear. An experimental new hotel concept founded in 2006 near Bangalore, India, called 'Our Native Village' claims to be 100% ecological, is constructed with bricks made from clay sourced on its own premises and strongly reflects a marriage of ideals about sustainability and the culture of the region in all aspects of design. Such design choices are hard, if not impossible for a chain like Hilton or Marriott to make.

The design from 'scratch' of a completely new hotel chain is rare and offers its own challenges. One could say that the *construction* of the citizenM hotels, granted the European Hotel Design Award 2008, is the core of its design. Its building blocks are, literally, its container-sized rooms, completely constructed in a factory with preinstalled bed, shower, toilet, lights and mirror, and then stacked one on top of another on site to create a hotel. The concept is a fusion of architecture and design involving high technology specifications, little space allowance, high levels of comfort, low staff levels and high levels of staff involvement (www.citizenm.com). In this case the design, from the mood-pad (control unit) in the room to the do-it-yourself check-in is essential for success. Since the design is based on the preferences of the so-called 'mobile citizen', the element of cultural differences is deliberately wiped from the design board.

The design of citizenM hotels and similar 'streamlined' hotel brands has similarities with the very clear-cut product and service design of airlines like easyJet or a fast food chain like McDonald's. This does not, of course, mean that the corporate values ask for similar design choices. Intercontinental Hotels Group (ICHG) developed the brand 'Hotel Indigo' launched in 2004. Steve Porter of ICHG made the following claim for the brand: 'For the first time in the hotel industry, we're defining customers by a mindset rather than a price point' (Ozler, 2004). According to one source, Hotel Indigo is based on a retail service model, 'provides a true balance of color and tranquility in its design ... and the flexibility to continually refresh the hotel décor in order to leave guests feeling welcomed, relaxed and renewed after each visit' (hospitalitynet.org, 2004).

CONCLUDING REMARKS: FUTURE DESIGN DEVELOPMENTS

Design processes are influenced as much by current social trends as by professional history and practice. As in the Aloft example, and thanks to the transparency of the internet, the wisdom of crowds (Surowiecki, 2004) can now be applied in design processes to improve the way hotels are developed. Information via websites like TripAdvisor® can be used quickly by hotels for immediate improvement. Co-creation (where companies and consumers co-operate in product creation) with other organizations in networks can lead to open innovation (where innovation processes are shared by more than one company) (Chessbrough, 2006). Design companies like IDEO in Palo Alto, California, and Flex in Delft, The Netherlands, have constructed ways to work together with potential customers to create their products. For example, IDEO introduced design-thinking as a way of developing the corporate strategy. It uses the guest journey as a tool for the design of the complete service. The Ritz–Carlton brand invited IDEO to help design the quality of the total guest experience. For that purpose, they used a scenographer to create a set of scenography workbooks (Saco and Goncalves, 2010).

As these examples suggest, design seems likely to remain an exciting and critical aspect of hotel brand development and differentiation in the foreseeable future.

FURTHER READING

Brown, T (2009) *Change by Design. How Design Thinking Transforms Organizations and Inspires Innovation*, New York: HarperCollins.
Riewoldt, O (2002) *New Hotel Design*, New York: Watson-Guptill Publications.
Rutes, W A, Penner, R H and Adams, L (2001) *Hotel Design, Planning, and Development*, New York: Norton.

REFERENCES

Chessbrough, H (2006) *Open Innovation: The New Imperative for Creating and Profiting from Technology*, Boston: Harvard Business School Press.
Hospitalitynet.org (2004) Interview with James F. Anhut, Senior Vice President, Brand Development InterContinental Hotels Group (discussing the New Lifestyle Brand from IHG: Hotel Indigo), www.hospitalitynet.org/news/4019492.html, last accessed 10 October 2011.

Ozler, L (2004) 'Hotel Indigo unveils novel design concept', www.dexigner.com/news/1762, last accessed 10 October 2011.

Saco, R M and Goncalves, A P (2008) 'Service design: an appraisal', *Design Management Review*, 19, 1: 10–19.

Surowiecki, J (2004) *The Wisdom of Crowds: Why the Many Are Smarter Than the Few and How Collective Wisdom Shapes Business, Economies, Societies and Nations*, New York: Doubleday.

West, A and Purvis, E (1992) 'Hotel design: the need to develop a strategic approach', *International Journal of Contemporary Hospitality Management*, 4, 1: 15–22.

Geoff Marée

Entrepreneurship in Hospitality

See also: Franchising; Industry structure and sectors in hospitality; Innovation in hospitality

Entrepreneurship derives from the word *entrepreneur*, which originated in seventeenth-century France and was applied to an individual who provided services associated with carrying out a commercial project for someone with capital to invest. In more recent times, it has been defined in numerous, often conflicting, ways with no single definition or interpretation being universally accepted. Morrison, Rimmington and Williams (1999: 4) state that efforts have been made to define entrepreneurship 'relative to: an economic function; ownership structure; degrees of entrepreneurship; size and life-cycle of firms; and a resource base'. Most modern interpretations of the term emphasize the role of entrepreneurship in the identification of environmental or market opportunities and processes of social and market change to create value for individuals and society as with, for example, the definition employed by the UK Government in a White Paper on Competitiveness (Department of Trade and Industry, 1998): 'Entrepreneurs sense opportunities and take risks in the face of uncertainty to open new markets, design new products, and develop innovative processes. In the knowledge driven economy this process is critical in large and small businesses alike' (see also Stokes and Wilson, 2006: 31). It is therefore apparent that entrepreneurship is a complex and multi-faceted phenomenon and grasping both the concept and practice of entrepreneurship is, as Wickham (2004: 6–7) notes, somewhat challenging.

THE 'NATURE' OF THE ENTREPRENEUR

One of the key debates within the general entrepreneurship literature relates to whether entrepreneurs are born or made or, to put it another way, whether entrepreneurs are a natural occurring phenomenon or whether they can be nurtured through education and training. The predisposition of a person to be entrepreneurial in terms of their personality is far from clear and is controversial but it does seem significant. However, environment, experience, acquired attitudes and learning all appear to additionally have a role. Thus most commentators conclude that entrepreneurs are both born and made.

The idea that key features of personality, background and actions must be common to all entrepreneurs and can be identified, measured and classified has proved very attractive to both researchers (especially psychologists) and lay persons. However, research investigating such diverse factors as entrepreneurs' motivations; elements in their backgrounds; their social and environmental roots; personality attributes (for example the needs for achievement, autonomy, to be in control of a situation, to take risks and to show leadership); behavioural characteristics; and the action roles of successful entrepreneurs, has shown that no common 'identikit' or stereotype emerges. Each entrepreneur appears to be essentially unique with different demographic, educational, cultural and professional features (see Bolton and Thompson, 2004: 14–24 and 27–35; Lee-Ross and Lashley, 2009: 3; Lowe and Marriott, 2006: 26–7 and 40; Minniti, 2006: 10–11; Morrison et al., 1999: 36–7; Stokes and Wilson, 2006: 43–6; Timmons, 1994: 191; Wickham, 2004: 17). This view is echoed by Richard Branson, the portfolio entrepreneur, who said that: 'Entrepreneurial success shows no respect for age, background, sex, race or class. It is open to anyone, all you need is the drive and personal ambition and a refusal to listen to those who do not share your vision' (Anderson, 1995: 3). It is also important to recognize that the nascent, or 'would-be', entrepreneur cannot be viewed in isolation and that external factors, sometimes termed the enterprise environment, and the existence of an enterprise culture, at a national or an organizational level, are also pertinent in considering entrepreneurial behaviour (Morrison et al., 1999: 50).

ENTREPRENEURSHIP AND HOSPITALITY

Entrepreneurs can be important and influential people, creating wealth not just for themselves but indirectly for the wider community. Successful entrepreneurs, by virtue of creativity and innovation, can also establish themselves as change agents in society. The global hospitality industry offers a rich seam of opportunity for entrepreneurs and entrepreneurship. The successes of corporate giants, such as those established by Charles Forte and Conrad Hilton, are well known, but entrepreneurs and entrepreneurship can also be key drivers of the development, success and survival of the many ubiquitous small and medium-sized firms that make up the majority of the industry. Low barriers to entry mean that independent entrepreneurship is a realistic prospect for individuals wishing to start up hospitality businesses while for established businesses, entrepreneurial approaches can be beneficial to their operation, development and growth. Such approaches in established businesses – whether large or small – are associated with what is increasingly termed 'intrapreneurship'.

The motivation for becoming a hospitality entrepreneur is both an individual and personal matter. Some are 'pulled' into becoming one through, for example the desire to work for themselves or the wish to turn a hobby (e.g. cooking) or previous experience (e.g. a college project) into a hospitality business while others are 'pushed' into being one through perhaps redundancy, dissatisfaction with their boss or the lack of opportunity to be innovative (Lowe and Marriott, 2006: 46–7; Stokes and Wilson, 2006: 37–8). Whatever the case, the possession of management competences and technical skills by both managers within an established business, and independent entrepreneurs, can also be vital to entrepreneurial success in the hospitality industry. Bringing together raw materials, people and premises, in a situation where production and service to customers most often occur simultaneously is a complex process and a wide range of management competences is required to achieve success. Such competences relate to marketing, finance and human relations functions and also include those that are especially entrepreneurial, for example opportunity identification, resource acquisition and networking. Technical skills related to the production and delivery of hospitality services and an understanding of the industry are also necessary, along with social skills, particularly given the human aspect of the hospitality industry.

The growing importance of entrepreneurship in the hospitality industry can be seen in the formation of specialist groups, such as the Entrepreneurs' Forum for Hospitality, Leisure, Travel and Tourism (founded in 2009), which engages in debate and knowledge exchange about entrepreneurial issues and practices (see www.epmagazine.co.uk). It is also reflected in the growth in importance of the concept of 'social entrepreneurship', which is an increasingly established aspect of many businesses (Peredo and McLean, 2006) and reflects the fact that entrepreneurship is increasingly being considered not just in terms of its economic significance, but in terms of its capacity to enhance personal development and help solve social problems. Within the hospitality industry, Ben and Jerry's (www.startup nation.com/business-articles/1296/1/social-entrepreneuship-ben-cohen.asp) and Jamie Oliver's 'Fifteen' restaurant chain have been cited as models of social entrepreneurship. In these the objective is not only to make a profit, as has traditionally been the case with entrepreneurship, but to be socially responsible and innovative for the achievement of social good. Social entrepreneurship involves using entrepreneurial skills for the public good rather than for private profit alone, employing imagination and creativity to identify new opportunities and to seek to bring them to fruition in order to effect social change.

Social entrepreneurship is, then, an important aspect of entrepreneurship in the hospitality industry. For example, catering is often an important element of economic development and regeneration initiatives, and the revitalization of inner cities and their communities is often linked with, and heavily reliant upon, ethnic minority entrepreneurship, which is traditionally concentrated in the catering industry (Deakins and Freel, 2003: 89) (women, the young and ethnic minorities are becoming increasingly important in entrepreneurship and whilst their activity rates, potential contribution and challenges experienced have been analyzed in the general entrepreneurship literature their role in the hospitality industry has not been so closely examined – see Ball, 2005: 3–4; Deakins and Freel, 2003; Lowe and Marriott, 2006; McClelland et al., 2005; Ram and Barrett, 2000; Welsch, 1998). There are also many unrecognized social entrepreneurs involved with hospitality activities who deliver not-for-profit services through an enterprise, for example pensioners' lunch clubs.

CONCLUDING REMARKS

There is increasingly broad agreement that the promotion of entrepreneurship is crucial for innovation, healthy economies, productivity gains, sustainable prosperity and job creation (Ball, 2005). As a consequence, emphasis upon entrepreneurial activities and approaches in policy and practice has grown in political, industrial, educational and other settings throughout the world and entrepreneurship has moved to the core of contemporary management thinking and action. *Politically*, the need for entrepreneurship has become the policy battle-cry of recent UK and other governments in their pursuit of a variety of economic, social and other objectives. *Industrially*, entrepreneurship is increasingly central to the activities of all types of organization, whether new start-ups seeking to establish in the marketplace, established businesses wanting to strengthen themselves, or governmental or non-profit organizations pursuing social or environmental goals using market-based strategies. *Educationally*, the relevance of entrepreneurship and desire of educationalists to encourage and develop enterprising minds is increasingly reflected in the design and delivery of courses of study from primary and secondary school levels through to higher education. In UK higher hospitality education, Ball (2005: 9) reported that thirteen universities offered mostly optional entrepreneurship modules, normally in the advanced stages of their programmes.

Entrepreneurship is a major area of inquiry within management studies. From the discussion above, it is clear that enterprising behaviour is central to the development of entrepreneurship yet no particular entrepreneurial profile exists. Entrepreneurs come from a variety of backgrounds and possess a variety of characteristics. They are not special people but are simply alert individuals who are willing to act by taking calculated risks upon a perceived opportunity in a somewhat innovative way. Entrepreneurs are particularly important within the hospitality industry, whose many small and medium-sized enterprises constitute the majority of operations within the industry. Although we know more about entrepreneurship and entrepreneurs now than at any time in the past, gaps in our knowledge continue to contribute to the fascination of these subjects.

FURTHER READING

Bosman, N and Levie, J (2009) *Global Entrepreneurship Monitor: 2009 Global Report*, www.gemconsortium.org/docs/265/gem-2009-global-report, last accessed 17 February 2012.

Morrison, A, Rimmington, M and Williams, C (1999) *Entrepreneurship in the Hospitality, Tourism and Leisure Industries*, Oxford: Butterworth–Heinemann.

REFERENCES

Anderson, J (1995) *Local Heroes*, Scottish Enterprise, Glasgow.

Ball, S (2005) *The Importance of Entrepreneurship to Hospitality, Leisure, Sport and Tourism*, Hospitality, Leisure, Sport and Tourism Network, May (see www.heacademy.ac.uk/assets/hlst/documents/projects/Entrepreneurship/ball.pdf).

Bolton, B and Thompson, J (2004) *Entrepreneurs: Talent, Temperament and Technique*, 2nd edn, Oxford: Butterworth–Heinemann.

Deakins, D and Freel, M (2003) *Entrepreneurship and Small Firms*, 3rd edn, London: McGraw-Hill.

Department of Trade and Industry (1998) *Our Competitive Future: Building the Knowledge Driven Economy: Analysis and Background*, Cm 4176, London: The Stationery Office, available from http://webarchive.nationalarchives.gov.uk/+/http://www.dti.gov.uk/comp/competitive/wh_ch2_1.htm.

Lee-Ross, D and Lashley, C (2009) *Entrepreneurship and Small Business Management in the Hospitality Industry*, Oxford: Butterworth–Heinemann.

Lowe, R and Marriott, S (2006) *Enterprise: Entrepreneurship and Innovation*, Oxford: Butterworth–Heinemann.

McClelland, E, Swail, J, Bell, J and Ibbotson, P (2005) 'Following the pathway of female entrepreneurs: a six-country investigation', *International Journal of Entrepreneurial Behaviour and Research*, 11, 2: 84–107.

Minniti, M (2006) 'The size and scope of entrepreneurial activity: evidence from a large cross-country dataset', paper prepared for *Exploring Rural Entrepreneurship: Imperatives and Opportunities for Research*, October 26–27, Washington, DC.

Morrison, A, Rimmington, M and Williams, C (1999) *Entrepreneurship in the Hospitality, Tourism and Leisure Industries*, Oxford: Butterworth–Heinemann.

Peredo, A M and McLean, M (2006) 'Social entrepreneurship: a critical review of the concept', *Journal of World Business*, 41, 1: 56–65.

Ram, M, Barrett, G and Jones, T (2000) 'Ethnicity and enterprise', in Carter, S and Jones-Evans, D (eds) *Enterprise and Small Business: Principles, Practice and Policy*, 2nd edn, Harlow: Pearson. pp. 192–207.

Stokes, D and Wilson, N (2006) *Small Business Management and Entrepreneurship*, 5th edn, London: Thomson.

Timmons, J (1994) *New Venture Creation*, Boston: Irwin.

Welsch, H (1998) 'America: North', in Morrison, A (ed.) *Entrepreneurship: An International Perspective*, Oxford: Butterworth–Heinemann. pp. 115–136.

Wickham, P A (2004) *Strategic Entrepreneurship*, 3rd edn, Harlow: Pearson.

entrepreneurship in hospitality

Stephen Ball

Food, Beverage and Restaurant Management

See also: Beverages and beverage management; Food production and service systems; Gastronomy and haute cuisine; The meal experience; Procurement in hospitality

'Food and beverage management' in the context of the hospitality industry describes the managerial processes of selection, procurement, storage and sale of food and beverages to achieve profit. Food and beverage managers may also be involved in any or all of restaurant and menu design, restaurant marketing and merchandising, and banqueting and convention business. In most hotels, the food and beverage manager or director is a member of the hotel's senior management team. In larger hotels s/he may be assisted by specialist banqueting managers, and beverage or bar managers.

Of course, restaurants are not only found in hotels and, in standalone enterprises, whether independent or part of a chain, the term 'restaurant management' perhaps enjoys greater currency than food and beverage management. The nature and scale of food, beverage and restaurant operations in an individual business unit determines the range and quality of managerial skills required as well as the number and type of managerial personnel – for example a large hotel with several restaurants may have individual restaurant managers for each outlet. Food and beverage management encompasses more than restaurant management – for example bars and snack outlets – but the restaurant is at the heart of food and beverage management. A restaurant sells food and beverage products and service and may sell much more – for example ambience, status and 'lifestyle'. Service styles vary across restaurant genres. Typically in today's restaurant marketplace the level of service is defined by the pricing strategy of the restaurant. Simply put, the more expensive the food and beverage items offered via the menu the higher likelihood of increased service levels and associated cost.

THE MENU

The menu is the central focus for all management that occurs within any restaurant and its relationship to other aspects of restaurant management. The menu defines the raw ingredients *purchased* by the restaurant which will subsequently be transformed into the advertised menu items. The menu items determine the *training and development* requirements required of service staff in order to best sell the menu to guests. *Profitability and financial control* embraces the pricing of food (menu) items and allows such key metrics as average consumer spend and turnover to be targeted. The design and layout of the menu may have an influence on *sales* via the customer's choice and propensity to order additional items whilst dining in the restaurant. More strategically, the menu can also be a key marketing tool for attracting guests to the restaurant in the first instance.

Recognizing the relationship of the menu to the successful management of a restaurant simultaneously requires a primary attention to menu development and monitoring. Effective food, beverage and restaurant management relies on the recognition that constant monitoring of the menu and its performance will allow changes to be made that will increase the profit either through an increase in the volume of sales or a decrease in overall food cost. There are a variety of documented models for new menu development and the best of these (see as an example Mooney, 1994) communicate the need for menu development to be a cyclical process; encourage realism about the complexities associated with implementation; and emphasize the need for continual monitoring of a menu's performance in order to obtain best results.

In respect of the last of these, menu analysis techniques provide a reasonably logical, managerial, approach to assessing performance and implementing change in a menu. Much of the theory associated with menu analysis was developed in the latter part of the twentieth century. Miller (1980), Kasavana and Smith (1982) and Pavesic (1983) all developed quadrant analysis techniques to allow the performance (principally in terms of sales and revenue) of menu items to be plotted against each other, providing managers with methodologies to identify better- or worse-performing menu items and provide justification for implementing menu changes. Quadrant analysis techniques generally employ measurement criteria such as menu item popularity, food cost percentage and contribution margins to generate the data on which analysis is based (data that, with the development of technologies, notably electronic point of sale technologies – EPOS – is now readily available). Hayes and Huffman (1985) adopt a somewhat different approach by taking into account fixed and variable costs and creating profit and loss statements for each menu item. They distribute equally the fixed costs attributable to the production of the menu amongst all menu items along with a percentage of variable cost allowing the actual contribution to profit made by each item to be calculated. Arguably, this technique allows management to make more confident menu changes based on which menu items are least profitable (see Taylor et al., 2009, for an outstanding review of the current literature in this field).

PURCHASING

Food cost control lies at the heart of good purchasing. Rapidly rising food prices globally suggest the need for more in-depth knowledge of food distribution systems together with purchasing strategies that minimize the cost of raw ingredients received. Competition in the restaurant market place means that wholesale food price rises often have to be absorbed by the restaurant, as passing the increase on to the consumer in the form of more expensive menu items risks the restaurant becoming less competitive. Restaurant chains can benefit from economies of scale by centrally purchasing all items and achieving bulk discounts. However, such savings are not available to most independent businesses, which essentially need to increase volume of custom if profit levels are to be sustained and food price rises absorbed.

Strategies for independent restaurants to counter this challenge can be in the form of consolidated purchasing, where they give more of their business to one supplier to attempt to achieve greater discounts. An alternative is to join forces with competitors in purchasing common items collectively. Without some form of consolidated buying, independent operators will eventually be faced with the prospect of passing food costs on to the consumer in the form of price rises in order to stay in business. If a restaurant competes primarily on price then in doing this it will be at a significant disadvantage in the marketplace and may have to seek to compete on aspects other than price.

SALES AND MARKETING

Customers are the lifeblood of any business. Restaurants primarily sell food and beverage products and associated service. This is, principally, what customers pay for. However, the concept of the meal experience originally evolved by Campbell-Smith (1967) also suggests that factors such as ambience, cleanliness and value for money may also play a part in encouraging restaurant patronage. What is clear for the discipline of restaurant management is that some awareness of the complexities of the motivation of the target market for a restaurant needs to be known and ultimately exploited through sales and marketing efforts.

For new restaurants a marketing assessment can reveal more about the needs and wants of those consumers most likely to make use of a new restaurant facility. This can help the restaurant to better align their product to these needs and subsequently appeal to customers through better targeted marketing efforts. Marketing efforts can take the form of newspaper adverts, websites, flyers, radio adverts, sample giveaways and so on. However, research suggests that positive word of mouth (PWOM) recommendations from previous customers remains arguably the most powerful marketing tool within services (Mangold et al., 1999). Longart (2010) found that the physical aspects of the meal experience are still the most important to generating PWOM, indicating that food and drink quality need to be either on or above the customer's expectation levels. Longart (2010) also suggests that restaurants' marketing efforts might be best employed in creating uniqueness or distinctiveness in some area of the 'meal experience' as this can help to differentiate a restaurant within its marketplace. It is interesting to note that we are again reminded of the importance of the menu items to the likely success of the restaurant rather than external marketing efforts. This is encouraging for the restaurant owner/manager as marketing budgets, if they exist at all, are unlikely to be extensive. Focusing on the core product and its service may be the most effective strategy to encouraging successful sales and marketing.

TRAINING AND DEVELOPMENT

In restaurant management the provision of quality service on a consistent basis represents a major challenge to managers. The restaurant industry is well known for its high staff turnover, low wages and unsociable working hours. In this context management need to devise systems that ensure that guest service standards never fall below the accepted or expected level. Training and development is one of the key strategies to assist in lowering labour turnover and improving the consistency of menu item provision to guests.

Food preparation employees, namely chefs, represent less of a challenge than those employees at the customer interface due to the fact that their skills are often acquired through a formal education prior to commencing work in the industry and are developed as a result of subsequent experience. The role of foodservice staff can be more problematic. Research suggests that within restaurants the role of waiting staff is often undervalued and training is at best informal if it occurs at all (Pratten, 2003). Pratten (2003: 832) notes that 'Training of waiting staff is minimal, yet they need technical skills, product knowledge and interpersonal skills'. Given the financial constraints on restaurants and the labour cost involved it is understandable that training is often neglected. However, training can be approached in an informal manner that allows staff to pick up the skills and knowledge necessary to perform effectively in their jobs.

The menu provides the basis for the product knowledge required and short training sessions on a daily basis can be incorporated into briefing sessions prior to service to augment and develop staff knowledge. This, coupled with short-term incentives such as rewards for upselling certain items or exceeding weekly sales targets, can have the effect of motivating service personnel. Technical skills can form part of the induction that each member of the team receives on commencement of employment, and interpersonal skills should arguably be part of the employment specification rather than a result of training. As product knowledge increases it is likely that interpersonal skills will improve as employees' confidence grows.

FINANCIAL CONTROL AND PROFITABILITY

As with most businesses, financial control and profitability are crucial to restaurant operations. The pricing strategy associated with the menu will dictate the gross profit available from the sale of food and beverage items. As discussed earlier, ensuring the lowest price of raw ingredients will be critical to maximising profit margins along with minimizing the fixed and variable costs associated with conducting business in a restaurant's location. Where margins are kept low due to competitive constraints on pricing policy then maximizing turnover within the restaurant will become the priority. Whichever strategy is adopted to maintain profitability, financial control and monitoring will be imperative to long-term success.

CONCLUDING REMARKS

The ability to bring competitive food and beverage items to the marketplace and offer them in an appropriate service environment involves knowledge and skills in several management areas. The menu is central to successful restaurant management and its construction and continual analysis pivotal to remaining profitable. Motivating and developing personnel through training and development represents no less of a challenge in an industry known for high levels of labour turnover and often unattractive terms of engagement. For these reasons the restaurant industry remains an exciting and challenging environment for managers.

FURTHER READING

Davis, B, Lockwood, A and Stone, S (2008) *Food and Beverage Management*, Oxford: Butterworth–Heinemann.

Ojugo, C (2009) *Practical Food and Beverage Cost Control*, New York: Delmar.

REFERENCES

Campbell-Smith, G (1967) *The Marketing of the Meal Experience*, Guildford: University of Surrey Press.

Hayes, D and Huffman, L (1985) 'Menu analysis, a better way', *Cornell Hotel and Restaurant Administration Quarterly*, 25, 4: 64–70.

Kasavana, M L and Smith, D I (1982) *Menu Engineering*, East Lansing: Hospitality Publications.

Longart, P (2010) 'What drives word-of-mouth in restaurants?', *International Journal of Contemporary Hospitality Management*, 22, 1: 121–8.

Mangold, W G, Miller, F and Brockway, G R (1999) 'Word-of-mouth communication in the service marketplace', *Journal of Services Marketing*, 13, 1: 73–89.

Miller, J (1980) *Menu Pricing and Strategy*, Boston: CBI.

Mooney, S (1994) 'Planning and designing the menu', in Jones, P and Merricks, P (eds) *The Management of Foodservice Operations*, London: Cassell. pp. 45–58.

Pavesic, D V (1983) 'Cost/margin analysis: a third approach to menu pricing and design', *International Journal of Hospitality Management*, 2, 3: 127–34.

Pratten, J D (2003) 'The importance of waiting staff in restaurant service', *British Food Journal*, 5, 11: 826–34.

Taylor, J, Reynolds, D and Brown, D M (2009) 'Multi-factor menu analysis using data envelopment analysis', *International Journal of Contemporary Hospitality Management*, 21, 2: 213–25.

Gareth Currie

Food Production and Service Systems

See also: Food, beverage and restaurant management; Gastronomy and haute cuisine; The meal experience; Operations management in hospitality; Procurement in hospitality

A food production and service system is a planned and integrated set of resources, processes and procedures designed to deliver one or more product and service offerings. Although aspects of hospitality food production and service systems have attracted some sporadic theoretical and empirical research attention (e.g. Pickworth, 1988; Rodgers, 2005) and are inevitably remarked upon in hospitality texts on the subject (e.g. Waller, 1996), one commentator – Peter Jones – has dominated contributions to this field of study over the last twenty years or so (see especially Jones, 1993, 1994a, 1994b; also Huelin and Jones, 1990; Johns and Jones, 1999a, 1999b, 2000; Kirk, 2000). In many ways, therefore, understanding current knowledge and the 'state of play' about hospitality food production and service systems involves understanding Jones' work.

MODELLING FOODSERVICE SYSTEMS

In his early work (e.g., Jones, 1993), Jones argued both that there was no widely accepted classification of foodservice systems and that conceptual clarity in discussing foodservice operations was impeded by the absence of agreed definitional frameworks. Much of his subsequent efforts have been directed towards rectifying this situation and have focused on the ways in which, traditionally, most food production and service systems have been conceived and implemented as unified systems with production and consumption taking place spatially and temporally more or less together. Of course, advances in technology have broken, or produced the potential for breaking, the direct link between production and consumption.

For Jones (1993: 4–7; see also Huelin and Jones, 1990), this is best illustrated by adopting a 'materials flow' approach to food production and service systems. He therefore begins by taking the traditional catering service delivery system that has its origins in nineteenth-century hotels. Identifying the flow of materials through the system, Jones generates eight essential stages, namely: storage; preparation; production (cooking); holding; service; dining; clearing; and dishwash. The development of food technologies, for example regenerative techniques based on food preservation (like cook–freeze, cook–chill and sous vide) allow various opportunities for configuring this classical model in different ways. The critical 'pivot' here is the ability to decouple production and service derived from the benefits that technologies present for lengthening the time that food can be held between the production and service stages – the 'holding' stage. Technology permits food production and consumption to be separated both temporally and spatially. Accordingly, Jones extends the eight-stage model to ten stages with the addition of 'transportation' and 'regeneration' thus: storage; preparation; production (cooking); holding; transportation; regeneration; service; dining; clearing; and dishwash.

According to Jones, some or all of these ten elements, which in effect constitute a generic model, can be combined in different ways, to produce various permutations that are representative of real food production and service contexts. For example the combination/permutation storage–preparation–cooking–service–dining–clearing–dishwash is operationalized as an à la carte restaurant where fresh commodities are employed and dishes cooked to order. Further, specific combinations and permutations arising from the generic can be classified according to a tripartite typology:

- integrated foodservice systems where production, service and consumption take place in the same location – in other words the 'traditional' concept of the restaurant;
- food manufacturing systems where a decoupling occurs between the production and service of meals and the role of transportation is emphasized; and
- food delivery systems where operations have little or no on-the-ground food production activities but rather centre on the assembly and/or regeneration and service of meals.

Further development of this model, Jones (1994b: 142) argues, should entail refinements based on the 'real world' mapping of various combinations/permutations of the generic type, perhaps making adjustments according to variations in any or all of a series of variables, including the type of raw materials employed by systems; inventory size; the product range offered; production capacity; production batch sizes; and flexibility.

LIMITATIONS IN THE STUDY OF FOOD PRODUCTION AND SERVICE SYSTEMS

In response to Jones and other writers on food production and service systems, Wood (2008) argues that there is a tendency to both over-descriptiveness and reductionism in existing analyses. In terms of over-descriptiveness, Jones' model as an example provides a basic template of analysis but does little to advance that analysis. Instead we are given a descriptive framework for the possible arrangement of technologies and a list of variables possibly influencing such arrangements without any further elaboration. Reductionism in the context of existing approaches to food production and service systems has three principal components, being:

a   a tendency to examine hospitality food production and service systems in isolation from wider economic, social and technological networks relating to food production, distribution and consumption;
b   emphasis on the micro rather than macro aspects of food production and service systems that leads to undue weight being given to the former, that is to localized food production systems, reducing consumption and the consumer in hospitality food production and service systems to that of an agent, or caricature that is acted upon by food systems rather than contributing dynamically to the form and performance of those systems; and
c   an implicit belief in the rationality of systems such that solutions to catering 'problems' are sought within the boundaries of the system(s) employed rather than by reference to the functioning of the system(s) in wider social, economic and technological contexts.

The reductionist dimensions to systems theory are well recognized. Kirk (2000: 55), writing in a hospitality context, notes that 'There is an argument that the term "systems" has become so general that its meaning is at best confused and at worst misused'. In fairness, this is not a criticism that can easily be applied to the work of Jones. Rather, the problems with food production and service systems writing relate more to preoccupation with the technocratic aspects of the 'systems concept' (point 'c' above) that detract from the location of food production and service systems in the wider network of such systems in terms of production, distribution and consumption (points 'a' and 'b' above). Most current work on hospitality food production and service systems is firmly entrenched in a narrow 'operations management' context and fails to make linkages to the very substantial body of research work that is to be found in agricultural studies, sociology and other interested disciplines.

An important consequence of this reductionism is that the role of human agency in influencing how systems operate, change and develop is constantly and consistently ignored. The very development of food production and service systems is an intentional human act designed to achieve a number of purposes. Intention, design and 'rational' planning do not, however, lead automatically to what is intended and designed *actually working*, in a rational or any other way. In current treatments of food production and service systems, deviations in performance that derive from human interaction *with* a system tend to be treated as dysfunctional, as something to be corrected by improving the system such that 'rogue' human influence is eliminated or minimized.

A systems theory/operations management approach to food production and service systems has obvious relevance but is also restricting. To develop the field it is necessary to analyze hospitality food production and service systems in a broader context by positioning analysis of such systems within the wider web of the larger food system (Wood, 2008). This might include examining hospitality food production and service systems in the light of the ever-increasing social scientific research on similar topics (e.g. Beardsworth and Keil, 1997). Any extended approach to the study of hospitality food production and service systems must redress the balance between the design and intentionality of systems and the role of people within those systems in terms of the expectations they bring to using systems and the impact that usage has upon the evolution of the system. Similarly, the impact of institutional factors on the design and intentionality of systems – for example the role of government legislation (itself often arising from a network of public concerns and sometimes vested interests) on enabling or constraining the operation of systems – could usefully be explored. Perhaps most important of all, however, is to recognize that precisely because hospitality food production and service systems are the product of human planning, design and intention, it is important to establish the range of factors that influence these activities. Planning and design are not 'neutral' or 'scientific' practices but respond to 'a brief' and are mediated by personal and professional values and beliefs. Understanding the content and mechanisms of these processes would immeasurably improve our knowledge and understanding of hospitality food production and service systems.

CONCLUDING REMARKS

Food production and service systems are a relatively neglected area of academic research interest within hospitality management given their crucial role in corporate investment decisions, operational integrity and, of course, guest satisfaction. Like so many aspects of human food consumption, it is as if they are a taken-for-granted aspect of existence that requires no elaboration. At the same time, it is undoubtedly the case that neglect of hospitality food production and service systems is, for better or worse, in part due to the shift that has taken place in hospitality education in the past forty years, a shift that has seen scientific components of the curriculum increasingly marginalized in favour of managerial orientations. With the increasing interpenetration of management and social scientific analysis, however, the potential exists for substantial elaboration of our knowledge about hospitality food production and service systems, presenting numerous opportunities for developing further a key area of interest within hospitality management.

FURTHER READING

Ball, S, Jones, P, Kirk, D and Lockwood, A (2003) *Hospitality Operations: A Systems Approach*, London: Continuum.

REFERENCES

Beardsworth, A and Keil, T (1997) *Sociology on the Menu: An Invitation to the Study of Food and Society*, London: Routledge.

Huelin, A and Jones, P (1990) 'Thinking about catering systems', *International Journal of Operations and Production Management*, 10, 8: 42–52.

Johns, N and Jones, P (1999a) 'Systems and management: mind over matter', *The Hospitality Review*, July: 43–8.

Johns, N and Jones, P (1999b) 'Systems and management: the principles of performance', *The Hospitality Review*, October: 40–4.

Johns, N and Jones, P (2000) 'Systems and management: understanding the real world', *The Hospitality Review*, January: 47–52.

Jones, P (1993) 'A taxonomy of foodservice operations', Paper presented at the 2nd Annual CHME Research Conference, Manchester, April.

Jones, P (1994a) 'Foodservice operations', in Jones, P and Merricks, P (eds) *The Management of Foodservice Operations*, London: Cassell. pp. 3–17.

Jones, P (1994b) 'Catering systems', in Davis, B and Lockwood, A (eds) *Food and Beverage Management: A Selection of Readings*, Oxford: Butterworth–Heinemann. pp. 131–44.

Kirk, D (2000) 'The value of systems in hospitality management', *The Hospitality Review*, April: 55–6.

Pickworth, J R (1988) 'Service delivery systems in the foodservice industry', *International Journal of Hospitality Management*, 7, 1: 43–62.

Rodgers, S (2005) 'Selecting a food service system: a review', *International Journal of Contemporary Hospitality Management*, 17, 2: 157–69.

Waller, K (1996) *Improving Food and Beverage Performance*, Oxford: Butterworth–Heinemann.

Wood, R C (2008) 'Food production and service systems', in Brotherton, B and Wood, R C (eds) *The Sage Handbook of Hospitality Management*, London: Sage. pp. 443–59.

Roy C. Wood

Franchising

See also: Entrepreneurship in hospitality; Industry structure and sectors in hospitality

Franchising can be divided into two major categories: business format franchising and product (or trade name format) franchising. Business format franchising is defined by the International Franchise Association (IFA) (2011) as a marketing method in which the owner of a product or service, known as the 'franchisor', offers the right to operate and manage their product and service to others, the 'franchisees', in return for a fee and ongoing royalty payments. Product or trade name format franchising is where the franchisor gives a right to the franchisee to distribute a product or use a trade name and is most commonly found in the soft drink, automobile and gasoline distribution industries.

Business format franchising is 4.3 times as prevalent as product or trade name franchising (PriceWaterhouseCoopers, 2004) and is the preferred format of franchising in the hospitality industry. It is designed to provide a formula for operating a successful business by supplying a uniform product and service concept, thereby offering to the consumer a recognized standard and a higher perceived value. A successful franchisor will, prior to launching a franchise programme, specify and test all product and service delivery systems. Franchisors will assist franchisees in the launch of their business and provide continuous product, concept and marketing assistance in order to ensure long-term success. As William Rosenberg, founder of Dunkin' Donuts, said, franchising is 'the epitome of entrepreneurship and free enterprise and is one of the most dynamic economic factors in the world today' (Rosenberg and Keener, 2001: 245).

DEVELOPMENT AND GROWTH OF HOSPITALITY FRANCHISING

The development of franchising as a business model is primarily an American phenomenon. One of the earliest examples of consumer goods franchising was when, in 1950, the Singer Sewing Machine Company granted agents the right to sell and repair its line of sewing machines within specific territories (Justis and Judd, 2008). Howard Johnson is recognized as the first person in the hospitality industry to use the franchising model. In the 1940s, he expanded his original ice cream business into the Red Roof coffee shops and later expanded further into motor lodges. In 1961, Ray Kroc acquired a limited-service restaurant from Dick and Mac McDonald for $2.7 million. Today, McDonald's operates over 32,000 restaurants in 100 countries (McDonald's, 2010), more than 80% of which are owned and operated by local business people.

Today, franchising is recognized as an established global business model. The French company Accor is Europe's leader of franchised hotels, with more than 4,250 budget to upscale hotels in 90 countries (Accor, 2011). The British brewing company Bass also entered the franchise market by acquiring established US brands such as Holiday Inn and InterContinental Hotels. InterContinental Hotels Group (ICHG) was spun off and now operates more than 4,400 hotels in 100 countries, with 3,768 units operating under franchise agreements or management agreements (InterContinental Hotels Group, 2010). Countries such as Japan, India, China, Australia and Brazil are also embracing franchising. Seven-Eleven, the world's largest chain of convenience stores, is now owned by a Japanese conglomerate and operates more than over 39,000 franchised outlets worldwide (Seven and i Holdings Co Ltd, 2011).

ADVANTAGES AND DISADVANTAGES OF FRANCHISING

Franchisee perspective

The primary advantages of franchising from the perspective of the franchisee are: (a) the provision of a recognizable consumer brand; (b) tested product and service concepts; (c) technical assistance in the areas of site selection, facility construction and interior design; (d) training; (e) marketing support; and (f) financial controls. In addition, it is often the case that franchisors will assist franchisees in obtaining one or more of financing, lease agreements and legal clearances in setting up their business. Although all business models encompass a certain amount of risk, proven franchise concepts experience a considerably reduced level of failure such that even individuals without extensive prior experience in the field of a chosen franchise can often acquire and successfully manage a franchise business.

The primary disadvantages of franchising from the perspective of the franchisee are that the franchisee must pay a royalty fee and comply with rigorous quality and control procedures established by the franchisor. Conflict may arise between the franchisee and franchisor when territorial exclusivity is breached or when trademark issues or renewal rights are disputed.

Franchisor perspective

The primary advantage of franchising from the perspective of the franchisor is that it enables a company to establish a large number of outlets in a relatively short period of time. Resource scarcity theory sees franchising as a solution to the capital, managerial and informational constraints that are faced by firms wishing to expand. The franchising model allows a business wishing to expand the opportunity to gain access to scarce capital (the franchisee's capital) in a cost-effective way. John Y. Brown, the former president of Kentucky Fried Chicken (KFC), estimated that it would have cost KFC $450 million to establish its first 2,700 stores, an amount of capital that was not available to KFC in the early stages of its expansion (Tikoo, 1996). Firms choosing to expand through franchising can have significant advantages over firms that grow through their own means. A study by Aliouche and Schlentrich (2009a) showed that US public franchised restaurants created more market value than their non-franchising competitors from 1993 to 2002.

A further advantage of franchising from the franchisor perspective is that although the franchisor provides the business concept, it is the franchisee that is required to obtain financing to pay for the land, physical facility, inventory and working capital. The franchisor's costs are primarily related to administrative and support expenses, such as pre-opening assistance, training and quality control. Franchise companies are therefore leveraged to a lesser degree and are less vulnerable to cyclical fluctuations.

The primary disadvantages of franchising from the perspective of the franchisor are that, as its system grows, it is difficult to maintain high standards and effective communication with franchisees. In addition, national and international growth often requires adaptation of the franchise system to local laws, culture and tastes. This is evident, for example, in the case of McDonald's, where certain core products have been replaced or supplemented by local 'specials' (in India, for example, where beef is generally not eaten).

THE ECONOMIC AND SOCIAL IMPACT OF FRANCHISING

According to a study on the economic impact of franchising commissioned by the International Franchise Association (PriceWaterhouseCoopers, 2007), franchising provides direct employment for more than 9.1 million Americans. The total direct and indirect jobs created from franchising is projected at more than 17.4 million, and more than 75 industry sectors use franchising to distribute goods and services to consumers in more than 8,000 establishments. Business format franchising has been the primary driver of the extraordinary growth of franchising. In response to economic downturn cycles and corporate restructuring, many individuals have successfully made the transition from employee to employer by acquiring a franchise. Franchising plays an important role in providing employment to individuals without a higher education or specialized skills. It also provides first-time job seekers with an entry into the business world.

EMERGING TRENDS

During the past twenty years, franchising has grown dramatically in the international marketplace, primarily as a result of saturation in the US market, and especially in the areas of hotels, fast food and personalized services. Many US-based franchise companies increasingly generate a large proportion of their revenue from foreign operations. However, expansion into foreign markets does not come without risk and American franchisors need to be aware of the importance of adapting their system to the local environment (Aliouche and Schlentrich, 2009b). In addition to American franchisors expanding their brands into foreign markets, foreign franchisors are increasingly creating their own franchises, with the hospitality industry leading the way. The Jumeirah Group in

Dubai, the Mandarin Oriental Hotel Group in Hong Kong, Mealia Hotels International in Spain, Taj Hotels, Resorts and Palaces in India and Kempinski Hotels in Germany are expanding internationally using franchising, leasing and/or management contracts.

Another recent franchising phenomenon is multi-branding, a strategy in which one company owns several franchise brands that it markets under one roof, for example in the food courts of malls, in airports or in gas stations. This strategy was pioneered by the US company Yum! Brands, proprietor of Kentucky Fried Chicken, Pizza Hut, Taco Bell, Long John Silver's and A & W. Although franchised fast food concepts have expanded rapidly worldwide, they have recently come under attack by consumers and government agencies for offering unhealthy, high calorie foods. This sector is now responding by offering healthier food options and consumer nutrition awareness programmes. In addition, new franchise concepts continue to emerge in response to changes in society. Child care, in-home care of the elderly, day spas and 'green' hotels and restaurants are areas in which the growth of new franchise concepts is presently occurring.

CONCLUDING REMARKS

The importance of a business phenomenon can often be judged in terms of the desire of governments to regulate that phenomenon, and in terms of the strength of its representative (and related) organizations. In these respects, franchising is unquestionably a key force in modern business. The economic significance of franchising can be seen in the extent to which in the USA (and increasingly elsewhere) governments feel the need to legislate to regulate the phenomenon, particularly in respect of protecting franchisees. The US Federal Trade Commission (2007) drafted the first regulations aimed at protecting franchise applicants. Franchisors are required to make an extensive disclosure document (the Franchise Disclosure Document or FDD) available to each potential franchisee before the franchisee signs a franchise agreement. The FDD covers twenty-three important disclosure statements that give details about a franchise system's business experience, any outstanding litigation, fee and investment requirements, franchisee and franchisor obligations, territory and trademark regulations, restrictions on what the franchisee may sell, renewal and termination clauses. Inaccuracies or misrepresentations by franchisors contained in FDD documents may result in civil and/or criminal penalties.

The International Franchise Association (IFA), based in Washington, DC, is the most important membership organization representing franchisors, franchisees and suppliers. The association was founded in 1960 and is the world's oldest, largest and most important franchise organization, with members in more than 100 countries. Its mission is to protect, enhance and promote all aspects of franchising. The association develops and administers education and certification programmes, conducts research and holds an annual convention. The William Rosenberg International

Centre of Franchising at the University of New Hampshire maintains the largest financial database of US and international publicly listed franchise companies. The Centre publishes a quarterly index that tracks the market performance of the top fifty US public franchisors and compares the performance of these companies against those in the S&P 500. The leading franchise research and educational centre in the Pacific Rim is the Asia Pacific Centre for Franchising Excellence at Griffith University in Queensland, Australia. The strength of these institutions and of the franchising concept itself is likely to ensure the continuing importance of this business model into the future.

FURTHER READING

Mendelsohn, M (2004) *The Guide to Franchising*, 7th edn, London: Cengage.

REFERENCES

Accor (2011) *Accor Company Profile*, www.accor.com/en/group/accor-company-profile.html, last accessed 17 February 2012.

Aliouche, E H and Schlentrich, U A (2009a) 'Does franchising create value? An analysis of the financial performance of US public restaurant firms', *International Journal of Hospitality and Tourism Administration*, 10, 2: 93–108.

Aliouche, E H and Schlentrich, U A (2009b) 'International franchise assessment model: entry and expansion in the European Union', *Entrepreneurial Business Law Journal*, 3, 2: 517–37.

Federal Trade Commission (2007) 'FTC issues updated franchise rule', Bureau of Consumer Protection, Washington, DC, www.ftc.gov/opa/2007/01/franchiserule.shtm, last accessed 24 January 2012.

InterContinental Hotels Group (2010) *Annual Report*, www.ihgplc.com/files/reports/ar2010/docs/IHG%20Review_Lo.pdf, last accessed 24 January 2012.

International Franchise Association (2011) 'Frequently asked questions about franchising', www.franchise.org/faq.aspx, last accessed 24 January 2012.

Justis, R T and Judd, R J (2008) *Franchising*, 4th edn, Cincinnati: Dame-Thomson Learning.

McDonald's (2010) *McDonald's 2010 Annual Report*, www.aboutmcdonaldscom/content/dam/AboutMcDonalds/Investors/investors-2010-annual-report.pdf, last accessed 24 January 2012.

PriceWaterhouseCoopers (2004) *The Economic Impact of Franchised Businesses, Vol. I*, Washington, DC: The International Franchise Association.

PriceWaterhouseCoopers (2007) *The Economic Impact of Franchised Businesses, Vol. III*, Washington, DC: The International Franchise Association.

Rosenberg, W and Keener, J B (2001) *Time to Make the Donuts*, New York: Lebhar-Friedman Books.

Seven & i Holdings Co Ltd (2011) *Annual Report*, www.7andi.com/en/ir/pdf/annual/2011_all.pdf, last accessed 24 January 2012.

Tikoo, S (1996) 'Assessing the franchise option', *Business Horizons*, May–June: 78–82.

franchising

45

E. Hachemi Aliouche and
Udo A. Schlentrich

See also: Accommodation, lodging and facilities management; Housekeeping management; Revenue management; Hotels and security

Together with housekeeping, the front office department is one of the two main departments or units within the rooms division of a hotel (Verginis, 1999). The front office itself consists of a number of sub-departments and a variety of positions that have particular roles and responsibilities within the organization. Depending on the size, service level and target customer groups of a hotel, the front office departmental size, structure and organization may vary. The department is led by the front office manager (FOM), who is traditionally responsible for reservation, reception, cashiering, night-audit, guest service and telephone switchboard activities.

Be it while making a reservation, checking in to the hotel, at various points during their stay, or when settling their account upon departure, nearly all guests have some contact with the front office department and its members of staff. These important contact moments are spread over all of the so-called 'guest cycle', an operational model of four sequential stages (pre-arrival, arrival, stay and departure) that drives the work of a front office department and not least its procedures for dealing with guest contact moments and the interaction of the front office with other departments in the hotel (especially the housekeeping, accounting and engineering departments or sub-units), which is often central to intra-hotel communications.

PRE-ARRIVAL – RESERVATIONS

With the introduction of the internet, guests have become less dependent on traditional travel agents for information about hotels or making hotel room reservations. Innumerable online travel agencies and other third party travel sites have emerged, leading to a major increase in the number of online bookings. At the same time the hotel room market has become more transparent, making it easier for customers to compare hotels, rooms and prices. Despite this, direct reservations, particularly by telephone, so called 'voice bookings', have not completely ceased to exist. Guests can make hotel room reservations without the involvement of intermediaries, by contacting a hotel directly, or via a central reservations department and its central reservations system (CRS). 'Voice reservations' are generally more labour-intensive and time-consuming than online bookings, which are usually automatically processed in a hotel's property management system (PMS), but are nonetheless an attractive booking source due to opportunities for up-selling (selling a higher product category, for example a better and more expensive room) and cross-selling (selling additional products or services from other categories). At the same time, direct bookings do not require commission payments to intermediaries and can therefore generate a larger profit margin.

Despite advances in technology applied to hotel room reservations and booking, the nature of reservation processing has changed little. Apart from the guest's details, the date of arrival, number of nights stay and preferred room type are noted together with information on special requests, for example as to transport requirements from an airport or other travel hub to the hotel, or for a particular type (for example smoking/non-smoking) or location of a room (for example lower floor/higher floor). In case of expected late arrival (usually after 10 p.m.) guests can choose to guarantee their booking, most commonly by providing the hotel with their credit card details. This means that the hotel has to make sure that the room is kept available for the guest at all times. A guest not making use of a booking and failing to cancel a guaranteed reservation within a set cancellation period may be charged for the first night or the entire stay: these terms are notified to guests at the time of booking. Reservations that have not been guaranteed by the guest have a so called 'deadline', a pre-determined moment on the day of arrival (for example 6 p.m.) after which the guest is no longer assured of a room at the hotel. Should the guest fail to cancel or not take up the booking (the latter is known as 'no-show'), s/he will not be charged by the hotel. Apart from processing reservations, booking confirmations may be sent out to the guest to ascertain that all booking details have been processed correctly. Furthermore, a variety of reports, holding information relating to advanced and past reservations, can be produced by the reservations department for the management of the hotel. This all helps the hotel in seeking to meet guests' expectations.

ARRIVAL – CHECKING IN

In larger, 'upscale' and some medium-sized hotels the first physical contact between guest and hotel is usually with a member of uniformed staff. Uniformed staff includes door attendants (who provide baggage service and traffic control at the entrance of the hotel); valet parking attendants (who provide parking services to guests who arrive by car); transportation attendants (who take care of guest transportation needs, such as arranging taxis, limousine services and airport shuttle transportation); and bell attendants, also known as bell boys or porters and led by the bell captain, who provide luggage services and in the process of rooming the guest may explain the functionality of various in-room facilities and appliances like lighting, air conditioning, television and safety box (in many upscale hotels these latter tasks may be handled by a guest services agent). Bell boys may also run errands; deliver messages, parcels and mail; be responsible for ensuring the hotel lobby is kept neat and tidy; and provide secure baggage storage for luggage when needed. In smaller hotels the range of these functions may be reduced and many might be performed by other front office or front/reception desk staff.

The front (or reception) desk is the heart of the front office department. It is not simply a place where guests check in and check out but often the focal point for any enquiries, and is normally open twenty-fours hours a day in medium- and large-sized hotels. Front desk activities are co-ordinated by the desk manager or supervisor, reporting regularly to the front office manager. Based on information found in the guest booking, a front office operative may allocate a particular room to a guest prior to that guest's arrival, communicating the same to other departments (for example housekeeping and room service) thus facilitating any special requests, ensuring the room is ready for the guest upon arrival and saving precious time during the check-in process. For guests who arrive without prior reservations, so called 'walk-ins', the guest room is allocated at the time of arrival. Unlike guests who hold reservations, walk-in guests' details are usually not known and need to be obtained on the spot. Regular guests on the other hand may enjoy a quick and/or dedicated check-in procedure as special requests are usually known and registration details are available from previous stays. Dedicated check-in facilities may also apply to guests who book executive floor rooms in those hotels providing them.

In addition to completing the registration details on the registration card, guests will need to guarantee payment and/or establish credit with the hotel either prior to arrival or at check-in, most commonly by providing the hotel with their credit card details. The final step in the registration process is registering the guest in the property management system (PMS) of the hotel. The PMS is a computer-based management information system that supports a variety of front, and back of house applications. Before handing the room key or key card to the guest, the receptionist ascertains that the data in the guest account are correct. Guests may then be escorted or given directions to their rooms.

STAYING AT THE HOTEL

By registering the guest in the property management system (PMS), the guest's folio is activated and in-house charges can be made. Charges from the hotel's restaurant or bar are manually posted in a point-of-sale (POS) unit and auto-matically transferred through an electronic interface to the guest folio in the PMS. Automatic charges may incur when making use of the telephone or an in-room entertainment system. Some hotels offer the possibility to (re)view the guest folio on the television screen in the room; the same system may be used for displaying guest messages.

Mail, messages and facsimiles may come from the front desk or from the hotel's switchboard or private branch exchange (PBX) operator. Besides answering and transferring external and internal telephone calls, the operator may assist hotel guests with setting up telephone connections, take care of guest paging and wake up calls, and co-ordinate emergency communications.

Special guest services are usually requested from a staff member at the front desk or from uniformed staff, which often in the case of the latter and in luxury hotels, will be the concierge. The concierge takes care of a wide variety of guest service needs, including reservations for transportation, tourist trips, restaurants or theatres. Top concierges are members of the international organization 'Les Clefs d'Or' and can easily be identified through the gold crossed keys on the lapel of their uniform jacket.

Although guests may call on the cashier (usually located at the front desk) for changing money, currency exchange or the printing of their bill, the front office cashier more importantly monitors and controls financial transactions throughout the guest cycle and maintains a large set of accounts (for example guest accounts, master accounts and house accounts), known as the guest ledger. A specific responsibility is credit monitoring to ensure that a guest's outstanding account balances stay within the established credit limits. At night the night auditor verifies the account transactions (charges, transfers, adjustments and settlements) of the previous day and makes sure that all front office accounts balance. The night auditor resolves any rate or room status discrepancies before closing the books of a particular business day, also known as the 'end of day'. Apart from looking for and correcting possible accounting errors, the night auditor produces a number of accounting and management reports, including occupancy and revenue statistics.

DEPARTURE – CHECKING OUT

Within the property management system of a hotel, various ledgers (a collection of accounts folios or bills) exist. The guest ledger, also known as the front office or transient ledger, consists of all the guest folios on which charges and payments are processed. Settling an outstanding bill and bringing the guest account balance back to zero (zero balancing) can be done in various ways. Payments in local or foreign currency as well as payments by bank card and cheques, which are all considered cash, are settled within the guest ledger. Guest folios that have been settled by credit card, travel agent vouchers, as well as guest accounts for which the invoice is sent (direct billing) are transferred from the guest ledger to the city ledger or non-guest ledger. Folios in the city ledger are maintained by the accounting department of the hotel who take care of the collection of outstanding city ledger balances.

Occasionally it happens that charges occur after the guest has settled his/her bill and left the hotel; these are so called 'late charges'. Collecting payments for such postings can be laborious and relatively costly. Guests who leave the hotel without making any arrangements for settlement of their account are called 'skippers' or 'walk-outs'. In the event the hotel is not able to secure payment for these accounts, they suffer a direct loss of revenue.

The check-out process changes the status of the guest room from occupied to vacant. The housekeeping department can service the room and prepare it for the next guest arrival. The property management system automatically creates or updates a guest history file that holds key information relating to the past stay of the guest. Room number and room rate as well as guest preferences are noted. The reservation department can access the guest history file when the guest makes his/her next reservation at the hotel, with that starting the next guest cycle.

Bardi, J A (2010) *Hotel Front Office Management*, 5th edn, New York: John Wiley and Sons.
Kasavana, M L and Brooks, R M (2009) *Managing Front Office Operations*, East Lansing: EIAHLA.
Vallen, G K and Vallen, J J (2009) *Check-In Check-Out: Managing Hotel Operations*, Upper Saddle River: Pearson Prentice Hall.
Walker, J R (2010) *Introduction to Hospitality Management*, Upper Saddle River: Pearson Prentice Hall.

REFERENCE

Verginis, C (1999) 'Front office management', in Verginis, C S and Wood, R C (eds) *Accommodation Management: Perspectives for the International Hotel Industry*, London: Thomson. pp. 97–113.

Simen Kooi

Gastronomy and Haute Cuisine

See also: Beverages and beverage management; Food, beverage and restaurant management; Food production and service systems; Innovation in hospitality; The meal experience

Definitions of the term 'gastronomy' are numerous, varied and sometimes controversial, ranging from gastronomy as an ancient understanding of the rules or regulations ('nomos') of how to treat one's stomach (gastro) to a more contemporary consideration of being a self-directed and sometimes artistic act of preparing, presenting and consuming food (Richards, 2002). Here, the latter, very general, definition is adopted. In hospitality and hospitality management, however, the term 'gastronomy' is more narrowly associated in the Western world with French haute ('high') cuisine. France has a long tradition of regarding both gastronomy and haute cuisine as matters of economic and cultural significance, as a result of which established and elaborate culinary practices and aesthetics have globally influenced chefs and the hospitality industry for over 400 years, an influence recognized in 2010 when UNESCO (United Nations Educational, Scientific and Cultural Organization) added the gastronomic meal of the French to its 'Representative List of the Intangible Cultural Heritage of Humanity' (UNESCO, 2010).

Since the fifteenth century, led by the French, European gastronomy and haute cuisine has witnessed three distinct culinary eras: the *ancien régime*, classical cuisine and nouvelle cuisine. At present there is much debate over whether we are entering a fourth era, of molecular cuisine, or avant-garde cuisine. This debate centres mainly on whether avant-garde cuisine can be considered as a new and distinct culinary era in its own right, a question that will be revisited later in this discussion. Whatever the case, it is important to recognize that the emergence of distinct culinary eras does not lead to the extinction of previous practices. Rather, the development of gastronomy and haute cuisine is gradual and cumulative, leading to substantial diversity in that field of culinary endeavour where, many believe, cooking meets art.

FROM *ANCIEN RÉGIME* TO CLASSICAL CUISINE

Essentially, the development from the French *ancien régime* to the era of the classical cuisine was a development that liberated both chef and cuisine and changed gastronomy from a purely elitist activity into an activity that could be enjoyed by many. During the French *ancien régime* of the fifteenth to the eighteenth century, meals for aristocratic and other elites were organized as spectacular banquets. Hierarchy and social status were of great importance and chefs were treated as bondsmen (essentially 'property') of the ruling echelon. The French Revolution of 1789 marked the end of this period and fostered a less extravagant, but freer and more commercially focused type of gastronomy (Ferguson, 1998; Rao et al., 2003)

The opening of public restaurants also fostered the profession of gastronomic journalist. Together with chefs, these groups began to organize a formal set of principles of French haute cuisine. This process included, for example, ways in which menus were organized; standards for the use and combination of ingredients; rules of cooking; and the creation of a gastronomic meta-language – all of which reinforced the professional status of chefs (Ferguson, 1998; Fischler, 1989, 1993).

One of the most prominent pioneers of these organizing efforts was Antonin Carême (1784–1833) who propagated the notion of haute cuisine as both science and art. His ideas were further developed by a new and more self-confident breed of chef, including Georges Auguste Escoffier (1847–1935) and Prosper Montagné (1865–1948). Carême's books are considered by many as the original foundation of writing on haute cuisine and Escoffier's *Guide Culinaire*, published in 1903, is seen as the natural extension of Carême's texts. Escoffier's guide became the principal reference for chefs during the era of classical cuisine and is still widely respected and used today (cf. Mennell, 1985; Rao et al., 2003).

FROM CLASSICAL CUISINE TO NOUVELLE CUISINE

In May 1968 France experienced its most widespread social unrest since the 1789 Revolution mentioned earlier. Protests against the prevailing economic, political and social system created a significant impetus for change in many aspects of French life and culture. While, arguably, very little changed in the long term in the economic and political system, this upheaval did influence cultural developments, notably in film-making, literature and the arts more generally, including the art of cookery. At the heart of these changes was an emphasis on critical self-reflection and a re-thinking of old and established values. In the culinary world this led slowly but steadily to the development of a new style of cuisine – nouvelle cuisine – that crystallized as a distinct phenomenon in the early 1970s (cf. Rao et al., 2003).

The underlying philosophy of nouvelle cuisine was based on four values: truth, lightness, simplicity and imagination (e.g. Rao, 2009: 86). Chefs started to question established culinary conventions and created new dishes by using the concepts of transgression and acclimatization. Transgression meant that old cooking techniques were combined with new ingredients, or old cooking techniques were combined with old ingredients in hitherto unacceptable ways, such as combining fish with meat or salads with foie gras. Acclimatization, on the other hand, meant adopting foreign cooking traditions, in particular through employing exotic spices and sea-soning (Fischler, 1993; Rao et al., 2003). In this sense, nouvelle cuisine introduced a more contemporary and self-expressive way of cooking. Chefs like Paul Bocuse, the Troisgros brothers Pierre and Jean, Alain Chapel and Michel Guérard were at the forefront of the nouvelle cuisine movement and their styles of cooking echoed the new liberal, moral and 'anti-establishment' ideals of France. These chefs acted as role models for the whole culinary world, encouraging others to both break free from the strict classical era rules of Escoffier's *Guide Culinaire*, and allow a greater degree of interpretation and creativity to enter their cooking (see Wood, 1991).

FROM NOUVELLE CUISINE TO AVANT-GARDE CUISINE

During the period of the nouvelle cuisine, in creative terms independence from Escoffier's *Guide Culinaire* was a major driving-force for chefs. In 1998 the Spanish chef Ferran Adrià, for example, published his book *Los Secretos de El Bulli* (*The Secrets of El Bulli*) in which creativity is described as an element of culinary practice. Another root for creativity to become accepted as a concept in culinary practice was laid by the Oxford physicist Professor Nicholas Kurti, who was interested in applying science to solve problems in the kitchen. In 1988, together with physical chemist Hervé This, he founded a new branch of food science under the name of molecular and physical gastronomy (This, 2006a). This name derived from a series of workshops about the physics and chemistry of cooking run by both scientists. In 1998, however, Hervé This decided after the death of Nicholas Kurti to use the simpler term molecular gastronomy that he had always favoured (This, 2006b). The basic intention of molecular gastronomy is to better understand the 'chemistry and physics behind the preparation of any dish' in order to gain knowledge that can help to produce healthier, more attractive and better food (This, 2006a: 1062).

Unfortunately, the term molecular gastronomy became fashionably misused by both the media and some chefs who, straining after effect, pursued a form of largely excessive hyper-creativity that took shape in such dishes as strawberry risotto with salmon and tended to emphasize the aesthetic (especially the photogenic) appear-ance of food over taste. However, it is not unusual to find such excessiveness in the early development of novel phenomena. Indeed, excessiveness could also be witnessed at the beginning of the nouvelle cuisine movement. Therefore, at this point in time it remains to be seen whether the development of avant-garde cuisine marks the beginning of a new, fourth, culinary era in its own right.

CONCLUDING REMARKS

Throughout the history of haute cuisine chefs have exhibited a clear tendency towards achieving greater freedom in the ways they can express themselves creatively through their cooking. The earlier-mentioned decision by UNESCO to inscribe the French gastronomic meal is in part recognition of this process of creative culinary liberation. This recognition by the world of culture is an honour for the French, but has strong implications beyond that country's borders, opening further the doors for haute cuisine to establish itself as a publicly accepted form of art. In fact, some chefs strongly emphasize the artistic nature of haute cuisine by using food beyond the spheres of cooking. For example the Austrian chef Roland Trettl creates fashion (FashionFood) and images (CookArt) (Trettl, 2011) through the use of food and speaks of a 'symbiosis between cook and photographer'.

The academic study of food, and in particular the study of haute cuisine, has generated considerable strength of feeling as to whether such inquiry is academically legitimate. In some views, the aspiration to the status of 'artist' that some chefs clearly covet has been the source of much scepticism, as has the very idea that food can be an art form (Wood, 2000b). Much sociological analysis of the work of professional chefs has been characterized by an over-emphasis on aspects of consumption, media and culinary celebrity, notably in the form of television cookery programmes (see, for example, Chapter 11 of Ashley et al., 2004). This has been at the expense of detailed studies of the processes at work in creating culinary artefacts and experiences. The question as to whether food can be an art form and (some) chefs artists, does not seem likely to go away but may, in the future, become a both more contested and interesting topic.

FURTHER READING

Becker, H (1978) 'Arts and crafts', *American Journal of Sociology*, 83, 4: 862–88.

Blanck, J (2007) 'Molecular gastronomy: overview of a controversial food science discipline', *Journal of Agricultural and Food Information*, 8, 3: 77–85.

Cousins, J, O'Gorman, K and Stierand, M (2010) 'Molecular gastronomy: basis for a new culinary movement or modern day alchemy?', *International Journal of Contemporary Hospitality Management*, 22, 3: 399–415.

Kurti, N and Kurti, G (1988) *But the Crackling Is Superb: An Anthology on Food and Drink by Fellows and Foreign Members of the Royal Society*, Oxford: Institute of Physics Publishing.

REFERENCES

Adrià, F (1998) *Los secretos de El Bulli: Recetas, técnicas y reflexiones*, Barcelona: Altaya.

Ashley, B, Hollows, J, Jones, S and Taylor, B (2004) *Food and Cultural Studies*, London: Sage.

Ferguson, P (1998) 'A cultural field in the making: gastronomy in 19th century France', *American Journal of Sociology*, 104, 3: 597–641.

Fischler, C (1989) 'La cuisine selon Michelin', in Piault, F. (ed.) *Nourritures: Plaisirs et angoisses de la fourchette*, Paris: Autrement. pp. 42–51.

Fischler, C (1993) *L'Homnivore*, 2nd edn, Paris: Odile.

Mennell, S (1985) *All Manners of Food: Eating and Taste in England and France from the Middle Ages to the Present*, Oxford: Blackwell.

Rao, H (2009) *Market Rebels: How Activists Make or Break Radical Innovations*, Princeton, NJ: Princeton University Press.

Rao, H, Monin, P and Durand, R (2003) 'Institutional change in Toque Ville: nouvelle cuisine as an identity movement in French gastronomy', *American Journal of Sociology*, 108, 4: 795–843.

Richards, G (2002) 'Gastronomy: an essential ingredient in tourism production and consumption', in A-M Hjalager and G Richards (eds), *Tourism and Gastronomy*, London: Routledge. pp. 3–20.

This, H (2006a) 'Food for tomorrow?', *European Molecular Biology Organization Reports*, 7, 11: 1062–6.

This, H (2006b) *Molecular Gastronomy: Exploring the Science of Flavour*, New York: Columbia University Press.

Trettl, R (2011) www.rolandtrettl.com/oben.htm, last accessed 22 October 2011.

UNESCO (2010) The gastronomic meal of the French (Decision 5.COM 6.14), www.unesco.org/culture/ich/en/RL/00437, last accessed 24 August 2011.

Wood, R C (1991) 'The shock of the new: a sociology of nouvelle cuisine', *Journal of Consumer Studies and Home Economics*, 15, 4: 327–38.

Wood, R C (2000b) 'Is food an art form? Pretentiousness and pomposity in cookery', in Wood, R C (ed.) *Strategic Questions in Food and Beverage Management*, Oxford: Butterworth–Heinemann. pp. 153–71.

Marc B. Stierand

The Hospitality Finance Environment

See also: Income statements in hospitality finance; Industry structure and sectors in hospitality; Investing in hotels

There can be few industries that demonstrate such slavish devotion to the vagaries of the business cycle as the hospitality industry. As economic activity rises, so does occupancy and RevPAR (revenue per available room). Conversely, when the economic climate becomes gloomier, then what is now deemed 'non-essential' expenditure is reduced and the hospitality sector suffers accordingly. Fluctuations in the business cycle are accompanied by wild swings in RevPAR, as evidenced by the three economic recessions of the 1980s, 1990s and late 2000s, each of which saw falls in RevPAR in the region of 10% (PriceWaterhouseCoopers, 2011b: 12–13).

This discussion examines the nature of this volatility and considers ways in which the hospitality industry attempts to accommodate it. First, the concept of 'beta' is examined. This is a measure of how a company's stock price fluctuates relative to overall market indices such as the Dow Jones, Hang Seng or Nikkei. Then, the capital asset pricing model (CAPM) and the weighted average cost of capital (WACC) are examined. The CAPM and the WACC are techniques by which investors and firms incorporate this riskiness or volatility into their investment decisions. This will tell us the relationship between the beta and an investor's/company's decision making, revealing that a more volatile environment makes investors/companies look for a higher return on any potential investment opportunity in order to compensate for higher potential risk. Finally we shall discuss operating leverage, which refers to the ratio of fixed costs relative to total costs. We shall see that a high fixed cost ratio causes a company's profits to fluctuate more than if there are relatively higher variable costs.

THE BETA

At its simplest, the value of a share reflects assumptions by financial markets regarding a firm's future profitability. If there is a general belief that prospects are good, more shares will be bought and the price will rise. If, however, the market is relatively pessimistic about the firm's future prospects, more shares will be sold and the price will fall. Beta is a measure of a company's risk relative to that of the overall market. The share price of a company with a beta of 1 will closely conform to the fluctuations of the stock market in which it is traded (for example the Dow Jones Industrial Average). Generally speaking, a 1% rise in the Dow Jones will cause the share price of a company with a beta of 1 to increase by 1%. A fall in the Dow will bring about a similar drop in the firm's share price.

If a beta is less than 1, the company trades in a relatively stable environment, and their goods or services are bought more or less regardless of economic circumstances. At the time of writing (early 2012), PepsiCo's beta is 0.52 and Walmart's 0.25, reflecting the fact that their products are relatively impervious to fluctuating income levels. Indeed, relative to the Dow Jones, Walmart's share price is, traditionally, relatively stable and in the positive economic circumstances prior to Autumn 2007, the Dow significantly outperformed Walmart. However, during the economic crisis of 2008–9, Walmart appeared relatively immune, even rising for a period of some 12 months from late 2007 as money poured into Walmart shares, seeking a safe haven from the carnage of the global stock markets. In contrast to this, the hotel industry does not operate in a particularly stable environment. As stated earlier, RevPAR follows a much more dramatic path and this is reflected in the betas of the larger hotel chains: Marriott is 1.48, IHG 1.61, while Starwood comes in at a whopping 1.99.

CAPITAL ASSET PRICING MODEL (CAPM)

Understanding the practical application of beta is aided by knowledge of two concepts: the capital asset pricing model (CAPM) and the weighted average cost of capital. The CAPM helps us understand much of the reasoning behind a firm's decision as to whether or not to invest in new projects by indicating what return potential investors would expect to make from a project – given the particular firm's beta – before they can be induced to part with their money. The key formula for the CAPM is: $r_e = r_f + \beta(r_m - r_f)$ where:

1 r_e = is expected return on the proposed investment;
2 r_f = is risk-free return;
3 β = beta; and
4 r_m = is overall market return.

The best example of a risk-free return (2 above) is government bonds, otherwise known as treasury bills. The potential investor could spend the same sum of money on the purchase of government bonds and enjoy a low, but safe, return every year for the life of the bond. The current return on a ten-year treasury bill is in the region of 3.5% per annum. The overall market return (4 above) refers to the average increase in a composite stock market index such as the FTSE 100 or Dow Jones over a prolonged period of time. Somewhat surprisingly given the volatility of recent times, the average return for the last 90 years or so is in the region of 11% per annum.

In order to induce investors to part with funds, a hotel chain with a beta of 1.60 would have to convince them that they could expect to realize a return of: $r_e = r_f + \beta(r_m - r_f)$. Working through the formula, this gives us $r_e = 3.5 + 1.6(11 - 3.5)$ which yields $r_e = 15.5\%$. So in this scenario, investors would require an expected return of 15.5% to induce them to part with their cash. To put this in context, they would only have to expect a return in the region of 5.4% to invest in Walmart which, it will be recalled, has a beta in the region of 0.25: $r_e = 3.5 + 0.25(11 - 3.5)$, yielding an r_e of 5.375%. It is hardly surprising that in tough economic times a lot of money market cash flees from the more risky, high beta investments into safer havens such as government bonds, Walmart and PepsiCo.

WEIGHTED AVERAGE COST OF CAPITAL (WAAC)

The weighted average cost of capital (WACC) is also known as the 'hurdle rate' as it tells us the level of projected return an investment must clear in order to be deemed viable by a company. Consider a hotel company with a debt equity ratio of 0.4 – that is, out of every €1,000 of borrowed capital, €400 comes from the banks and €600 is raised from shareholders. Let us also assume that interest on the bank loans is 7% while dividend payments (to the shareholders) are the equivalent of 15.5% interest (remember the return on equity we calculated for the CAPM above). The WACC equals $(r_{debt} \times \%_{debt}) + (r_{equity} \times \%_{equity})$ so WACC = $(0.07 \times 0.4) + (0.155 \times 0.6)$ which yields WACC = 12.1%.

This means our hotel company will be looking for a return on investment of over 12% before seriously considering committing to a new project. Potential investors require a high average return in order to compensate them for possible times of economic hardship. In tough economic times this level of return may be hard to find. On the other hand, Walmart, our low beta example, given the same debt equity ratio, would have a WACC of 6.025%, i.e. $(0.07 \times 0.4) + (0.05375 \times 0.6)$. Our low beta firm would happily consider any appropriate project that had a potential return of only a little over 6%. Clearly this hurdle rate is not nearly such an impediment to investment as that confronting our hotel chain.

OPERATING LEVERAGE

The concept of operating leverage (not to be confused with financial leverage) refers to a firm's ratio of fixed to variable costs. If a firm has high fixed costs and relatively low variable costs it is said to have high operating leverage. Conversely, if the firm has low fixed costs relative to variable costs, it has low operating leverage. Companies with high operating leverage, i.e. relatively high fixed costs, tend to have more volatile profits in the face of fluctuating revenues, while those with a lower operating leverage have more stable profits. If we consider two medium-sized hotel chains, one with a high (Firm A) and one with a low (Firm B) operating leverage, we can see the difference.

	Firm A:	Firm B:
Revenue =	€120m	€120m
Total costs =	€100m	€100m
Of which fixed costs (FC) =	€80m	€30m
Of which variable costs (VC) =	€20m	€70m
Profit =	€20m	€20m

In one year each company sells 1 million hotel rooms at an average price of €120 per night, generating profits of €20m. For Firm A, variable costs work out at €20 per guest (€20m/1m rooms), while for Firm B they are €70. From the relative fixed and variable cost figures, we can see that Firm A has high operating leverage while Firm B is low. Assume that in the following year both companies experienced a fall in revenues to €96 million reflecting a drop in rooms sold from 1m to 800,000. We keep the average price and variable costs constant.

	Firm A:	Firm B:
Revenue =	€96m	€96m
Total Costs =	€96m	€86m
Of which fixed costs (FC) =	€80m	€30m
Of which variable costs (VC) =	€16m	€56m
Profit	€0	€10m

We can see that, given the same fall in revenues, Firm A now breaks even, making neither a profit nor a loss, while Firm B, though also experiencing hard times, still manages to turn a profit of €10m. Why should this be? Think of fixed costs as an indigestible lump that refuses to go away. Regardless of a company's fortunes, it still has to pay property taxes and insurance, as well as the mortgage or rent and sundry other expenses. Firm A has to pay €80m per year irrespective of how many rooms it sells in a year, whereas Firm B has to find only €30m. Put in the context of breakeven Firm A has to sell 800,000 rooms per year in order to break even, while Firm B has to sell only 600,000, i.e. Break-even number of rooms = Fixed costs ÷ (Price − Variable cost per room). For Firm A by substitution this is break even rooms = €80m ÷ (€120 − €20) = 800,000 and for Firm B it is Break-even number of rooms = €30m ÷ (€120 − €70) = 600,000. This puts Firm A in a relatively vulnerable position. With its current cost and pricing structure it must sell 800,000 rooms in any given year before it can think of making a profit, whereas Firm B is in the money after selling only 600,000 rooms.

CONCLUDING REMARKS

The major, practical, consequence of perception of risk in the hospitality financial environment in recent years, and not least the high level of operating leverage, has been the tendency for hotel chains to divest themselves of their property portfolios in an effort to eradicate wild fluctuations in profits from one year to the next. In essence, many hotel companies now confine themselves to managing hotels, the land and buildings of which are owned by others. For example, one of the world's leading hotel companies, Four Seasons, does not own hotels but manages them according to strict standards (Segal, 2009, see also Story, 2007). This approach has been complemented by expansion strategies that entail a hotel company franchising or directly managing properties under a management contract, properties that are, however, constructed and owned by others. In a 2012 interview, Sir David Michels, former group Chief Executive of Hilton, comments: 'Hotels have got more numerous and larger, and now the City of London and Wall Street prefer hotel companies to manage hotels rather than own them …[.] In the vast majority of cases, large hotels are now owned by wealthy individuals, pension funds, banks, investment companies or property houses' (Walker, 2012: 24–5). The concepts of beta, the CAPM, the WACC and operating leverage offer some insight into how the state of affairs described by Michels has come about.

FURTHER READING

Brealey, R A, Myers, S C and Marcus, A J (2009) *Fundamentals of Corporate Finance*, 6th edn, New York: McGraw-Hill.

REFERENCES

PriceWaterhouseCoopers (2011b) *UK Hotels Forecast 2011 and 2012: How big a party for hotels in 2012?* www.pwc.co.uk/en_UK/uk/assets/pdf/uk-hotels-forecast-2011-2012.pdf, last accessed 10 March 2012.

key concepts in hospitality management

Segal, D (2009) 'Pillow fights at the Four Seasons', www.nytimes.com/2009/06/28/business/global/28four.html, last accessed 10 March 2012.

Story, L (2007) 'Blackstone to buy Hilton Hotels for $26 billion', www.nytimes.com/2007/07/04/business/04deal.html, last accessed 28 August 2012.

Walker, B (2012) 'The Institute's new President', *Hospitality*, Issue 25, Spring.

John Mackillop

Hospitality and Hospitality Management

See also: Hospitality management education; Industry structure and sectors in hospitality; Service, service industries and the hospitality sector

People intuitively understand what 'hospitality' and 'management' are because they have experienced both as recipients and practitioners. It is not difficult to recognize when we provide or receive hospitality or when we manage our own lives and activities or are managed by others. This implies that if a wide range of people were asked to describe or define the meanings of hospitality and management there would be considerable agreement in their responses. Unfortunately, evidence tends to suggest that this contention may be illusory. Two basic perspectives have been used to define hospitality's nature and meaning. One may be described as the 'behavioural' perspective. The second may be described as the 'industry' or 'provider' view.

BEHAVIOURAL DEFINITIONS OF HOSPITALITY

Definitions rooted in this tradition focus on the types and nature of the behaviour(s) exhibited by those providing hospitality for others. This is reflected in dictionary definitions of hospitality. The *Oxford English Dictionary* defines hospitality as: 'the act or practice of being hospitable; the reception and entertainment of guests, visitors, or strangers, with liberality and goodwill', and the *Collins Concise English Dictionary* as: 'kindness in welcoming strangers or guests'. These definitions may accord with everyday notions of what hospitality entails, but are one-dimensional, vague and could equally be applied to other types of human activity and interaction that would not normally be regarded as constituting the existence or provision of hospitality. Nevertheless they indicate and emphasize one important dimension of hospitality, namely the type(s) of behaviour necessary for hospitality to exist. The existence of hospitable behaviour, or 'hospitableness', is a vital prerequisite for the provision of hospitality in its fullest sense because other components of hospitality that people might experience could be seen as ordinary, general or even inhospitable in the absence of hospitable behaviour from the provider.

However, the existence of hospitable behaviour alone is not a sufficient condition to claim that hospitality exists. Consider the following examples to illustrate these points. Most people would associate hospitality with a place where food, drink, or accommodation and possibly some form of entertainment is provided. Being invited for dinner at a friend's house, going to a bar for a drink or to a restaurant for a meal would all be reasonably expected to involve hospitable behaviour in the delivery of the product/s and experiences these situations embody. On the other hand, food, drink and accommodation are provided to prisoners in prisons but no one would claim these are provided in a hospitable manner or environment. Therefore, one might conclude that while the more physical, tangible elements of hospitality may be *necessary* for hospitality to exist they are certainly not *sufficient* for it to do so.

Alternatively, while hospitable behaviour is a necessary condition for hospitality to exist it is not, in and of itself, sufficient. People can behave hospitably in a wide variety of circumstances that have nothing to do with the provision of hospitality. It is quite possible to be welcomed, treated kindly and in a friendly manner, to be given respect and shown goodwill, to be looked after, in the workplace, in shops, in the street, in hospitals, on a train, an airplane or bus, or in a sports centre or entertainment complex. However, few, if any, would conclude that, what most people would define as hospitality is being provided or received in these circumstances.

INDUSTRY/PROVIDER DEFINITIONS OF HOSPITALITY

Industry/provider definitions emphasize the physical, tangible elements of hospitality. It is common in economics and business to define types of economic activity on the basis of the technologies and processes used to supply particular end products. In everyday parlance reference to the car, computer or banking industries is a simple and easily understood way of differentiating between these types of economic activity. Historically, the same approach has been taken to defining the 'hospitality industry' and, from this, to defining hospitality itself. This has proved to be a flawed process because hospitality constitutes a far more amorphous collection of commercial and non-commercial activities. Unlike many other forms of economic activity, hospitality can be provided in non-commercial contexts (within the home for example), whilst also existing as the primary activity of a business or as very much a secondary one. Because of the wide variety of forms it can take, and the range of environments and circumstances in which hospitality can be provided, it is not as easily delimited as many other forms of economic activity although, constituting as they do reasonably homogeneous business activities, it may be sensible to talk of a hotel industry, a restaurant industry, a bar or pub industry, or even a fast food or catering industry.

What, then, is hospitality? Hospitable behaviour is one dimension; certain physical products (food, drink and accommodation) constitute another; hospitality also has a spatial dimension because it occurs within a physical location or place; and a temporal dimension that is manifested in the types of occasion when it is provided. Human interactions entailing hospitality are also usually entered into voluntarily and are 'temporary' in nature – there is no transfer of ownership of any kind of resource or asset for future use or consumption as there are in many other consumer transactions. Thus, hospitality is essentially a rental or leasing transaction. Whether it occurs in a commercial or non-commercial context, the recipient is given temporary permission to occupy a physical locality, for example a seat in a restaurant or someone's home, or a hotel bedroom within which they receive the behavioural and physical elements of the hospitality being provided and pay 'rent' to the owner of the space – this rent being, for example, the room rate or restaurant bill in a commercial context, and the obligations of reciprocity in a non-commercial context.

With these dimensions in mind and following from Brotherton (1999), we can say that hospitality is a contemporaneous delivery-consumption exchange, entered into voluntarily, that generates mutual benefits and obligations on the part of its participants and which only occurs discontinuously within the contexts of a physical place and an occasion. The existence of hospitable behaviour and provision of accommodation and food and/or drink are the features that distinguish and differentiate hospitality from other types of exchange.

HOSPITALITY MANAGEMENT

It is self-evident that we have to manage how we conduct our lives and, invariably, have others managing aspects of our lives within particular contexts. In both respects there are certain core considerations and activities. Almost a century ago Henri Fayol (1930) proposed five generic, core management roles: planning, organizing, coordinating, controlling and commanding (or leading). If this is true of management *per se* then it is true of any context within which management takes place, including that of hospitality – i.e. it is reasonable to conclude that the core aspects of management and managing are generic in nature. Therefore, managing the production and provision of hospitality in any context involves a combination of these five elements. Naturally, within both the academic management and business worlds, the relative weight that should be attached to each of these elements is debated. It is equally self-evident that not all management and managers are the same. Although the basic principles and elements endure across differing managerial contexts, additional specialist knowledge, skills and experience may be required to be an effective manager. For example, a financial manager would need to have specialist financial knowledge and skills to be able to function effectively. The question therefore arises as to what, if any, similar specialist attributes are required by hospitality managers?

Any answer is necessarily ambiguous. There are two issues here: the nature of the specialism and the level of the managerial task. It can be argued that a shop and a restaurant are different types of business requiring different types of manager. It is equally possible to contend that they are both businesses with many things in common. Therefore a good shop manager could be a good restaurant manager, and vice versa. The issue centres upon whether it is necessary for a manager to have specialist skills and experience relating to the context s/he is operating in or whether managerial skills and experience are generic and therefore transferable between differing contexts. Some argue that such specifics are desirable, because they supposedly provide the manager with a deeper understanding of the nature of the context in which s/he operates and this, in turn, makes the manager more effective. Others take the view that although the underlying processes and dynamics in any context may differ in content and scale they are essentially the same and hence require the same generic managerial skills. In short, a good manager can be a good manager wherever s/he is managing.

From a functional perspective the transferability of specialist skills relating to the functional areas of a business, for example finance, marketing and sales, human resource management and, in hospitality, food and beverage and accommodation management, are well documented. Functional specialists are valued for their skills in that function and hence may move from company to company across differing industrial and commercial boundaries. Indeed there are many finance, marketing and human resource managers employed in hospitality businesses who have come to these posts from other industries. Similarly, for example, food and beverage managers may move between different types of food and beverage contexts but this type of contextual specialism is more limited than that of the generic function.

On the issue of managerial level it is probably fair to say that, at departmental, unit and possibly area/regional level, many companies view context-specific skills and experience as highly desirable, although by the very nature of the managerial roles these levels embody, specialist skills are starting to become less important because the managerial context is now much broader in scope and larger in scale. These are features that require, at the very least, a re-ordering of managerial emphasis, priorities and action. At higher, corporate/executive levels some would contend that the necessity for managers to have a context-specific background becomes less important. Indeed, some suggest it is a positive disadvantage because it may encourage insularity, and there are certainly many examples of hospitality companies employing senior managers with backgrounds in different industries.

Management can thus be considered as both generic and context/level specific. Does this mean hospitality management is unique or different from management in other contexts or essentially the same? It is both. Clearly Fayol's basic management elements are context-independent or generic. In this sense management *per se* is generic and therefore the management of hospitality is no different to management in other contexts. However, the level of management holds implications for the relative emphasis and priority of Fayol's elements. For example, the elements of commanding and leading assume greater importance for senior executives, whereas organizing and controlling have a similar priority for departmental and unit level managers. Similarly, the 'additionality' of specialist hospitality knowledge/skills may be helpful, if not entirely necessary, for managing hospitality operations.

CONCLUDING REMARKS

All of the above said, it may be reasonable to conclude that the relatively transitory and context-dependent nature of the hospitality encounter and experience can be enhanced by the personal and experiential insight and skills of managers who are both aware of this feature and capable of creating memorable (for the right reasons) hospitality experiences for their guests or customers. Good managers can perform effectively on Fayol's elements in almost any context but to excel in the management of commercial hospitality may just take a little something extra.

FURTHER READING

Brotherton, B (2005) 'The nature of hospitality: customer perceptions and implications', *Tourism and Hospitality Planning and Development*, 2, 3: 139–53.
Brotherton, B and Wood, R C (2000) 'Defining hospitality and hospitality management', in Lashley, C and Morrison, A (eds) *In Search of Hospitality – Theoretical Perspectives and Debates*, Oxford: Butterworth–Heinemann. pp. 134–56.
Brotherton, B and Wood, R C (2008b) 'The nature and meanings of hospitality', in Brotherton, B and Wood, R C (eds) *The Sage Handbook of Hospitality Management*, London: Sage. pp. 37–61.

REFERENCES

Brotherton, B (1999) 'Towards a definitive view of the nature of hospitality and hospitality management', *International Journal of Contemporary Hospitality Management*, 11, 4: 165–73.
Fayol, H (1930) *Industrial and General Administration*, London: Pitman.

Bob Brotherton

Hospitality Management Education

See also: Hospitality and hospitality management; Industry structure and sectors in hospitality; Service, service industries and the hospitality sector

hospitality management education

Hospitality management education is that form of post-school educational provision preparing people for management careers in the hospitality industry as opposed to careers in any of the mainly functional occupational specializations of the sector (for example those of engineer and chef). Initial education in hospitality management is increasingly at the 'first degree', bachelor's level, although this is not invariably the case. Those who graduate from courses in hospitality management and remain and develop within the industry may in time reasonably expect to achieve unit manager and/or strategic management positions, or become specialized in some key functional management role, for example human resources, sales and marketing.

Hospitality management education has a long and variable history. The oldest schools dedicated to hotel management were founded, respectively, in Lausanne, Switzerland, in 1893 and at Cornell University in the USA in 1922. In Britain, creation of The Scottish Hotel School, in Glasgow in 1944, was an attempt to fuse the emerging disciplines of management with the practical skills of schools such as Lausanne (Gee, 1994). Incorporated into the University of Strathclyde in 1964 on that institution's formation, The Scottish Hotel School was, however, closed by the University in 2009. The reputations of the Lausanne and Cornell schools endure but many others have developed similarly high international profiles, not least those in The Hague, Netherlands, and in Hong Kong (the Polytechnic University). Of equal note is the observation that, for many, a single country, Switzerland, with its myriad number of (mainly private) hotel schools, is believed, whether accurately or not, to represent a benchmark for excellence in international hospitality education.

Contemporary provision of higher-level hospitality management education around the globe for the most part follows one of two models (Brotherton and Wood, 2008a). Whether in private or public sector, the first model is where a hotel management school is part of a larger educational organization, usually a university, and emphasis is placed on both the teaching of students and the conduct and dissemination of academic research. This model is found extensively in the UK, Australia and New Zealand, where the majority of institutions are, in fact, in the public or 'state' sector – that is, higher education is funded by government (in America provision is distributed over a range of institutions including public and private universities and colleges, see Barrows, 1999). Another feature of these systems is that, often, many of the institutions offering hospitality management education have only relatively recently become universities, having previously had the status of polytechnics or colleges.

The second model of delivery is principally teaching-focused and is mainly found in the private sector alone. Schools in the second category often partner with foreign universities and colleges who validate their diploma and degree programmes. Countries such as the UK have relatively little private provision whereas, as already noted, in Switzerland it is extensive. Other countries evidence 'mixed' provision, for example Malaysia and India. Elsewhere, hospitality education has been largely excluded from 'state' universities, being viewed and confined as a subject to be taught in vocational colleges (whether private or public) as, for example, in France (Lominé, 2003).

HOSPITALITY MANAGEMENT EDUCATION IN 'TRADITIONAL' HIGHER EDUCATION INSTITUTIONS

Within 'traditional' higher education institutions, hospitality management currently faces two pressures. *First,* and especially in the English-speaking academic world where research as a measure of performance has become an obsession, the quantity and quality of hospitality research output is frequently viewed (on the basis of often questionable criteria, it must be noted) as inferior to that of other, related, subjects. This has led in the UK and elsewhere (see O'Mahony, 2009) to many separate university hotel management schools being closed and/or merged into other units, notably business schools (for a more detailed discussion of these issues see Brotherton and Wood, 2008a).

Secondly, there persists in some quarters a sentiment that hospitality management education really has no business being provided in a traditional higher education context as it is a form of specialist professional training rather than an academic discipline. Of course, hospitality management has experienced debates similar to those in several other fields about whether it is a 'discipline' (and rather more importantly an 'academic' discipline) or a subject, or a field of study. Such debates have tended towards sterility except where they grapple with core conceptual matters. In the last decade or so there has been modest discussion of the nature of hospitality and hospitality management (see Brotherton and Wood, 2008a; Pizam and Shani, 2009), but this has had little impact on the subject area as a whole. Indeed, there has been some resistance to the notion that the subject field requires such conceptual reflection at all (Jones and Lockwood, 2008).

Brotherton and Wood (2008a) identify four reasons as to why hospitality management experiences difficulties within a traditional higher education setting. *First* is the career status of the hospitality industry, which is generally low because of the sector's reputation for low-quality conditions of employment, especially in terms of work–life balance, and the fact that in certain countries at least the hospitality industry has a poor record of retaining and developing graduates (Wood, 1997). *Second* is the expense of providing hospitality education in traditional higher education environments. For much of its history, the view has been taken by educators and endorsed by employers that the credibility of hospitality management education requires a strong practical component to programmes, normally reflected in the requirement for at least a training restaurant and kitchen as part of a school's provision of facilities. This is often seen by universities as an undesirable expense despite the acceptance of the need for laboratories in the natural sciences. *Thirdly,* industry support for advanced hospitality education in many countries has been and remains highly variable. There has been a persistent unease in the relationship between education and industry, the latter feeling that university graduates in hospitality are ill equipped with the practical skills the sector requires. The intellectual ambitions of traditional higher education institutes are such that there is reluctance to place too much emphasis on such skill development as opposed to 'more academic' content. The *final* reason why hospitality management education fares poorly in the traditional higher education sector is

hospitality management education

65

the rather more intangible intellectual and other forms of snobbery that it faces, probably because of hospitality's historical associations with (domestic) service. As Brotherton and Wood (2008a: 10–11) note: 'There can be no reasonably well attuned hospitality academic who has not encountered the astonishment of the uninitiated in comments of the "You teach students to be waiters – in a university?" kind'. Though existence of such snobbery is difficult to document empirically (and, of course, equally difficult to refute), it is a phenomenon to which we should remain alert.

THE CHALLENGE OF THE PRIVATE SECTOR

Despite the generally accepted global economic significance of the interdependent tourism, transport and hospitality sectors, it can be seen that the presence of hospitality management in traditional higher-level educational institutions is both contentious and contested. In contrast, there is an *impression* that private sector provision is thriving although the research evidence is far from categorical on the point.

There are at least two plausible reasons to think that the private school sector may become the dominant provider of hospitality management education in the future. *First*, any decline of hospitality management within traditional public higher education is likely to benefit private school enrolments if demand for student places remains unchanged or increases. In the developing world and emerging economies, the inability of an increasingly cash-strapped public sector to meet demand for hospitality education when combined with the growth of the moderately affluent middle-class (from which most students of hospitality management are drawn) may, in the short term at least, continue to ensure a steady stream of students from these countries to overseas schools. At the same time, however, any growth in demand for hospitality education is also likely to stimulate the creation of home-based private sector institutions (a notable phenomenon, for example, in India, see Gupta and Wood, 2008). Since most developing and emerging economies enjoy cost advantages over mature economies, this may, in the long term, lead to declining demand for hospitality management education in the latter. Further, many developing and emerging economies place considerable emphasis upon the importance of formal educational credentials, even for access to what would be regarded in the developed world as relatively modest labour market positions. Because the state sector cannot satisfy the volume of demand for such qualifications, private sector provision is the only alternative, at least in the short term.

Secondly here, private schools, rarely having the requirement or desire to undertake research, can potentially focus resources more effectively on pedagogic processes, not least those valued, or perceived to be valued, by students and potential employers. A well-worn ideological objection to this view is that education is about more than graduate employability. Few would dispute this view (despite its popularity with many students!), but there are no persuasive reasons for accepting that teaching-led vocational relevance based on sound pedagogy is somehow inferior to research-led curricula, at least not in undergraduate programmes.

CONCLUDING REMARKS

To summarize, whilst higher level hospitality management education is facing difficult times in this, the early part of the twenty-first century, it is perhaps worth observing as a corrective to unnecessary pessimism that most of these difficulties are not being experienced in a uniform manner save in the public sector education provision of some countries (Barrows and Johan, 2008). Elsewhere, especially in developing and emerging economies, hospitality management education gives a distinct impression of growth, social and academic acceptance, and increasing complexity – all entirely appropriate to the context of a huge and vibrant industry that increasingly touches all our lives.

FURTHER READING

Barrows, C W and Johan, N (2008) 'Hospitality management education', in Brotherton, B and Wood, R C (eds) *The Sage Handbook of Hospitality Management*, London: Sage. pp. 146–62.

Brotherton, R and Wood; R C (2008b) 'The nature and meanings of hospitality', in Brotherton, B and Wood, R C (eds) *The Sage Handbook of Hospitality Management*, London: Sage. pp. 37–61.

Wood, R C (2004a) 'Hospitality education: they think it's all over … it is now', *The Hospitality Review*, 6, 2: 16–18.

Wood, R C (2004b) 'Public sorrow, private joy', *The Hospitality Review*, 6, 4: 23–7.

REFERENCES

Barrows, C W (1999) 'Introduction to hospitality education', in Barrows, C W and Bosselman, R H (eds) *Hospitality Management Education*, New York: Haworth Press. pp. 1–20.

Barrows, C W and Johan, N (2008) 'Hospitality management education', in Brotherton, B and Wood, R C (eds) *The Sage Handbook of Hospitality Management*, London: Sage. pp. 146–62.

Brotherton, B and Wood, R C (2008a) 'Editorial introduction', in Brotherton, B and Wood, R C (eds) *The Sage Handbook of Hospitality Management*, London: Sage. pp. 1–34.

Gee, D A C (1994) 'The Scottish Hotel School – the first fifty years', in Seaton, A V, Jenkins, C L, Wood, R C, Dieke, P U C, Bennett, M M, MacLellan, L R and Smith, R (eds) *Tourism: the State of the Art*, Chichester: Wiley. pp. xvi to xxiii.

Gupta, S and Wood, R C (2008) 'Human resource challenges in the Indian hotel sector', *Asian Journal of Tourism and Hospitality Research*, 2, 2: 87–96.

Jones, P and Lockwood, A (2008) 'Researching hospitality management: it's OK to use the 'm' word', *The Hospitality Review*, 10, 3: 26–30.

Lominé, L L (2003) 'Hospitality, leisure, sport and tourism in higher education in France', *Journal of Hospitality, Leisure, Sport and Tourism Education*, 2, 1: 105–12.

O'Mahony, B (2009) 'University kitchen nightmares enter a new ERA', *The Hospitality Review*, 11, 4: 5–7.

Pizam, A and Shani, A (2009) 'The nature of the hospitality industry: present and future managers' perspectives', *Anatolia*, 20, 1: 134–50.

Wood, R C (1997) *Working in Hotels and Catering*, 2nd edn, London: Thomson.

Roy C. Wood

Hotels, Hospitality and Sustainability

See also: Design for hotels; Innovation in hospitality

Sustainable development is usually defined as development that meets the needs of present generations without compromising those of future generations expressed in the so-called 'three Ps' of sustainability: people, planet and profit. In its most naive form this implies that industries should, as far as possible, pursue their business in a manner that ensures they create a healthy profit whilst simultaneously seeking to minimize harm to people and the environment. Achieving sustainable behaviour is problematic, not least in a business where the paramount concern tends to be the potential (negative) effect of every activity on the 'bottom line', i.e. profit. This problem is made more complex by the very real issues entailed in establishing criteria related to the 'three Ps' that can differentiate between sustainable and less sustainable types of behaviour.

SUSTAINABILITY

Sustainability is an important social issue. Changes in the behaviour of 'nature' as a result of human action over the centuries have led to concerns about rising carbon dioxide (CO_2) emissions and sea levels, climate change and decreasing biodiversity. Although specific details are often scientifically controversial, there is agreement that specific actions by individuals, groups, companies, industries and nations can seriously affect the world we live in now as well as for many years to come. Making a contribution to decreasing, minimising or even solving these problems is usually referred to as being environmentally friendly, environmentally responsible, or acting sustainably.

Sustainability, however, refers to more than just 'saving' the environment. The 1987 report *Our Common Future* by the United Nations World Commission on Environment and Development (UNWCED), often referred to as the Brundtland Report, is seen by many as the official launch of sustainability as a concept. The assignment given to this commission by the United Nations Secretary-General in 1983 was to develop 'a global agenda for change' (UNWCED, 1987: 11) and seek 'ways in which global development can be put on a sustainable path into the 21st Century' (UNWCED, 1987: 23). The UNWCED defined sustainable development as 'development that meets the needs of the present without compromising the ability of future generations to meet their own needs. It contains [...] two key concepts: (1) the concept of "needs", in particular the essential needs of the world's poor [...]; and (2) the idea of limitations imposed by [...] the environment's ability to meet present and future needs' (UNWCED, 1987: 54).

Sustainability, therefore, encompasses environmental, social and utility components. Sustainable development is closely linked to the so-called 'triple bottom line' (Elkington, 1997), the logic of measuring organizational success based on a combination of economic, ecological and social criteria. Nowadays, this triple bottom line is often simply referred to as people, planet, profit, with the latter sometimes replaced by 'prosperity' to show that profit is not necessarily expressed in money value. Early opinion was that sustainability requirements (and notably the environmental aspects of sustainability) and business goals were irreconcilable (Walley and Whitehead, 1994). Now, both champions of sustainability and business managers seem to agree that win–win situations can actually be created (Dean and McMullen, 2007; Geyer and Jackson, 2004; Meisner Rosen, 2001). Success stories in manufacturing industry have often come about as a result of applying well-known and widely available tools from the quality management field to develop 'best practices' in reducing waste and losses, thereby contributing to companies' ecological and economic performance.

SUSTAINABILITY AND THE HOTEL AND HOSPITALITY INDUSTRY

While some industries have made progress regarding the triple bottom line, one could argue that the hospitality sector is lagging behind. Some hospitality industry leaders are sceptical about the prospects for achieving greater sustainability in the industry. Bohdanowicz (2005: 188) studied European hoteliers' attitudes towards addressing environmental issues and concluded that 'environmental stewardship has taken a backseat to other operational concerns in many cases'. One hotelier who participated in the survey commented: 'The environment is important for tourism, but not in the centre of Paris' (Bohdanowicz, 2005: 192).

Nevertheless, there are examples of hospitality companies that have managed to incorporate sustainable practices in their business processes. One of the earliest instances of a company that addressed sustainability on a corporate level and implemented sustainable practices leading to financial success is Scandic Hotels (Bader, 2005; Bohdanowicz, et al., 2005; Goodman, 2000). In the early 1990s Scandic was on the verge of financial collapse. To save the company, two business principles were introduced: (1) decentralized management and (2) sustainable development. Scandic introduced sustainability as a core business principle in all its strategic thinking and many of the innovative 'sustainability practices' subsequently implemented resemble the type of solutions and innovations that we usually see in manufacturing industry. These included technological innovations (such as low-flush toilets and special shower heads to save water) and energy-saving equipment (such as special systems for heating, ventilation and air conditioning). Scandic also sought to create partnerships with employees, guests and suppliers focusing specifically on sustainable practices, enabling them, among other things, to create rooms almost exclusively constructed and furnished with recyclable and eco-labelled materials. These eco-labels, of which there are many different ones, represent labelling systems applied by manufacturers and suppliers to inform customers of the fact that those materials comply with specific standards with respect to sustainability.

Scandic Hotels is not the only example of sustainable practices being applied in the hospitality industry. The Orchid Hotel in Mumbai, India, has introduced and maintained a number of sustainable practices, such as water and energy usage-reducing technologies and equipment, and a number of other measures to create a 'five star eco-friendly' hotel (www.orchidhotel.com). Within the conference centre sector, the Sånga Säby Conference and Study Centre in Sweden is one of the leading hospitality businesses when it comes to applying renewable energy sources, such as marine and geothermal energy for the heating and cooling of buildings (www.sanga-saby.se). Other early adopters have shown how comprehensive environmental management programmes, waste reduction and recycling schemes and employee environmental education programmes can be implemented successfully (Enz and Siguaw, 1999). Currently, many established major hotel brands are announcing environmental programmes, and new hotel brands often stress their environmental friendliness (Butler, 2008). What is more, in recent years we have witnessed the rise of ecotourism – a specific niche market that focuses on maintaining or protecting the integrity of the land and people visited (Butcher, 2008) – which has been accompanied by a growing number of so-called eco-hotels and eco-resorts to accommodate tourists 'sustainably'. However, the nature of ecotourism and its contribution to sustainable development has been questioned (Butcher, 2008; Ryan and Stewart, 2009).

A discussion on sustainability within the hospitality industry would not be complete without mentioning towels. Not washing towels and bed linen every day saves energy, water and (pollution caused by) cleaning detergent. Throughout the hospitality industry this is probably the most commonly applied sustainable practice, with hotels placing information cards in guest rooms urging them to consider the effects of the laundering of towels on the environment. Interestingly, relatively little is known about how effective such general appeals to guests' environmental conscience are, although a study by Goldstein et al. (2008) shows that guests actually respond as if socially connected to other guests that have used the room before them: if other guests have not had their towels washed every day and new guests are aware of this, this is the factor that will most likely convince new guests to do the same. In other words, it is not so much the option offered to the guest, but much more the way in which this is communicated that determines whether guests will behave in a specific way and choose the sustainable alternative.

SUSTAINABILITY, HOSPITALITY AND THE FUTURE

The preceding discussion shows that the hospitality industry can introduce sensible and pragmatic environmental measures. It is therefore surprising that these, and other strategies, are not more widespread. One possible explanation for this lies in the largely undeveloped relationship between knowledge of sustainable practices and knowledge of the benefits such practices can bring in terms of environmental friendliness and business performance. As reported by Scanlon (2007: 722), currently 'many [...] operators and engineers [in the hospitality industry] are still unaware of the savings to be realized' by implementing sustainable practices. Furthermore, the adoption of environmental measures, especially in the small hospitality firms which dominate the industry, is, according to Tzschentke, Kirk and Lynch (2008: 126) subject to 'personal, socio-cultural and situational factors' that result in a situation where the implementation of sustainable measures tends to be *ad hoc* and 'outwith the parameters of a specific business strategy'.

This is not the only complicating factor with respect to the link between sustainability and hospitality. Even though progress has been made with respect to the environmental component of sustainability, the current state of the hospitality industry does not represent the triple bottom line approach that is required for sustainable development. This is not just related to the need for further progress related to the environmental component of sustainability, but also, and especially, to the questionable reputation of the industry when it comes to the 'people' component of sustainability. Kusluvan, Kusluvan, Ilhan and Buyruk (2010) reported that 'together with a [high] physical and emotional workload, hospitality employees [still] face perceptions of low social status and prestige, along with poor employment conditions and unsocial and irregular working hours'. Furthermore, the contribution of hospitality firms to the social development of the communities they are located in has, so far, also been limited (Chung and Parker, 2010).

CONCLUDING REMARKS

All of the above means that with respect to the question whether hospitality and sustainability are truly reconcilable, the current state of the hospitality industry represents a 'hung jury' at best. Quite a few businesses within this industry have made progress regarding the environmental component but, for the industry as a whole, the verdict is somewhat more ambiguous, especially when considering all of 'planet, people, and prosperity', that together represent sustainability. From this perspective, it would be overly optimistic or, more precisely, inaccurate to claim that the hotel industry is truly realising a triple bottom line (yet).

FURTHER READING

Chen, J, Sloan, P and Legrand, W (2009) *Sustainability in the Hospitality Industry: Principles of Sustainable Operations*, Oxford: Butterworth–Heinemann.

REFERENCES

Bader, E E (2005) 'Sustainable hotel business practices', *Journal of Retail and Leisure Property*, 5, 1: 70–7.
Bohdanowicz, P (2005) 'European hoteliers' environmental attitudes: greening the business', *Cornell Hotel and Restaurant Administration Quarterly*, 46, 2: 188–204.
Bohdanowicz, P, Simanic, B and Martinac, I (2005) 'Environmental training and measures at Scandic Hotels, Sweden', *Tourism Review International*, 9, 1: 7–19.
Butcher, J (2008) 'Ecotourism as life politics', *Journal of Sustainable Tourism*, 16, 3: 315–26.
Butler, J (2008) 'The compelling "hard case" for "green" hotel development', *Cornell Hospitality Quarterly*, 49, 3: 234–44.

Chung, L H and Parker, L D (2010) 'Managing social and environmental action and accountability in the hospitality industry: a Singapore perspective', *Accounting Forum*, 34, 1: 46–53.

Dean, T J and McMullen, J S (2007) 'Toward a theory of sustainable entrepreneurship: reducing environmental degradation through entrepreneurial action', *Journal of Business Venturing*, 22, 1: 50–76.

Elkington, J (1997) *Cannibals with Forks: The Triple Bottom Line of 21st Century Business*, Oxford: Capstone.

Enz, C A and Siguaw, J A (1999) 'Best hotel environmental practices', *Cornell Hotel and Restaurant Administration Quarterly*, 40, 5: 72–7.

Geyer, R and Jackson, T (2004) 'Supply loops and their constraints: the industrial ecology of recycling and reuse', *California Management Review*, 46, 2: 55–73.

Goldstein, N J, Cialdini, R B and Griskevicius, V (2008) 'A room with a viewpoint: using social norms to motivate environmental conservation in hotels', *Journal of Consumer Research*, 35, 3: 472–82.

Goodman, A (2000) 'Implementing sustainability in service operations at Scandic Hotels', *Interfaces*, 30, 3: 202–14.

Kusluvan, S, Kusluvan, Z, Ilhan, I and Buyruk, L (2010) 'The human dimension', *Cornell Hospitality Quarterly*, 51, 2: 171.

Meisner Rosen, C (2001) 'Environmental strategy and competitive advantage: an introduction', *California Management Review*, 43, 3: 8–15.

Ryan, C and Stewart, M (2009) 'Eco-tourism and luxury – the case of Al Maha, Dubai', *Journal of Sustainable Tourism*, 17, 3: 287–301.

Scanlon, N L (2007) 'An analysis and assessment of environmental operating practices in hotel and resort properties', *International Journal of Hospitality Management*, 26, 3: 711–23.

Tzschentke, N A, Kirk, D and Lynch, P A (2008) 'Going green: decisional factors in small hospitality operations', *International Journal of Hospitality Management*, 27, 1: 126–33.

UNWCED (United Nations' World Commission on Environment and Development) (1987) *Our Common Future*, New York: United Nations.

Walley, N and Whitehead, B (1994) 'It's not easy being green', *Harvard Business Review*, 72, 3: 46–52.

Frans Melissen

Hotels and the Internet

See also: Information technology in hospitality; Marketing in hospitality; Revenue management

Growth in consumer adoption of the internet has had a profound effect on how hotels market, promote and distribute their product. This discussion examines how internet-based distribution has changed hotel operations, and speculates on how current developments will affect the sector in the future.

THE CASE FOR WEB DISTRIBUTION

The highly perishable nature of the hotel product makes effective distribution particularly important, as any unsold room cannot be stored and subsequently consumed at a later date. Thus, selling every room every night at an optimum price is critical to profitability (O'Connor, 1999). Hotels have traditionally made extensive use of multiple distribution channels to help sell their products. Initially, these were composed of networks of intermediaries such as travel agents and tour operators, who acted as middlemen between hotels and the market. As technology developed, use was made of electronic systems (primarily the airline-focused Global Distribution Systems or GDS) to facilitate this process, with the result that electronic distribution became a key characteristic of the hotel sector.

However, the development of the Web as an informational and commercial medium in the mid-1990s began a revolution in travel distribution. Instead of working through constricting and expensive intermediaries, the Web offered the potential to reach out and establish direct contact with customers. As internet penetration grew across the globe, travel quickly emerged as one of the most frequent products searched for, and sold, online. According to the Pew Internet and American Life Project (2010), searching for travel information is now one of the most popular online activities and, while actual online revenue estimates vary, most analysts agree that spending on travel is approximately one-third of total online business-to-consumer (B2C) transactions. Internet analyst company PhoCusWright (2010) valued the size of the US online travel market in 2008 at over US$95 billion. Estimates from Karl Marcussen at the Centre for Regional and Tourism Research, Denmark, place the equivalent European figure at approximately US$79 billion, while Asia lags considerably, with travel revenues estimated at less than US$30 billion (PhoCusWright, 2011).

While suppliers in other sectors of the travel industry were quick to exploit this opportunity, setting up consumer-focused websites with information and transactional capabilities, the highly conservative hotel sector reacted more slowly, questioning whether the trend towards direct bookings would continue. In addition, the fragmented nature of the hotel sector, with its high incidence of independent, owner-managed, properties, also contributed to adoption delay. Intermediaries, however, were quicker to react, setting up their own websites, while a number of other companies also spotted online travel's potential, entering from outside the sector and quickly introducing new business models and challenging existing practices. Thus began the rise of online travel agencies (OTAs).

THE RISE OF THE ONLINE TRAVEL AGENT (OTA)

With few preconceived ideas or legacy relationships, these new online travel agent (OTA) companies quickly evolved and captured consumers' imaginations. In most cases, their key selling point became choice, both in terms of selling multiple brands and offering a comprehensive product range on a single site. Most became one-stop-travel-shops for the time-starved, information-overloaded, consumer, allowing them to source information about and make bookings for all of their travel needs on a single site. While this role does not differ greatly from that of a traditional high street travel agent, OTAs also offered the convenience of 24-hour access, gave consumers instantaneous access to up-to-date content, provided powerful aggregation facilities and promised lower prices (even if the latter often only represented perception rather than reality, see Buhalis and O'Connor, 2006). As a result, consumers quickly turned to this new type of site for their booking needs and OTAs quickly gained control over travel distribution.

As the power of OTAs grew, many became more demanding in terms of how they worked with suppliers, forcing the latter to switch from the traditional commission-based agency business model to the more constricting merchant model (Carroll and Siguaw, 2003). Instead of selling hotel rooms for a predefined fixed commission, OTAs demanded allocations of inventory at highly discounted prices (known as a net rate). These were then marked up by varying amounts in response to market demand, with the OTA's margin being the difference between the net rate and whatever they could achieve as the retail rate. While good for the OTA, the merchant model was less attractive to hotels as, irrespective of the distribution cost element, it meant that they did not have control over their own pricing and inventory. Industry pushback, most notably from Intercontinental Hotels in 2004, led to the gradual adaption of a modified merchant model which allowed hotels to take advantage of the market reach of OTAs at a more acceptable cost and with better control over pricing. However, exact conditions depend on negotiating power, and while many hotel chains have more favourable terms, most independents still remain on the more restrictive merchant model.

DIRECT DISTRIBUTION

Although OTAs make a valuable contribution, the original potential of Web distribution remains. By reaching out using the Web, hotels can interact with customers directly and bypass intermediaries (be they online or offline). However, while most hotels have a Web presence (of varying quality), few are devoting sufficient time and resources to fully exploit this opportunity. This is particularly true for independent hotels, whose websites for the most part remain little more than electronic brochures, and which suffer from low conversion rates as they fail to merchandise effectively. Booking engines are in most cases primitive, and pages rarely updated. In comparison with the more professional OTAs, hotel sites typically fail to resonate with the customer and under-deliver in terms of bookings.

Even where hotels have developed an acceptable website, major challenges exist in terms of gaining visibility in the crowded online marketplace. The vast majority of travellers now use the major search engines such as Google and Yahoo!® as a key data source, making where and how a hotel is positioned in search engine results an important issue. The vast majority of searchers do not look past the first page, so having a favourable position in search result listings is vitally important for anyone wishing to gain exposure to the online consumer. However, achieving a high ranking requires investment, skills and commitment in search engine optimization (manipulating site structure and content in order to be naturally ranked highly under particular search terms) or search engine marketing (paying for positioning). While hotel chains typically perform well in terms of search engine optimization (with their website appearing on the first page of organic listings on searches for the hotel's name and location), in most cases their success is being compromised by third parties (primarily OTAs) bidding on their trade names in paid search, appearing more prominently and diverting business (O'Connor, 2007). Independent hotels, with fewer financial resources and little technical expertise, tend in general to perform less well, with their efforts swamped by the professional techniques of the OTAs and their affiliates. As a result, despite a desire to drive bookings directly, the majority of online bookings continue to flow through OTAs, particularly for smaller, unbranded properties.

THE SOCIAL MEDIA REVOLUTION

While developing and implementing an effective online distribution strategy remains a critical issue, the growth in social media and user-generated content also needs attention from hotel companies. As discussed above, historically, customers typically relied on travel agents or other intermediaries to guide them to the best places to go and the most exciting things to do. However, as the latter are commercially motivated, this created potential for distrust as customers questioned their impartiality and wondered whether recommendations were genuine or based on payments or other incentives. While the Web added greatly to the quantity of information available, the challenge of credibility remains (Chen, 2006). Much Web-based travel information has its origins as marketing material produced by suppliers or intermediaries and is thus highly suspect. Further, while some offline travel guides have made the jump to the online world, in many cases they have struggled to adapt to an online business model, and the information they provide, particularly for free, is limited.

Social media potentially help address these issues. Since travellers enjoy talking about their experiences and seeking the recommendations of others, social media sites (such as blogs, online review sites and social networks) have become important information resources. Most provide consumers with easy access to high-quality, topical and unbiased information, generated not by commercial interests but by other consumers (Estis-Green, 2008a, see also Estis-Green, 2008b). This 'wisdom of the crowd' provides a credible alternative to marketing orientated content, helps reduce, if not eliminate, the credibility issue and is thus gaining increasing traction as a key source of travel information for today's consumers.

However, social media channels need to be actively managed. Just being present typically results in little return. Social media users also typically do not respond well to overt selling messages, with the result that traditional broadcast marketing is unlikely to work. O'Connor (2011) has proposed a four-stage 'social media management continuum' running from *monitoring* through *presence* and *activity* to *engagement*. Hotels need to begin by actively monitoring what is being said about them across the social media space and, without joining the channel(s) in question, employing automated procedures to track mentions or comments in key systems. Hotels then need to create a minimum account on selected channels. This passive presence means that they will be found when searched for by the customer, and also allows 'vanity' names (for example www.facebook.com/marriott) to be claimed before they are grabbed by third parties. Once a presence has been established, the hotel can start to generate activity and interact with customers. This may be reactive (by systematically responding to comments posted on the system, thus showing customers that they are listening and care about what is being said) or proactive (with the hotel starting conversations and reaching out to their community with comments, information and offers). At the highest level, the brand tries to engage with community members. However, this can only happen once prior stages have been well implemented. When successful, community members accept the hotel as an equal partner, and in effect work as brand advocates for the hotel, implicitly promoting it to their own sub-networks. Achieving engagement takes time and effort, but can bring major benefits in terms of publicity, goodwill and ultimately increased sales.

CONCLUDING REMARKS

As can be seen from the above discussion, today's distribution environment has become complex and convoluted. Hotels need to manage pricing, inventory and content on multiple, competing channels of distribution, striking a balance between working effectively with OTAs and driving business directly. An entirely new skill set, encompassing a comprehensive understanding of the distribution environment, electronic marketing techniques, pricing, merchandising and how to manage online image, is needed to ensure that hotels maximize bookings, at an optimum price, from each and every electronic point of sale. Such skills and knowledge are difficult to acquire, and rapidly evolving as technology and consumer behaviour change, but are essential if hotels are to successfully exploit the ever-expanding potential of the internet.

FURTHER READING

O'Connor, P and Piccoli, G (2003) 'Marketing hotels using global distribution systems revisited', *Cornell Hotel and Restaurant Administration Quarterly*, 44, 3: 105–14.

REFERENCES

Buhalis, D and O'Connor, P (2006) 'Information and communications technology – revolutionising tourism', in Buhalis, D and Costa, C (eds) *Tourism Management Dynamics – Trends, Management and Tools*, Burlington: Elsevier. pp. 196–210.

Carroll, B and Siguaw, J (2003) 'The evolution of electronic distribution: effects on hotels and intermediaries', *Cornell Hotel and Restaurant Administration Quarterly*, 44, 4: 38–50.

Chen, C (2006) 'Identifying significant factors influencing consumer trust in an online travel site', *Information Technology and Tourism*, 8, 2: 197–214.

Estis-Green, C (2008a) *Sales and Marketing in a Web 2.0 World*, New York: HSMAI Foundation.

Estis-Green, C (2008b) *Demystifying Distribution 2.0*, New York: HSMAI Foundation.

O'Connor, P (1999) *Electronic Information Distribution in Hospitality and Tourism*, London: CAB International.

O'Connor, P (2007) 'An analysis of hotel trademark abuse in pay-per-click search advertising', in Sigala, M, Mich, L and Murphy, J (eds) *Information and Communications Technology in Tourism 2007*, New York: Springer. pp. 435–46.

O'Connor, P (2011) 'A benchmark of social media adoption by international hotel companies', *Proceedings of the e-CASE and e-Tech 2011 Conference, Tokyo, International Business Academics Consortium, January*.

Pew Internet and American Life Project (2010) *Online Product Research* www.pewinternet.org/Reports/2010/Online-Product-Research.aspx, last accessed 4 July 2011.

PhoCusWright (2010) 'US online travel penetration stalls as corporate market leads recovery', http://phocuswright.us/library/pressrelease/1484, last accessed 18 February 2012.

PhoCusWright (2011) 'One third of world's travel sales to be booked online by 2012', http://phocuswright.us/library/pressrelease/1603, last accessed 7 March 2012.

Peter O'Connor

Hotels and Security

See also: Accommodation, lodging and facilities management; Front office management; Housekeeping management

All businesses in the hospitality industry have a general interest in (and sometimes legal obligation for) safety and security issues and this is particularly true of the hotel sector, not least because of the targeting of hotels in recent terrorist attacks, although such events have undoubtedly contributed to a heightened sensitivity about safety among hotel operators and users (Pizam, 2010). 'Security' can be defined as a systematic effort to afford as complete a protection and level of safety as is possible to the hotel as a physical entity, and to all its stakeholders – employees, guests and other users – from threats and hazards that may arise due to external or internal factors. Broadly speaking, security is concerned with human and technical systems that combine material and psychological elements. These include such things as the evacuation plan placed on the inside of a guest room door; illuminated emergency exit signs; metal detectors and other screening devices at the main entrances to hotels; and teams of (sometimes but not always) uniformed guards that patrol the public areas and, in some countries, guest room floors, whose function is to discourage negative behaviour.

THE HOTEL SECURITY DEPARTMENT

Hotel security services have typically been viewed by hotel managements as an ideal service for outsourcing to the many specialist external agencies that operate in the field. This is because security is a non-revenue-generating department and is thus perceived as an expense to be minimized. According to the (UK) Institute of Hospitality (2010: 12): 'There has historically been a problem in persuading some hotel owners of the importance of security; they may question what the return on investment is of installing expensive security equipment.' Generally, the number of permanent security staff in a hotel is nominal. Many hotels will have a relatively senior member of staff (often a security manager) who is responsible with other senior personnel for identifying suitable service providers, and providing and monitoring security training specific to a hotel's requirements. Recent terrorist attacks on hotels have done little to alter this basic operational model, although in-house monitoring of externally contracted staff has arguably become more sophisticated not least in terms of the biographical checks undertaken on employees.

In addition to outsourcing, another development of note in the last quarter of a century or so has been the expansion of the responsibilities of this department to include loss prevention (indeed the function of the security department or sub-unit in a hotel is often described in terms of 'security and loss prevention'). In this context, loss prevention is just as much about the protection of a hotel's assets as it is those of guests and therefore embraces a bi-polar policing function – i.e. crime prevention *and* detection (Gill et al., 2002).

Finally here, there has been some suggestion that hotel and security loss prevention departments have acquired an increasing responsibility for health and safety, broadly defined (Groenenboom and Jones, 2003). Health and safety may include such areas as food hygiene, the application and monitoring of external (legal) and internal (corporate) standards and requirements for the safe performance of work and, almost always, fire prevention (Graham and Roberts, 2000; Roberts and Chan, 2000). Increasingly, these areas, together with more general asset protection, are included in the key result areas of security and loss prevention department personnel.

PRINCIPAL SECURITY PROCEDURES

Surveillance, access control and emergency response are the three most important security procedures in most hotels. All of these are underpinned by the need for effective, and well-regulated and co-ordinated communication between personnel, and between personnel and other hotel users, principally guests. Advances in personal technology have greatly increased the possibilities for such communication: mobile telephones, pagers, two-way communication devices and personal digital assistants (PDAs) are now widely used for security purposes. It is important, however, to note that even the most advanced communication technologies are limited unless there is a holistic approach to security premised on the notion that a security and loss prevention department does not function alone but enlists as far as possible the assistance of all building users, including in the case of hotels, employees and guests.

Surveillance

Physical surveillance of hotel properties by authorized personnel is still a major feature of security strategy but increasingly it has been deemed necessary to complement human physical presence with surveillance technologies, notably closed circuit television (CCTV) the presence of which may be easily detected by an observer; may be actively notified to them (as in signs of the 'This area is under CCTV surveillance' kind); or may be deliberately disguised to obviate such intrusiveness. Advertising (or at least not disguising) the presence of surveillance equipment not only points to the physical measures being taken to ensure security but plays to psychological factors – a person who may be disposed to committing a criminal act can be discouraged from doing so if they know they are being watched either by a camera or by a security operative. Advertising the presence of surveillance also represents a clear commitment on the part of the hotel to the prevention of undesirable activities. CCTV recordings are typically monitored from a security control room and are preserved for a defined period before being wiped.

Access control

Access control is principally concerned with the physical and social *entitlements* of access to parts of a building. In the case of a hotel this includes the entitlements of both guests and personnel. On the personnel side, access control is usually underwritten by the rule of 'everyone in their place'. In traditional (and usually large) hotels this is perhaps easier to design and enforce than in hotels that employ various forms of multi-tasking and multi-skilling. Thus, in the case of the former, a front office receptionist who is not supposed to be in a guest corridor of the hotel need not be there. However, where receptionists also have the responsibility for showing guests to their rooms and assisting with baggage, this becomes more problematic.

Programmable electronic key card systems have been the major means of access entitlement control in the hotel sector. Increasingly they not only allow guests access to their rooms but also are required for operation of elevators, such a system discouraging access to guest floors for non-residents. In many hotels, guest key cards need to be inserted into a reader in the guest room in order to activate lighting. More sophisticated use of this technology is possible, for example the use of a card can register on a computer monitoring system. Personnel may also have such cards pre-programmed to allow access to some but not all areas of the hotel.

Emergency response

A central element of security procedure is emergency response. An emergency response procedure is necessary for ever-present dangers such as fire and death in a hotel as well as more extreme events such as terrorist attacks, natural disasters, bomb threats and the effects of localized civil disturbance. Of course, in many parts of the world affected by the last of these, or by, for example, ongoing armed conflict, the 'extreme' is the norm. Being able to respond effectively and efficiently to an emergency situation is critical. All personnel should be adequately trained in human and technical methods for dealing with emergencies. Once procedures are established, regular drills are required to reinforce such training.

It is increasingly the case that hotels establish Emergency Response Teams (ERT). These may be departmentally or cross-functionally based and include all personnel. Alternatively there may be a single ERT consisting of a representative number of staff members from different departments within a hotel who receive additional training in the co-ordination and supervisory skills necessary for dealing with emergencies. As many emergency situations involve external agencies such as the police, fire and ambulance service, not to mention the media, the Crisis Management Team (CMT) complements the ERT. The Crisis Management Team comprises higher level management staff with the authority and responsibility to issue public statements in an emergency situation.

SECURITY POLICY AND DEPARTMENTAL RESPONSIBILITIES

Security is a general responsibility that needs to be embraced by all departments in an effort to optimize secure hotel premises. Monthly or quarterly training audits can usefully be conducted to monitor the preparedness of each department for emergency situations. More generally, hotels require a security policy which, amongst other things, highlights general and specific responsibilities of departments for security and loss prevention. These might include, for example (for a more extensive discussion see Ellis and Stipanuk, 1999): the human resource department performing proper background checks on all those to be hired as employees; all operational departments – rooms division and food and beverage in particular – ensuring performance of all functions to legal standards and accurate recording of guest transactions; and appropriate training in security and safety for all personnel, including fire security and identification of 'suspicious' human behaviours.

CONCLUDING REMARKS: SECURITY VERSUS HOSPITALITY

Most hotels are round-the-clock businesses and this means that tension between the provision of hospitality and the provision of security is always at the core of hotel security operations (Groenenboom and Jones, 2003). However, the targeting of hotels by terrorists in recent years has led to adoption of supposedly more stringent security measures, with these sometimes being promoted as part of a company's marketing and sales strategy despite such measures being in any case normatively expected by guests. A core value of hospitality is the (reasonable) protection of those to whom it is extended. Nevertheless, as Paraskevas (2010) notes, when it comes to terrorism, a more strategic approach to the entire security function is required. This is a sensible prescription. Reactive 'bolt-on' approaches to terrorist threats to security are unlikely to be successful in the long term given the ease-of-access public nature of hotel buildings. Rather, an integrated and strategic approach to all aspects of security, safety and loss prevention is required. This increases both the moral and financial burden on hotel companies; presents operational dilemmas in terms of the provision (in-house or outsourced?) and control of security; and requires the integration of new skills in risk assessment and management into both strategic and operational decision-making.

FURTHER READING

Ellis, R C and Stipanuk, D M (1999) *Security and Loss Prevention Management*, 2nd edn, East Lansing: EIAHMA.

REFERENCES

Ellis, R C and Stipanuk, D M (1999) *Security and Loss Prevention Management*, 2nd edn, East Lansing: EIAHMA.

Gill, M, Moon, C, Seamna, P and Turbin, V (2002) 'Security management and crime in hotels', *International Journal of Contemporary Hospitality Management*, 14, 2: 58–64.

Graham, T L and Roberts, D J (2000) 'Qualitative overview of some important factors affecting the egress of people in hotel fires', *International Journal of Hospitality Management*, 19, 1: 79–87.

Groenenboom, K and Jones, P (2003) 'Issues of security in hotels', *International Journal of Contemporary Hospitality Management*, 15, 1: 14–19.

Institute of Hospitality (2010) 'Is security ever compromised by investment decisions?', *Hospitality*, Issue 20: 12.

Paraskevas, A (2010) 'Mind games and security tactics: six steps to tackle the terrorist threat to hotels', *Hospitality*, Issue 19, 36–9.

Pizam, A (2010) 'Hotels as tempting targets for terrorism attacks [Editorial]', *International Journal of Hospitality Management*, 29, 1: 1.

Roberts, D and Chan, D H-W (2000) 'Fires in hotel rooms and scenario predictions', *International Journal of Contemporary Hospitality Management*, 12, 1: 37–44.

Protyush Banerjee

Housekeeping Management

See also: Accommodation, lodging and facilities management; Design for hotels; Front office management; Revenue management

Housekeeping consists of a set of processes for the cleaning, repair and maintenance of accommodation, most notably in hospitality organizations, in hotels (Nitschke and Frye, 2008). Housekeeping activities focus mainly on guest rooms and public areas but may also include 'back of house' areas. Processes specify both daily and periodic tasks to be performed, as well as the methods, techniques, cleaning materials and equipment by which these tasks will be executed. Processes incorporate both legally required and (voluntary) agreed standards relating to health and safety; quality control; cost control; and the recruitment, training and motivation of personnel (Rawstron, 1999).

NATURE AND ROLE OF THE HOUSEKEEPING DEPARTMENT

Accommodation is the mainstay of most hotels. A guest's first impressions of a hotel (impressions that may positively or negatively influence the rest of their stay) include the standard, appearance and cleanliness of the property's public areas and guest rooms (Harris and Sachau, 2005). Room sales typically generate most of a hotel's revenue. According to the British Hospitality Association (cited by Powell and Watson, 2006), hotel room sales count for approximately 55% of total revenues while food revenue represents 23% and beverages 19% of the total hotel revenues. In addition, the operating costs of the hotel rooms department are on average 26% of room sales, compared to food and beverage expenses being 65% of food and beverage sales. These statistics underline the importance of the accommodation function.

In larger hotels, the housekeeping department together with front office and maintenance departments constitute the 'rooms division' and their respective heads (the executive housekeeper, front office manager and chief engineer) will report to the rooms division manager. A central issue in hotels is achieving co-ordination between these units: ineffective co-ordination is not unusual and can be highly problematic, negatively impacting on guest satisfaction (Frapin-Beaugé et al., 2008).

The role played by the housekeeping department varies according to the hotel's size and market position. The size of the property affects the amount of work to be done. The market position (from the highest – whether classified as 'five star', deluxe or upscale, or full service – to the lowest, such as one-star, budget or restricted service) influences the nature and level of service offered. Different service levels imply greater complexity and higher standards in the overall operation of a hotel, including the housekeeping department.

PLANNING OF HOUSEKEEPING TASKS AND ACTIVITIES

Careful planning of housekeeping tasks and activities is essential to efficiency and cost-effectiveness. A useful way of framing the planning process is to pose four simple questions – what, when, how often and who. The question 'what?' refers to defining those areas of the hotel that it is the housekeeping department's responsibility to maintain. The question 'when?' refers to the timing of cleaning and maintenance whereas 'how often?' specifies the frequency of these activities. A frequency schedule is established taking into consideration the extent of contamination and the number of users of a certain area and any legal responsibilities imposed by statute (for example matters relating to health and safety). For instance, a sanitary area will be cleaned at least once a day but windows could be cleaned once per month. A frequency schedule will include all cleaning and maintenance tasks together with specifications as to whether they should be undertaken daily, weekly, monthly or after some other, specified, period. The last of these – periodic tasks – includes special projects and deep cleaning (for a further comment on deep cleaning, see the following section).

There are two aspects to the question 'how'. First is how and how well surfaces are cleaned (what is the desired quality) – this is otherwise known as the performance standard. The second aspect is how much time particular types of cleaning should take – otherwise known as the productivity standard. Performance standards should specify appropriate cleaning methods, cleaning agents, equipment and techniques; and the frequency of performing the tasks according to the frequency schedule (Raghubalan and Raghubalan, 2007). The setting of productivity standards will take into account the type and age of property; distances between service and working areas; amount of traffic in the working areas; the nature of the cleaning task (some are more complicated and/or time-consuming than others); the degree of contamination; and the kind and availability of cleaning supplies and equipment.

The question 'who?' refers to the quantity and type of labour required to perform housekeeping tasks. It also embraces the nature of the sources of labour employed – whether 'in house' (employees of the hotel) or external contractors employed for specific, specialized and, usually, periodic tasks for which the hotel lacks the skilled personnel and/or equipment).

CLEANING PROCEDURES

Performance and productivity standards are increasingly integral parts of hotels' standard operating procedures (SOPs), which cover all departments and processes. Unfortunately, as Frapin-Beaugé et al. (2008) note, important and worthy as they are, SOPs sometimes fail to take account of the way in which work is actually performed (as opposed to how it should be performed). Nevertheless, hotel lore is a powerful force, not least in housekeeping, and typical and general (and very sensible) processes for the cleaning of guest rooms (and other areas) have evolved as standards. These include the following:

- work from the 'inside out' in sanitary areas (for example clean the inner part of a sink first);
- work from high to low surfaces (specifically, dust and otherwise clean higher 'top' surfaces and move to lower surfaces);
- work from 'back' to 'front' of a room or area (for example when cleaning a guest room start at the point furthest from the entrance);
- use appropriate protective clothing (for example when working with detergents, wear gloves); and
- use cleaning agents sparingly to prevent waste and for cost and environmental reasons.

Deep cleaning refers to the process of 'gutting' a room or area and ensuring that all materials and surfaces are more or less simultaneously subject to maintenance, cleaning and treatment as appropriate: for example carpets are shampooed; curtains, duvets and pillows laundered, dry cleaned and/or otherwise maintained and/or refurbished/repaired; mattresses are cleaned; and sanitary areas decalcified. For obvious reasons, deep cleaning is undertaken less frequently than other types of cleaning, and is usually scheduled on a 'rolling' basis with due regard for a hotel's occupancy levels. It is, however, an absolutely necessary process, the neglect of which can reduce asset value, negatively affect guest comfort and create hygiene and health problems (for example, at the time of writing there is increased concern about the growth of 'bedbugs' in hotels, see http://bedbugregistry.com/).

OUTSOURCING

Outsourcing (the contracting of specific tasks to external specialists) is increasingly common in the hotel industry, and the housekeeping department has been one area in which considerable interest in outsourcing has been shown (Gee, 1999). In addition, contracting out of tasks can stop short of 'full' outsourcing, as in, for example, employment agencies providing flexible numbers of staff on a temporary basis. A principal criterion employed in decisions to outsource housekeeping is the clarity of the required standard of service. Thus, Lamminmaki (2007) argues that room cleaning for business guests in high-class Australian hotels is predictable and as such facilitates outsourcing. To avoid complications and disputes, and ensure that external agencies deliver the hotel's required standards, careful contracting is required to ensure inclusion of all specifications and standards. Also, decisions are required as to matters of policy, for example as to whether the hotel or external contractor provides equipment and supplies. The outsourced service(s) need to be properly monitored by designated personnel within the hotel to ensure compliance.

HUMAN RESOURCE ISSUES

According to Wood (cited in Powell and Watson, 2006: 298): 'chambermaids rank amongst the lowest of the low in hotel work, treated as cheap and easily replaceable resource by employers and often spurned by other fellow employees'. The job of room attendant is generally considered as one that 'everyone can do', with simple, repetitive (but physically demanding and dirty) tasks, low development opportunities and high turnover. In fact, in hotels it requires medium to occasionally high levels of skill, there is a high level of task complexity (not least in effectively cleaning to quality standards) and housekeeping staff must respond to guests' needs and wants, be knowledgeable of safety regulations, possess knowledge and skills of cleaning methods and techniques, at least basic knowledge of computer systems and maintenance issues of diverse fixtures, etc. On top of that, room attendants are expected to show initiative and feeling of responsibility, as usually they perform their tasks alone.

Housekeeping employees also face greater health and safety issues than others. According to the Canadian Centre for Occupational Safety and Health (Liladrie, 2010: 60), 'a hotel housekeeper changes body position every three seconds while cleaning a room. The average cleaning time for each room is 25 minutes, which means that a housekeeper assumes 8,000 different body postures every shift'. Furthermore, the work is forcing body postures that lead to constant pain associated with work, as for example reported in a survey of 600 housekeepers in several big cities in North America (Liladrie, 2010). Examples of daily routine tasks linked to those associations are lifting heavy mattresses, tucking in layers of sheets, vacuum cleaning and cleaning tiles. Hotel employees are reported to be 48% more likely to be injured while working than any other worker in the service sector (Liladrie, 2010).

CONCLUDING REMARKS

Effective housekeeping management is critical to creating a positive hotel guest experience and thus to the overall success of a hotel business. Frequently marginalized in the study of hospitality management because of its apparently mundane qualities and lack of 'glamour', it is rarely acknowledged that the theory and practice of housekeeping management require a considerable degree of both complex knowledge and skills. Hotel housekeeping work, which is often included in that category of functions and tasks described in the industry as 'back of house', lacks visibility within hotel organizations, but the 'products' of housekeeping – clean and comfortable guest rooms and clean public areas – are all too visible to guests. Meeting and exceeding guest expectations are no less a part of the housekeeping function than any other aspect of hotel management.

FURTHER READING

Nitschke, A A and Frye, W D (2008) *Managing Housekeeping Operations*, East Lansing: EIAHLA. (see especially Chapter 1, pp. 3–36.)

Raghubalan, G and Raghubalan, S (2007) *Hotel Housekeeping Operations and Management*, New Delhi: Oxford University Press.

REFERENCES

Frapin-Beaugé, A J M, Verginis, C S and Wood, R C (2008) 'Accommodation and facilities management', in B Brotherton and R C Wood (eds) *The Sage Handbook of Hospitality Management*, New York: Sage. pp. 383–99.

Gee, D A (1999) 'Facilities management and design', in Verginis, C S and Wood, R C (eds) *Accommodation Management: Perspectives for the International Hotel Industry*, London: Thomson. pp. 172–82.

Harris, P B and Sachau, D (2005) 'Is cleanliness next to godliness? The role of housekeeping in impression formation', *Environment and Behaviour*, 37, 1: 81–101.

Lamminmaki, D (2007) 'Outsourcing in Australian hotels: a transaction cost economics perspective', *Journal of Hospitality and Tourism Research*, 31, 1: 73–110.

Liladrie, S (2010). 'Do not disturb/please clean room': hotel housekeepers in Greater Toronto',
Race and Class, 52, 1: 57–69.

Nitschke, A A and Frye, W D (2008) *Managing Housekeeping Operations*, East Lansing: EIAHLA
(see especially Chapter 1, pp. 3–36.)

Powell, P H and Watson, D (2006) 'Service unseen: The hotel room attendant at work',
International Journal of Hospitality Management, 25, 2: 297–312.

Raghubalan, G and Raghubalan, S (2007) *Hotel Housekeeping Operations and Management*, New Delhi:
Oxford University Press.

Rawstron, C G (1999) 'Housekeeping management in the contemporary hotel industry', in
Verginis, C S and Wood, R C (eds) *Accommodation Management: Perspectives for the International
Hotel Industry*, London: Thomson. pp. 114–27.

Marina Brinkman-Staneva

Human Resource Management in Hospitality

See also: Organizational behaviour in hospitality; Service, service industries and the hospitality sector; Women, gender and hospitality employment

Human resource management (HRM) concerns itself with the practices and policies used to manage employees within organizations. These include issues like new staff recruitment, remuneration and reward systems, evaluation of performance, training and development and employee participation. Most companies, with the exception of the smallest organizations, will employ HRM specialists who develop and operate the human resource systems. But line managers are also involved in delivering HR strategies, for example by selecting new staff, coaching and mentoring them, and appraising their performance.

HRM, as an approach, assumes that employees are assets that need to be managed effectively in the same way as any other resources. To do this, it is important to try to understand the link between HRM practices and organization performance. This is not straightforward. One debate is whether there is 'best practice' that can be applied in all circumstances or whether there are 'bundles' of policies that are appropriate in certain types of organization and in certain types of conditions. It is also useful to distinguish between two broad approaches to HRM: 'hard' HRM, where the main focus is on controlling and minimizing the cost of staff *resources*, and 'soft' HR, where the main focus is on keeping commitment from and improving the quality of the *human* resources (Storey, 1992).

HRM policies and practices need to be compliant with relevant employment law and other regulations. Obviously, this will vary according to the country in which the company is based. In many countries, employment law is becoming more complex and wide-ranging. For example, where equal opportunities legislation was originally focused on preventing discrimination against women, and on the grounds of race or ethnicity, in many countries legislation now covers a wide range of dimensions including religion, sexual orientation and age. Other regulations that impact hospitality organizations include those relating to working time; minimum wages; dismissal; redundancy pay entitlements; and maternity/paternity rights. Immigration regulations are also relevant for global organizations wishing to move staff from country to country or for organizations trying to cope with local staff shortages by recruiting migrant labour.

HRM PRACTICES IN THE HOSPITALITY INDUSTRY

The hospitality industry is a labour-intensive industry and one where a large proportion of staff are classified as unskilled or semi-skilled. It is also an industry where there are often large fluctuations in demand: according to season of the year or across the week. An increase in demand for service translates directly into a need for more staff, whilst if there is a decrease in demand for some reason, it is helpful to be able to reduce staff quickly. Thus flexibility of staffing is crucial for many organizations if they are to keep control of labour costs.

The most obvious way to increase and decrease staffing to reflect increases and decreases in demand is through 'numerical' flexibility, i.e. by varying the number of staff employed and/or the hours that staff work. The use of casual staff and of temporary contracts is widespread in the industry. The high level of labour turnover, which is a feature of many parts of the industry, can also be used as a mechanism of numerical flexibility, i.e. by not replacing staff that leave during quiet periods. Another approach to flexibility is through 'distancing', where work is sub-contracted: for example hotels often use agency staff for cleaning, and operations like car parking and leisure centres are often sub-contracted. This places the contracting company at less risk because the responsibility for varying staffing is placed on the contracted company. Finally here, 'functional' flexibility involves asking staff to multi-task rather than stick to one narrow functional role: for example a receptionist might help clean rooms after the morning check-outs are over. One of the most common forms of 'functional' flexibility is when managers 'trade down' and help out with operative tasks in busy periods (Baum, 2006, provides a fuller description of the different approaches to flexibility). 'Numerical' flexibility and 'distancing' are used with 'peripheral' groups of staff, that is, with those staff who have do not expect long-term careers with the company and do not require much training. 'Functional' flexibility tends to be expected of those 'core' staff who are more skilled and more committed to careers within the company.

It has been argued that the hospitality industry is a graphic example of the way 'hard' HRM works in practice (Lucas, 2002). The argument is that whilst a small 'core' of skilled and committed staff may be managed using 'softer' HRM practices, most staff are poorly paid and poorly skilled 'peripheral' workers. But one of the paradoxes of a strategy of staffing hospitality organizations with so-called 'peripheral' staff is that they are the staff likely to be in contact with the customer, doing jobs such as waiting and bar work, or doing work that directly impacts customer satisfaction, such as less skilled kitchen work or cleaning rooms. If they are uninterested and untrained, it is customer satisfaction and ultimately the company's bottom-line that will suffer. Some authors argue therefore that organizational performance would be better if there was more emphasis on 'soft' HRM practices of engaging and training staff so they become more committed to the organization and empowered to find ways of delivering better service (Hughes, 2002). Conversely, others point out that a 'hard' cost-driven approach makes perfect sense in stand-ardized operations (for example McDonald's), where jobs can be simplified and scripted so they require little training or skill (Lashley, 2001).

There is a debate about the extent to which HRM practices in the hospitality industry are not just 'hard' but also poor, in the sense that they are unsophisticated, with little input from professional HR specialists and not linked to any strategic goals. An example is the way that recruitment at the operative level is often man-aged in informal ways through word of mouth rather than through using more systematic methods. However, there is evidence that practices in the largest organizations are formalized and sophisticated and there is increasing use of well-qualified HR professionals (Hoque, 1999). Further, even if there is evidence that practices in the hospitality industry tend to be 'harder' than in other industries, it is not clear that employees are particularly dissatisfied with the way they are managed (Lucas, 2002).

MANAGING INTERNATIONALLY

Hospitality is an industry that operates across the world, in both developed and developing countries. Many large companies, for example international hotel and restaurant chains, operate across the world. But even if one considers small, nation-ally based organizations, there is a strong tradition of using migrant labour in this sector. Thus international human resource management practices and cross-cultural management are important considerations for the hospitality industry.

A challenge for international hospitality companies is whether they develop a home-oriented strategy, where key positions in other countries are held (using the categorization of Perlmutter, 1969) by 'home' country nationals (an *ethnocentric* strategy); whether they develop a localized strategy, where 'local' nationals hold key positions (a *polycentric* strategy); or whether they develop a 'globalized' strat-egy, where a truly global culture is built and where the right person may come from anywhere in the world (a *geocentric* strategy). Perlmutter's categorization has been employed in a number of studies of practices within different hospitality companies (see Nickson, 2007 for a useful summary). Even for those companies that are ostensibly trying to operate geocentric strategies, it is difficult to avoid the subtle influence of a company's national origins and the ways that people with certain national backgrounds tend to have an advantage in career terms. The use of expatriate managers from developed country backgrounds to manage hospital-ity units in developing countries is a broader political issue in some of these countries as it limits the opportunity for locals to develop and use their management and higher-level skills (see Baum, 2006, for a further discussion).

Whilst managers from more developed countries are frequently found working in developing countries, the opposite flow tends to happen at the operative level, particularly during times of economic prosperity when migrants are brought in to do jobs that locals find unattractive. For HR professionals, there are issues in ensuring that migrant employees are properly registered and legally permitted to work in the country. Beyond this, there are likely to be additional training needs, especially in relation to the expectations of local customers. Finally, there are the challenges of operating in a multi-cultural environment.

EMERGING ISSUES

One emerging issue for HR professionals is well-being in the workplace. At the minimum level, that involves keeping workplaces safe, managing stress at work and reducing absence through illness. As Lucas and Deery (2004) observe, for hospitality organizations, there is the issue of how to manage an around-the-clock work environment and the impact of shift work on well-being and, in relation to international companies, the issue of how to manage the safety of employees working in dangerous environments (for example in countries with high crime rates and/or a risk of civil disorder). A number of studies have shown how frontline operative staff in the hospitality industry are vulnerable to harassment from customers (see Guerrier and Adib, 2000). The problems can be exacerbated when alcohol is involved and, of course, employees who are serving alcohol to others can be tempted to drink heavily themselves at the end of a shift. (The danger to staff from secondary smoking has reduced following the introduction of smoking bans in many countries.) But well-being is not just about preventing harm; it can also be about encouraging better health and wellness at work.

CONCLUDING REMARKS

It is important to remember that generalizations about HRM in the hospitality industry that hold true in certain sectors within the industry and in certain parts of the world are not universally true. Most of the researchers who have written about HRM practices in the hospitality industry have written about the developed world and have focused on certain parts of the industry, particularly hotels and, to a lesser extent, chain restaurants. Thus the industry is characterized as being plagued by high turnover of staff: yet it is possible to find establishments where there is very low turnover. The industry is characterized as un-unionized: yet there are parts of the world where there is high unionization.

But, wherever they exist, hospitality organizations depend on their employees for success. All organizations need to develop strategies for attracting, developing and retaining staff that strike a balance between, on the one hand, the need to control costs and use staff efficiently and, on the other hand, the need to motivate and engage staff so they provide the best service to the customer. This remains the key challenge for the hospitality industry in the twenty-first century.

FURTHER READING

Baum, T (2006) *Human Resource Management for Tourism, Hospitality and Leisure*, London: Thomson.
Nickson, D (2007) *Human Resource Management for the Hospitality and Tourism Industries*, Oxford: Butterworth–Heinemann.

REFERENCES

Baum, T (2006) *Human Resource Management for Tourism, Hospitality and Leisure*, London: Thomson.

Guerrier, Y and Adib, A (2000) '"No, we don't provide that service": the harassment of hotel employees by customers', *Work, Employment and Society*, 14: 4, 689–705.

Hoque, K (1999) 'New approaches to HRM in the UK hospitality industry', *Human Resource Management Journal*, 9, 2: 64–76.

Hughes, J C (2002) 'HRM and universalism: is there one best way?', *International Journal of Contemporary Hospitality Management*, 14, 5: 221–8.

Lashley, C (2001) *Empowerment: HR Strategies for Service Excellence*, Oxford: Butterworth–Heinemann.

Lucas, R (2002) 'Fragments of HRM in hospitality? Evidence from the 1998 workplace employee relations survey', *International Journal of Contemporary Hospitality Management*, 14, 5: 207–12.

Lucas, R and Deery, M (2004) 'Significant developments and emerging issues in human resource management', *International Journal of Hospitality Management*, 23, 5: 459–72.

Nickson, D (2007) *Human Resource Management for the Hospitality and Tourism Industries*, Oxford: Butterworth–Heinemann.

Perlmutter, H (1969) 'The tortuous evolution of the multinational corporation', *Columbia Journal of World Business*, 4, 2: 9–18.

Storey, J (1992) *Developments in the Management of Human Resources*, Oxford: Blackwell.

Yvonne Guerrier

Income Statements in Hospitality Finance

See also: Franchising; The hospitality finance environment; Investing in hotels

People choose a career in hospitality management for various reasons – for example the 'romance' of hotels, and the prospect of an international career. Whatever the case, it is essential to recognize that hospitality businesses are, with few exceptions, like any other – they exist to make money for their stakeholders. It is therefore essential that managers and owners are financially literate and able to correctly interpret financial data to answer questions such as: are hotel guest rooms being sold at reasonable rates? Are the personnel of the organization deployed efficiently? Is the organization selling the right meals and beverages (namely those that contribute most to profit)? Financial management is the effective management of all organizational resources to optimize revenues and create surplus thereby ensuring the continuing existence of the organization. The discussion in this entry confines itself to certain financial characteristics of hospitality operations via the medium of what is, for a manager, arguably the most important financial statement: the income statement.

THE INCOME STATEMENT: REVENUES AND EXPENSES

Revenues are loosely defined as gains in value from the sale of goods or services. Expenses are the other side of the coin: losses of value incurred in selling goods and services. Expenses subtracted from revenues give us the profit, or 'net' value gained by an organization in a given period. All of these are represented on a statement called the income statement, also often referred to as the profit and loss ('P & L') statement. The Uniform System of Accounts for the Lodging Industry or 'USALI' (Hotel Association of New York City, 2006), offers a standard format for a hotel income statement which, though developed in the USA, is increasingly used by many hotels in different parts of the world. There also exist other such 'uniform systems' (e.g., for restaurants, see National Restaurant Association, 1996). Because it is extensive, including as it does most hospitality products and services imaginable, the USALI format is something of an 'ideal type' and employed in this discussion to present some financial issues typical to hospitality.

UNIFORM SYSTEM OF ACCOUNTS FOR THE
LODGING INDUSTRY (USALI)

The USALI offers the reader of a property's income statement a high level of detail in respect of showing where (in what department) revenues are generated and expenses incurred, and is made up of three sections: (a) the revenues and expenses of the operated departments (operated in the sense that revenue is generated in and by these departments, which are also known as profit centres); (b) the expenses of service departments (referred to in USALI as 'undistributed operating expenses'); and (c) other expenses, for example management fees and fixed charges. The 'Summary Income Statement' (for each department, USALI also provides a more detailed statement, or 'schedule') is shown in Table 2. The profit level expressed by the first two sections (total revenue of all operated departments minus all departmental *and* all undistributed operating expenses) is called gross operating profit (GOP). It is important to appreciate the fact that this level of profit, rather than net income, is the primary focus of most hotel general managers as this represents the part of the income statement they are responsible and accountable for.

Table 2 USALI Summary Income Statement

	Net revenue	Cost of sales	Payroll and related expenses	Other expenses	Income (loss)
Operated Departments					
Rooms					
Food					
Beverage					
Other Operated Departments					
Rentals and Other Income					
TOTAL Operated Departments					
Undistributed Operating Expenses					
Administrative and General					
Sales and Marketing					
Property Operation and Maintenance					
Utilities					
TOTAL Undistributed Expenses					
Gross Operating Profit					
Management Fees					
Income Before Fixed Charges					
Rent, Property Taxes and Insurance					
Depreciation and Amortization					
Interest					
Income Before Taxes					
Income Taxes					
Net Income					

Section 1: Revenue and Expenses of Operating

Section 2: Expenses of Service Departments

Section 3: Other Expenses

Other expenses more down the line in terms of their position on the income statement, such as depreciation of the hotel building, may be the consequence of decisions taken by the owners or company directors long before a general manager took up his/her position.

In the first section of the income statement, the profit for each department is calculated by deducting the following from the net revenues of the department in question: cost of sales; payroll and related expenses; and other expenses. Not all departments have *cost of sales*, as not all departments sell tangible goods, the prime example being the rooms department. *Payroll and related expenses* refers to the staff salaries, payroll taxes and benefits. Hospitality fundamentally being a service industry, these expenses can amount to quite large a percentage of total revenue. Of course this would very much depend on the type of establishment – for luxury hotels it would be much higher than for limited-service hotels. *Other expenses* may include operating supplies, laundry and dry cleaning, training and costs of staff uniforms.

The second section of the income statement in the USALI, called Undistributed Operating Expenses, consists of only payroll and related expenses and other expenses: there is no revenue generation and, hence, no cost of sales for each of the four service centre categories in this section of the income statement which are: administrative and general; sales and marketing; property operation and maintenance; and utilities (electricity, gas, water and so on).

WHAT CAN THE INCOME STATEMENT REVEAL ABOUT KEY ASPECTS OF HOTEL AND HOSPITALITY FINANCE?

In most hotels, the sale of rooms to guests will generate the largest share of overall revenue. Even in resorts where there are many non-rooms revenues, such as spa treatments and golf green fees, it is not uncommon for rooms to account for around 50% of total revenues (Hales, 2010). Room revenues will almost invariably be subjected to seasonality, the pattern of which largely depends on location, hotel concept and the business segment mix. Occupancy levels and average rates can vary widely throughout the year as well as throughout the week (working days versus weekends). Forecasting sales for this department is essential as many non-rooms products and services are spin-offs of the lodging product. Many hospitality managers therefore use forecasts of (guest or banqueting) rooms occupancy to forecast cross-selling into other departments such as food and beverage (Schmidgall, 2011).

The rooms department can also be considered to be an important contributor to profit, as the expenses incurred directly in running this department are relatively small. One obvious reason for this is the lack of cost of sales, as there is no physical 'good' sold. Housekeeping, or the expense for cleaning the rooms, is often outsourced to third parties, usually for a prearranged price per room cleaned that is typically but a relatively small percentage of the room rate.

Another important characteristic of (at least part of) the hospitality industry becomes apparent when studying the rooms department: the perishability of certain products and services. There is no making up for not being able to charge someone for using part of the fixed capacity of a property (number of available rooms in this case) on any given night: that revenue is lost forever. The key notion of a fixed capacity that should yield as much revenue as possible is driven home in what is probably the most-used and most important measurement in the hotel industry as a whole: RevPAR, or revenue per available room. It is calculated by dividing total rooms revenue in a given period by the number of rooms available for sale in that period. Doing so provides management and owners with better management information than just occupancy percentages or average room rates, as each of these ratios ignores the importance of the other. In other words, using RevPAR encourages managers to enhance rooms' revenue by focusing on price (rates) as well as on volume (occupancy).

In the USALI income statement, food and beverage are two separate operated departments. What they have in common is that profitability is notoriously difficult to achieve. A mix of (often labour-intensive) service and product, food and beverage service operations experience not only substantial payroll expenses, but also food and beverage cost of sales that may run up to 35% or more of revenue. Many food and beverage operations have historically been managed, at least financially, by monitoring and keeping these food and beverage cost percentages below a target level, thereby aiming to ensure sufficient gross margin – the difference between selling price and cost of sales – to cover all other expenses involved in providing food and beverage service. The departmental income statement for food also includes the revenues from the rental of conference (or banqueting) rooms.

Other operated departments can include a range of revenue centres, for example telecommunications, spas, fitness and health centres, and golf courses. One operated department merits some explanation: rentals and other income. An oft-encountered example of rental income would be the lease payments from third-party operated commercial establishments within the hotel, such as shops in the hotel lobby, or spa facilities.

Undistributed operating expenses

As noted earlier, the second section of the income statement is expenses only. A large part of it will be payroll and related expenses of employees. 'Administrative and General' includes the expenses of most back of house departments that are not in the other three service departments in this section of the income statement, such as human resource management, accounting and general management. Noteworthy are some expense categories in this section that reflect the credit nature of much of the hospitality industry: depending on the concept, much of the revenue generated by a hospitality operation will not be received straight away. Hence, for example, the 'provision for doubtful accounts', 'credit and collection' and 'credit card commissions' expense lines that would be found in the detailed schedule for this heading. 'Property Operation and Maintenance' and 'Utilities' each having their own line in the USALI clearly highlights the importance of the (expenses associated with the) built environment in which hospitality is delivered. 'Sales and Marketing' includes not only expenses of staff involved in marketing the products and services of the organization, but also of sales materials and franchise fees, if the hotel is franchised.

Management fees and fixed charges

To grasp the concept of management fees, it is important to consider a fundamental characteristic of the hotel industry. Many well-known international hotel chains, such as Hilton and Four Seasons, do not actually own that many hotels, just as that well-known hospitality conglomerate McDonald's owns less than 20% of 'its' restaurants (McDonald's, 2011). Many establishments that go by the above-mentioned names are actually franchises – that is, they just use the brand name and reservation system of the chain – or are managed for the owner by the chain under a so-called management contract. In the latter case, the owner pays the chain a management fee. The fee is mostly a percentage of revenues (base fee) plus another percentage of GOP (incentive fee).

In the remainder of the third and last part of the income statement, the so-called fixed expenses or fixed charges, are represented: rent, property taxes and insurance; depreciation and amortization, and interest. Fixed expenses are something all organizations, be they in the hospitality industry or not, incur in doing business. Very often, they are related to the lease, ownership and/or financing of real estate and furnishings, fixtures and equipment. As such, it should not come as a surprise that for many hospitality operations, especially those offering lodging, fixed expenses are often a very high percentage of overall costs.

Finally then, we arrive at the 'bottom line': the hotel's net income after all expenses have been subtracted from revenue.

CONCLUDING REMARKS

The importance of an income statement showing the financial results of a hotel operation can hardly be overrated. Hospitality managers should be able to correctly read and interpret its content. A thorough understanding of its overall structure and department-specific revenue and expenses can contribute to managers ensuring that all personnel behave in ways that will have a positive impact on the bottom line.

FURTHER READING

Harris, P and Mongiello, M (2006) *Accounting and Financial Management: Developments in the International Hospitality Industry*, Oxford: Butterworth–Heinemann.

REFERENCES

Hales, J A (2010) *Accounting and Financial Analysis in the Hospitality Industry*, Harlow: Prentice Hall.
Hotel Association of New York City (2006) *Uniform System of Accounts for the Lodging Industry*, 10th edn, East Lansing, EIAHLA.
McDonald's (2011) www.aboutmcdonalds.com/mcd/our_company.html, last accessed 3 October 2011.
National Restaurant Association (1996) *Uniform System of Accounts for Restaurants*, 7th edn, Washington, DC: NRA.
Schmidgall, R S (2011) *Hospitality Industry Managerial Accounting*, East Lansing: EIAHLA.

Rob van Ginneken

Industry Structure and Sectors in Hospitality

See also: Accommodation, lodging and facilities management; Food production and service systems; Hospitality and hospitality management; Service, service industries and the hospitality sector

In the last decade or so there has been growing debate over how both the nature and the concept of 'hospitality' should be defined. A social scientific view, at the heart of which is concern with host/guest relationships and human interaction, offers definitions of hospitality beyond 'commercial' contexts to include 'social' and 'private' dimensions alike (Brotherton, 1999; Lashley, 2000a). Whilst remaining conscious of these wider debates, hospitality is defined here as the (principally commercial) provision of food, beverage and/or accommodation services in public spaces, provision motivated by the attainment of profit maximization. The hospitality industry is heterogeneous, comprising a range of industry sectors catering to various customer needs (Clarke and Chen, 2007). There is no universally accepted and standardized scheme for classifying the numerous sectors of this or other industries. Some scholars have shown interest in mapping industry sectors according to the various venues and spaces where hospitality service provision occurs. David Bell (2009), for instance, subdivides the hospitality industry into 'foodscapes', 'drinkscapes' and 'restscapes' but other commentators (e.g. Lugosi, 2008; Slattery, 2002) have argued that this approach conceives the hospitality industry as overly concerned with satisfying basic needs such as 'tiredness', 'hunger' and 'thirst' while ignoring issues such as 'social interaction', 'enjoyment' or 'entertainment', which often form part of satisfactory hospitality experiences.

By far the simplest classification of the industry found in the hospitality literature is the simple bi-polar distinction between the *foodservice sector* and the *lodging sector*, neatly encapsulating the two distinctive features for which the industry is known. Foodservice establishments range from individually owned and operated fine-dining restaurants, to chain-affiliated quick-service operations such as McDonald's or Burger King, to simple takeaway restaurants, as well as catering outlets within institutions such as hospitals or schools, which may not be driven by the profit motive. The lodging sector offers a large variety of accommodation products catering to diverse targets. An overlap between foodservice and lodging disciplines occurs in hotels, which, in Bell's (2009) terms, typically house hospitality 'foodscapes', 'drinkscapes' and 'restscapes' under one roof. Both foodservice and lodging businesses are also primarily location-bound. As such, they are frequently affected by external factors difficult for management to control. These include everything from daily and seasonal fluctuations in demand to economic downturns, political unrest or natural disasters (see Yu, 2008: 65).

THE FOODSERVICE SECTOR

The term 'food service' or 'foodservice' is widely used to define businesses responsible for preparation and service of meals outside the home whether these are restaurants or other forms of catering business. The term *restaurant* generally defines 'an establishment where refreshments or meals can be obtained, usually for money by the public' (Ball and Roberts, 2008: 34). Dining out is a global phenomenon. In the UK, for instance, the value of household spending on eating out overtook spending on food sector products for home consumption for the very first time in 2004 (UK Statistics Authority – Office for National Statistics, 2006). Various approaches to segmenting restaurant operations exist. Ownership structure, restaurant concept (including target market and menu offering) and brand affiliation represent commonly used classifiers for modern-day restaurant establishments.

In terms of *ownership structure*, independently owned (and usually small) restaurant businesses dominate the global restaurant industry. However, a desire for consistency, value and accessibility has brought about growth in corporate chain restaurants in recent decades. Defined by Wyckoff and Sasser (1978: 185) as 'two or more eating establishments at separate locations under common ownership or related through other legal entities (e.g. franchising)', multi-unit chain restaurant businesses now account for more than 50% of restaurant sales in major markets such as the USA. In terms of *concept* (including also target market and menu offering), restaurants are frequently labelled as 'ethnic', 'fine dining', 'casual dining', 'mid-scale', 'quick-service' or 'themed'. However, these categories are increasingly fluid as businesses embrace aspects associated with more than a single concept. Restaurant operations may also be classified based on whether they are *brand-affiliated* or not. In a competitive business environment branding is frequently perceived as a means to achieve instant recognition, increased repeat business, and greater customer loyalty.

Catering usually differs from restaurant-based foodservice in so far as (a) food preparation and service/delivery are in line with specific contracts and (b) food production and service processes can be separated, with food prepared in one place and then transported for service to a second location for any or all of brief final cooking, reheating or assembly (Mattel and The Culinary Institute of America, 2008). A distinction can also be made between *institutional* and *social* caterers. The former typically practise business-to-business relationships and serve large corporations, convention centres, country clubs, healthcare organizations, retirement homes, military and correction facilities, transportation businesses (e.g. air, rail and cruise lines) and higher education institutions that for reasons of cost and efficiency have chosen to outsource their on-site foodservice operations. Foodservice is delivered at the respective institutions themselves and the target market may, in some cases, be literally or metaphorically 'captive'. In the last quarter century, this segment has seen the emergence of a handful of truly global players, such as ARAMARK, Compass Group plc, Groupe Elior and Sodexho. In contrast to institutional catering, the *social catering* segment is composed of usually smaller, less capital-intensive, frequently independently owned, catering firms that provide food and beverage services at parties, gala dinners, weddings or other similar events. It is common for these events to be 'one-off' rather than regular and venues may vary from banquet halls to private households and other event locations.

THE LODGING SECTOR

Over the last fifty years there has been substantial global growth in demand for overnight accommodation. As with most products and services, lodging properties are highly diversified in terms of market orientation and segmentation, serving different types of traveller. Prices charged generally reflect the quality and/or range of products and services included in the purchase offer. Lodging properties are typically classified according to (a) their class of quality of facilities and services; (b) their location; or (c) their facility type (see Rushmore and Baum, 2001).

In respect of *class and the quality of facilities and services*, numerous formal and semi-formal rating schemes of lodging establishments exist. Formal rating schemes include those of the American Automobile Association (AAA) and *Forbes Travel Guide*. Semi-formal schemes include internet-based services such as TripAdvisor® where reviews are contributed by customers and guests themselves. Luxury hotels impress by their range of facilities, quality of finishes, design, (brand) name and services and cater for elite travellers with high spending power. Such properties are generally limited in supply and concentrated in gateway cities and prime locations. Commonly associated brands in this segment include Four Seasons, Ritz Carlton, St Regis and Waldorf Astoria. Products within the upscale and midscale hotel segments typically cater to a wide group of travellers and a full range of competitively priced services and facilities is offered. In contrast, economy hotels represent a value-oriented option for the travelling population where services offered are typically limited. The budget hotel segment provides minimal facilities and no notable types of services. Rates charged by these establishments are the lowest within the industry and mark the entry hurdle for hotel accommodation. Examples of brand providers in this segment include, Etap, Travelodge, Days Inn and Premier Inn.

Hotels may also be categorized based on their *location*. Distinctions among establishments that serve guests in transit from one destination to another and among establishments that are located at a specific destination (or in fact represent a destination themselves) can be made. The first of these groups generally describes properties located along highways or at railway stations, ports and airports. The second group refers to properties located at particular destinations (e.g. city centres, exhibition complexes, resorts, etc.) which house certain commercial or leisure demand generators. In addition to categorization according to rating class and location, lodging properties are frequently grouped by the *type of facilities and service amenities* they offer – business, resort, conference and boutique hotels, bed and breakfast and guest house establishments and serviced apartments.

Business hotels are typically found in close proximity to central business districts or industrial parks with facilities normally including several dining outlets, meeting space and retail and spa areas. This type of hotel usually experiences peak occupancy rates between Monday and Thursday, when commercial demand is high. Built specifically to accommodate leisure guests, resorts are usually located close to attractions such as beaches, mountains, scenic spots and other points of interest. Various resort sub-categories emphasize activities such as skiing, golf, gaming, and spa and wellness. Business and support facilities are often limited at resort properties and certain resort developments (e.g. beach or ski resorts) may be constrained by seasonality patterns. Conference hotels usually feature large, standardized room inventories which are accompanied by sizeable meeting facilities in order to cater to group and event demand. Functions such as fairs, exhibitions, congresses, incentives, banquets and occasionally weddings are held at this type of hotel. Boutique hotels are stylish and chic, offering design and technology-driven facilities and innovative service solutions, normally at a premium price. In the original sense of the term 'boutique' as applied to hotels, properties were frequently individually owned and small in scale, thus normally lacking the marketing force associated with chain hotels. Then and now, many such properties affiliate with marketing consortia and booking networks such as Designhotels, Hip Hotels or Kiwi Collection to more effectively sell their inventories. Although often neglected by industry literature on account of their small scale, their owner-operated nature and their frequent lack of professional management, bed and breakfast and guest house accommodations account for a significant share of accommodation supply worldwide. Serviced apartments and extended-stay accommodations represent a hybrid model between a typical hotel and a traditional apartment or residence. Guests frequenting this type of accommodation are usually on temporary assignments and the duration of their stay may range from a few weeks to several months and even years. Furnished interiors, basic services and flexibility in length of stay offer an additional level of comfort and allow for price premiums to be charged over normal residences. Given their reduced guest turnover and limited public facilities, significantly fewer employees are required in serviced apartment properties as compared to traditional hotels, hence resulting in lower operational costs and elevated profit margins.

To conclude, the lodging industry is, for the most part, highly capital-intensive. Project finance is often tight, and development a complex and challenging process. Yet owners, investors and operators continue to seek development opportunities that fit their risk profiles and expansion strategies.

FURTHER READING

Yu, L (2008) 'The structure and nature of the international hospitality industry', in Brotherton, B and Wood, R C (eds) *The Sage Handbook of Hospitality Management*, London: Sage. pp. 62–89.

REFERENCES

Ball A, and Roberts, L (2003) 'Restaurants', in Brotherton, B (ed.) *The International Hospitality Industry*, Oxford: Butterworth–Heinemann. pp. 30–58.
Bell, D (2009) 'Tourism and hospitality', in Jamal, T and Robinson, M (eds) *The Sage Handbook of Tourism Studies*, London: Sage. pp. 19–34.
Brotherton, B (1999) 'Towards a definitive view of the nature of hospitality and hospitality management', *International Journal of Contemporary Hospitality Management*, 11, 4:165–73.
Clarke, A and Chen, W (2007) *International Hospitality Management: Concepts and Cases*, Oxford: Butterworth–Heinemann.
Lashley, C (2000a) 'Towards a theoretical understanding', in Lashley, C and Morrison, A (eds) *In Search of Hospitality: Theoretical Perspectives and Debates*, Oxford: Butterworth–Heinemann. pp. 1–17.
Lugosi, P (2008) 'Hospitality spaces, hospitable moments: consumer encounters and affective experiences in commercial settings', *Journal of Foodservice*, 19, 2: 139–49.

Mattel, B and The Culinary Institute of America (2008) *Catering: A Guide to Managing a Successful Business Operation*, Hoboken: Wiley.

Rushmore, S and Baum, E (2001) *Hotels and Motels: Valuations and Market Studies*, Chicago: Appraisal Institute.

Slattery, P (2002) 'Finding the hospitality industry', *Journal of Hospitality, Leisure, Sport and Tourism Education*, 1, 1, 19–28.

UK Statistics Authority – Office for National Statistics [Online], News Release: Input-Output Analyses, August 2006, www.statistics.gov.uk/pdfdir/ioa0806.pdf, last accessed 30 January 2011.

Wyckoff, D and Sasser, E (1978) *The Chain Restaurant Industry*, Lexington: Lexington Books.

Yu, L (2008) 'The structure and nature of the international hospitality industry', in Brotherton, B and Wood, R C (eds) *The Sage Handbook of Hospitality Management*, London: Sage. pp. 62–89.

Michael Schwarz

Information Technology in Hospitality

See also: Hotels and the internet; Marketing in hospitality

Information technology (IT-) based systems are widely used in service industries in general, bringing benefits such as higher productivity and efficiency; improved service quality; increased customer satisfaction; better organizational integration; reduced costs and thus higher profitability. However, the adoption of IT-based systems by hospitality companies has been somewhat problematic. Effectively managing IT is consistently cited as one of the most troublesome issues for hospitality managers (Enz, 2001). IT-based systems within the hospitality sector are perceived as being overreliant on closed IT-architectures and proprietary technologies. In addition, there is an absence of commonly agreed technology standards for inter-system communication, leading to the challenge of 'islands of isolation'. Staying up to date with new developments is difficult, which, coupled with the rapid pace of change, makes selecting appropriate systems difficult, risky and confusing.

As a result, the hospitality sector as a whole has been slow to adopt IT-based systems (Wang and Qualls, 2007). In the mid-1990s, the sector's total global spending on IT-based systems was approximately 2% of revenues. Since then, both the penetration and the sophistication of systems have grown, with spending increasing to approximately 5% of industry revenue (a figure comparable with other industries in the service sector). IT-based systems have become integrated into hospitality management and operations. However, for the most part these systems remain unsophisticated in terms of functionality. While the hospitality sector purports to have a customer-centric approach, the range of information technology-based systems deployed tends to focus on improving back of house productivity rather than enhancing guest satisfaction. Very few IT-based systems are strategic in scope, and in general are perceived as operational and transactional in nature. This is particularly true outside the United States, where the predominance of small and independent hotels exacerbates the challenges associated with justifying and implementing technology-based systems.

USING IT-BASED SYSTEMS FOR HOSPITALITY MANAGEMENT AND OPERATIONS

Despite these challenges, the use of IT-based systems has increased dramatically over the past decade, with most hotels adopting an expanding portfolio to help in management and operations. For the most part growth has been driven by wider hotel chain penetration. With their standardized methods of operations, more professional management approach and more stringent reporting requirements, chains have driven technology adoption. In many cases, they mandate the use of particular IT-based systems and thus technology penetration has grown. Another driver has been the switch from family to company (i.e. investment funds, banks, private equity) ownership, with the latter typically having more stringent reporting requirements than the more *laissez-faire* family businesses, while guest demand has also been a key issue, particularly with regard to the adoption of in-room technologies.

As a result, a variety of different IT-based systems are now commonly used in hotel management and operations. At a basic level these can be divided into three categories: distribution systems; hotel-facing systems; and guest-facing technologies. Distribution systems (examples include the hotel chain's central reservation system or CRS, as well as its yield management systems and Web bookings engine) reach out towards the customer to market and sell the hotel's rooms – an issue that is vitally important due to the perishable nature of the hotel product. Hotel-facing systems, on the other hand, are used internally by hotel management and staff to more effectively run operations. These may be further subdivided into front of house systems (such as, for example, property management systems (PMS) or energy management systems) and food and beverage systems (such as stock control systems, recipe costing systems, electronic point of sales (EPOS), sale and catering systems and e-procurement systems). Such systems tend to be primarily administrative in nature, focusing on improving the efficiency of day-to-day operations. Guest-facing systems, on the other hand, refer to technologies used directly by the client within the property and particularly within the guest room. As such, this includes audio-visual systems such as the television; telephone-based systems; in-room refreshment systems; wired and wireless high-speed internet access; electronic door locks; and guest self-service kiosks. Adoption in this latter area is increasingly being driven by 'wired' customers who typically use state-of-the-art entertainment and communications systems within their own homes and expect similarly sophisticated technology-based systems to be available during their hotel stay. In addition to providing the IT-based systems themselves, hotels also need to provide the right infrastructure to support the technology, and populate it with appropriate content at a selling price that both justifies the investment but is not off-putting to the guest.

ISSUES AND CHALLENGES

While hotels now make use of a portfolio of IT-based systems to help manage their operations, for the most part these remain relatively basic in functionality. Few challenge traditional methods of operations, and innovation within the sector is very limited. One reason behind this is that hospitality software tends to be both proprietary (developed specifically for a user) and legacy (from a previous generation in programming terms) in nature, and often does not have the flexibility and connectivity needed to function effectively in today's business environment. Such applications are often written in cumbersome programming languages which, in contrast to other sectors where more open architectures abound, make passing data from one application to another (particularly one supplied by a different vendor) highly problematic. This challenge is amplified by a lack of commonly agreed technology standards for sharing data between applications. Despite several attempts by industry representative bodies to agree technical standards to address this issue, integration between dissimilar systems remains problematic.

Software vendors have been reluctant to address this problem, preferring instead to lock customers into proprietary solutions or require the purchase of costly interfaces. This reflects a general lack of responsiveness by vendors to industry needs. With a small number of vendors dominating the market, system providers are in high demand. Most are so preoccupied attempting to cash in on servicing additional installations that they are not investing in research and development, with the result that there is little innovation in the solutions being offered or in development. In short, their focus on installing 'more of the same' means that they have no resources available to invest in developing the next generation of hospitality information systems.

Despite these challenges, hospitality IT-based systems continue to mature, driven primarily by the global hotel chains that see technology as a way of differentiating themselves from their competitors. Systems are evolving from being property-based (contained and used within a single hotel property) to intra-organizational (implemented seamlessly through a chain). In effect the objective is to develop these systems into a digital nervous system for the organization as a whole, allowing management more visibility and tighter control over operations by providing a consolidated, holistic view of what's happening throughout the organization. While greatly expanding the scope of hospitality IT-based systems, such developments give rise to an additional range of challenges, particularly as chains implement such systems outside of their US bases to more heterogeneous international markets. Where the business environment is multi-lingual, multi-currency and multi-cultural as well as multi-country (as is the case in the hotel sector), systems implementation is highly complex: for example having access to an appropriate communications infrastructure is important as companies move their core operational systems above property level. However, outside the USA, getting access to such facilities at an acceptable price becomes challenging as no single supplier can provide services on a global basis. Hotel companies thus have to work with different vendors in different countries, many of whom are state monopolies and often unresponsive to customer needs. Such increased complexity results in both frustration and higher costs, and may act as a brake on further penetration of innovative systems.

FUTURE PERSPECTIVES

Justifying the cost of investing in IT-based systems seems to be a permanent challenge in the hospitality sector, despite the fact that the capital required is perceived as negligible in comparison to the benefits accrued. The rapid pace of change means that technology investments must be made on an on-going basis. However, many of the benefits from implementation are difficult to quantify. Many are soft and accrue across multiple departments and functions, and thus tend to be difficult to evaluate using conventional payback or internal rate of return techniques. The problem is exacerbated by the ownership/management/branding split that typifies the hotel sector. While technology investments are suggested or mandated by management companies or franchisers wishing to implement standardized solutions across all properties within their chain, investments are typically funded by owners or franchisees with many conflicting calls on their capital. Given the aforementioned difficulty in assessing such investments using conventional investment appraisal techniques, getting the latter to approve such capital spending can be a daunting task.

Part of the challenge of justification may be that hotel IT-based systems have traditionally been limited in scope. Wang and Qualls (2007) feel that this is because most technology solutions adopted by hotels tend to be product- rather than process-orientated. Process-orientated technologies refer to applications that are revolutionary in that they introduce new ways of conducting business and transform business practices. However, organizations tend to favour product-orientated innovations as adoption is more straightforward than with process-orientated innovations, which by their nature require changes throughout the entire organization. Research by Siguaw and Enz (1999) highlights how hospitality organizations tend to focus on limited, product-orientated systems rather than trying to implement more comprehensive systems that might improve business processes but require substantial transformation and integration within the entire organization. Product-orientated systems tend to generate immediate and short-term benefits, but have little impact on enhancing strategic positioning and building core competencies (Namasivasyam et al., 2000). Most focus on issues such as streamlining operations, speeding information dissemination and increasing employee productivity rather than on more strategic applications that might result in enhanced revenues and more satisfied guests.

CONCLUDING REMARKS

Most authors agree that a more strategic approach to selecting, implementing and using hospitality IT-based systems is needed. Key systems need to be selected not based on short-term needs with limited scope, but to help build competitive advantage by identifying and responding to competitive forces and customer needs. IT-based systems are not a panacea for all ills, and a thorough revision of operational and strategic management practices must be carried out if substantial benefits are to be achieved. Developing Porter's competitive forces model in the context of the impact of information technology, Cho and Olsen (1998) propose that IT-based systems could help hotel companies to build barriers to entry, create switching costs, change the basis of competition, change the balance of power in supplier/customer relationships or generate new products. However, the current lack of vision as to the power of IT-based systems to contribute to strategic goals that typifies the industry makes such benefits impossible. In the long run, only by aligning the applications of IT-based systems with the overall goals of the organization can hotel companies hope to be successful.

FURTHER READING

Beldona, S and Cobanoglu, C (2007) 'Importance-performance analysis of guest technologies in the lodging industry', *Cornell Hotel and Restaurant Administration Quarterly*, 48, 3: 299–312.
O'Connor, P (2004) *Using Computers in Hospitality*, 3rd edn, London: Thomson.
O'Connor, P (2008b) 'Managing hospitality information technology in Europe: issues, challenges and priorities', *Journal of Hospitality and Leisure Marketing*, 17, 1–2: 59–77.

REFERENCES

Cho, W and Olsen, M (1998) 'A case study approach to understanding the impact of information technology on competitive advantage in the lodging industry', *Journal of Hospitality and Tourism Research*, 22, 4: 376–94.
Enz, C (2001) 'What keeps you up at night? Key issues of concern for lodging managers', *Cornell Hotel and Restaurant Administration Quarterly*, 42, 2: 38–45.
Namasivasyam, K, Sigaw, J and Enz, C (2000) 'How wired are we?', *Cornell Hotel and Restaurant Administration Quarterly*, 40, 5: 31–43.
Siguaw, J and Enz, C (1999) 'Best practices in information technology', *Cornell Hotel and Restaurant Administration Quarterly*, 40, 9: 58–71.
Wang, Y and Qualls, W (2007) 'Towards a theoretical model of technology adoption in hospitality organizations', *International Journal of Hospitality Management*, 26, 3: 560–73.

key concepts in
hospitality management

Peter O'Connor

Innovation in Hospitality

See also: Design for hotels; Entrepreneurship in hospitality

Innovation is defined as the acceptance of something new by those other than the creator. From a strategic management perspective innovation can be a major source of competitive advantage, but in the hospitality industry innovation is currently and largely viewed as problematic. A report on innovation activity across fourteen British industries found hotels and restaurants to be among the least innovative (Robson and Ortmans, 2008). Similar results are reported from North America, showing that the foodservice sector tends to be reactive, making few advances in current practice 'until a period of crisis arises' (Enz, 2004: 5).

Of course, innovation comes at a cost. The potential rewards of an innovation can be extremely high, but so are the risks, because most inventions will never become innovations yet often require huge amounts of resources for research and development. There are two principal reasons why most inventions fail. The first is that innovation is essentially the result of creativity but creativity – the creation of a new and potentially useful idea – is a cognitive process about which little is understood. Indeed, one leading commentator of creativity, Boden (1990: 41), suggests that it is 'not just improbable, but impossible' ever to understand the creative process. In terms of applications to business or any other sphere of activity, this means that creativity cannot be learned following a structured and streamlined process. The second reason why most innovations fail relates to the fact that innovations are normally only accepted and therefore recognized by the desired target audience when the audience can recognize the usefulness of the new idea. Put another way, there is an inbuilt tension in the innovation acceptance process – by definition an innovation must be rule-breaking enough to be considered as new and original, but to be accepted it must obviously have significant appeal to existing potential users who are often conservative (reluctant to change). It is thus not enough that the creator remains the only person who thinks that his or her idea is an innovation. Innovation requires the recognition of its usefulness by the audience for which the idea was developed.

WHERE DOES CREATIVITY HAPPEN?

As a result of the above-mentioned doubts that exist over the possibility of ever defining creativity successfully, one of the field's leading researchers, Mihály Csíkszentmihályi (1997: 27–8) suggests trying to understand *where* creativity happens instead of *what* creativity is. He distinguishes between Creativity (with a capital C) and personal creativity. Creativity is a system of three inter-related parts. The domain and the field comprise the physical and cultural 'locations' where creativity takes place (Creativity with a capital C). The *individual* is normally

innovation in hospitality

105

where personal creativity is found. To better understand these three parts and their inter-relationships, it is helpful to consider the example of chefs.

In the world of chefs the *domain* represents the culinary trade, which has both culture-related rules and practices (how to behave) and technical rules and practices, such as, for example, how to prepare a Sauce Béchamel, its variations, and with what food the sauce can be served. The *field*, on the other hand, are all those parties that have a 'gatekeeper' position that allows them to judge and recommend to the trade whether the work of a particular chef is consistent with the domain's understanding of usefulness, quality and value. Additionally, these gatekeepers tend to be the judges of innovation – as to whether claims by an individual chef as to the originality of new dishes, processes or systems of food preparation actually merit such claims. Gatekeepers include various food guides, particularly those consensually regarded as being of a certain calibre, for example Michelin's *Guide Rouge*, which can both make and break the reputations of the world's 'leading' chefs. The *individual*, on the other hand, with his or her talents and goals and immediate environment, such as family and collaborators, is the source of personal creativity, the type of creativity that is concerned with the actual cognitive act of creating something new and potentially useful.

INNOVATION IN HOSPITALITY

Joseph Schumpeter (1883–1959), acknowledged by most as the 'godfather' of the economic theory of innovation, argued that innovations are waves of 'creative destruction' that can revolutionize a whole market. The Organization for Economic Co-operation and Development (OECD, 1997: 28) proposed a distinction between five types of innovation based on Schumpeter's (1911) original work: the introduction of new products; the introduction of new methods of production; the opening of new markets; the development of new sources of supply for raw materials or other inputs; and the creation of new market structures in an industry.

In the hospitality context, an example of the *introduction of a new product* is 'The Soyer Field Stove'. The chef of the London Reform Club, Alexis Soyer (1809–1859), developed a stove for the British troops during the Crimean War in order to centralize food production. Following just a few minor modifications, his stove was used by the British Army until the 1980s (Cousins et al., 2010; Soyer, 1857).

A more recent product development that relies to some degree on *new uses of established methods of production* (rather than new methods of production *per se*) is the hotel group citizenM. With its slogan 'affordable luxury for the people', the company creates boutique budget hotels through a clever concept of pre-fabricated room units that can be assembled into an entire hotel in very short time. The chief operating officer of citizenM, Michael Levie, (2010) says that based on market research his company has learned that their potential guests expect first class when it comes to, for example, materials used in the room, such as bed linen, but that they do not mind to have smaller rooms if the rooms are designed in a clever and convenient way. As a result, citizenM created exactly this: a luxury hotel that makes use of cost savings due to reduced room space and standardized room cubicles that are manufactured in a plant in Great Britain. These cost savings, on the other hand, allow citizenM to charge lower prices to their guests and to open hotels next door to the big names of the luxury hotel trade.

In this sense, citizenM is also an example of *the opening of a new market*. A further example that presents both a new method of production as well as an opening of a new market is 'sous vide' (under vacuum) cooking. The science of sous vide, that heat can be transmitted through a vacuum, was originally discovered at the end of the eighteenth century. However, it was not until 1974 that the method was introduced to the restaurant industry by the French chef Georges Pralus (Xie, 2000).

There are numerous historical examples from within hospitality of the development of *new sources of supply* for raw materials or other inputs from the gaining of access to certain foodstuffs through enhanced cultivation, preservation and transportation techniques, to the vertical integration of food and related supply and production in such companies as McDonald's.

The creation of *new market structures* in the hospitality industry comprises such past examples as franchise and timeshare business models. A more recent example of a change in market structure may include the emergence of molecular gastronomy. While it remains to be seen whether molecular gastronomy can be regarded as a distinct culinary movement (Cousins et al., 2010), it clearly disrupted the established haute cuisine restaurant sector by challenging more conservative and classical-oriented chefs and by creating a media profile that regularly promoted an excessive view of creativity in cooking (see more on this issue at Adrià et al., 2006).

An interesting side-development of molecular cooking, and a recent example for a new method of production, is the application of the 'creative workshop' concept in restaurants. A creative workshop, such as El Taller, which has been the creative playground of the Spanish chef Ferran Adrià and his team of the former restaurant El Bulli, is nothing else than the workshop of an artist where, sometimes together with a team of artists, new pieces of art are produced. Using this concept in a business context has the advantage that the unpredictable phases of trial-and-error, creativity and research and development happen within a confined space and are only released once they are 'waterproof' and can be integrated in the overall daily production process in a kitchen that must adhere to strict quality control mechanisms. In other words, creative workshops are '"homes" for knowledge workers ... for sharing tacit knowledge, creating concepts, or prototype building' (von Krogh et al., 2000: 170).

Earlier it was said that the poor understanding of the cognitive process of creativity is one of the reasons for the high failure rate of many inventions. However, by looking closer at the aforementioned examples of innovations in the hospitality industry, an interesting commonality emerges. CitizenM, sous vide cooking, the creative workshop concept, and molecular gastronomy all share the same characteristic of having emerged at an intersection between two domains. CitizenM applies technology from the building industry to the hospitality industry, the science behind sous vide cooking comes from physics, the creative workshop concept applies elements from the working environment of an artist to a business context, and the foundations of molecular gastronomy emerged in food science. Johansson (2006) calls this effect of 'discovering' innovations at the intersection between two domains the 'Medici Effect' in recognition of the famous Florentine banking family who funded many creative people in fifteenth-century Italy, thus generating a real burst of creativity.

CONCLUDING REMARKS

It is important to recognize that the potential rewards of an innovation can be extremely high, but investing in innovation is risky: the financial investment and development costs are often significant, and most inventions will never become innovations. As the Italian Renaissance writer Niccolò Machiavelli (cited in Rogers, 1962/2003: 1) noted: 'there is nothing more difficult to plan, more doubtful of success, nor more dangerous to manage than the creation of a new order of things'. This may perhaps go some way to explaining why the hospitality industry views innovation as problematic and is often reactive rather than proactive in times of change.

FURTHER READING

Rogers, E (1962/2003) *Diffusion of Innovations*, 5th edn, New York: Free Press.

REFERENCES

Adrià, F, Blumenthal, H, Keller, T and McGee, H (2006) 'Statement on the "new cookery"', *The Observer*, www.guardian.co.uk/uk/2006/dec/10/foodanddrink.obsfoodmonthly, last accessed 18 January 2012.
Boden, M (1990) *The Creative Mind*, London: Weidenfeld & Nicolson.
Cousins, J, O'Gorman, K and Stierand, M (2010) 'Molecular gastronomy: basis for a new culinary movement or modern day alchemy?', *International Journal of Contemporary Hospitality Management*, 22, 3: 399–415.
Csíkszentmihályi, M (1997) *Creativity: Flow and the Psychology of Discovery and Invention*, New York: HarperCollins.
Enz, C (2004) 'Issues of concern for restaurant owners and managers', *Cornell Hotel and Restaurant Administration Quarterly*, 45, 4: 315–32.
Johansson, F (2006) *The Medici Effect. What Elephants and Epidemics Can Teach Us About Innovation*, Boston: Harvard Business School Press.
Levie, M (2010) 'Innovation in hospitality', Keynote speech presented at EuroCHRIE Conference, Amsterdam, October 25–28.
OECD (1997) *Proposed Guidelines for Collecting and Interpreting Technological Innovation Data (The Oslo Manual)*, 2nd edn, Paris: Organization for Economic Co-operation and Development.
Robson, S and Ortmans, L (2008) 'First findings from the UK Innovation Survey 2007', *Economic and Labour Market Review*, 2, 4: 47–53.
Rogers, E (1962/2003) *Diffusion of Innovations*, 5th edn, New York: Free Press.
Schumpeter, J (1911) *The Theory of Economic Development*, Boston: Harvard University Press.
Soyer, A B (1857) *Soyer's Culinary Campaign*, London: Routledge.

von Krogh, G, Ichijo, K and Nonaka, I (2000) *Enabling Knowledge Creation: How to Unlock the Mystery of Tacit Knowledge and Release the Power of Innovation*, New York: Oxford University Press.

Xie, G (2000) 'Comparison of textural changes of dry peas in sous vide cook–chill and traditional cook–chill systems', *Journal of Food Engineering*, 43, 3: 141–6.

Marc B. Stierand

Investing in Hotels

See also: Franchising; The hospitality finance environment; Income statements in hospitality finance; Industry structure and sectors in hospitality

Investing in hotels is potentially both lucrative and complex. This is because a hotel is a business with various activities and various investment stakeholders. There are typically three (and sometimes more) investment stakeholder groups. The main three are: the owner(s); lending institutions (banks, mortgage societies, private equity funds and so on); and the hotel management company (often referred to as the operator). While many smaller hotels are owned and operated by their owners, the majority of internationally branded hotels are owned by an owner, or a group of owners, and managed (operated) by a hotel management company (such as Intercontinental, Hilton or Marriott). In this case there is a clear separation between ownership and management. The above-mentioned stakeholders often have different objectives in terms of investment timeframe, return expectations and other, general, risk considerations.

In respect of *investment timeframe*, owners invest both in the short- and long-term and prefer the flexibility to sell a hotel if the right buyer comes along. Owner investment timeframes vary by owner(s) and location. In some regions long-term investments (10+ years) are perfectly normal, while in others anything over five years is untypical. Hotel management companies normally have much longer timeframes; typical hotel management contracts range in duration between 15 and 25 years. Lender timeframes vary significantly from one country to the next but can be as short as 5 years and as long as 30 years (or more in exceptional cases).

Turning now to *return expectations*, it is generally the case that the riskier the hotel investment then the higher is the return expectation of all the stakeholders. Investment risk is a complex topic, but in general the key issues with any hotel investment are: country risk (the risk associated with doing business in a particular country – some countries are less stable and/or more volatile than others therefore increasing the element of risk); industry risk (that risk associated with investing in one industry as opposed to some other – for example investing in the hotel industry as opposed to retail or banking); and currency risk (the risk associated with fluctuations in the value of currency – of particular interest to international investors). A rational investor will not take on risk without the possibility of being compensated for so doing – in other words the higher the perceived risk, the higher the return expectations (Beals and Denton, 2004).

Finally here there are other, *general risk considerations*. The principal risk considerations of owner(s) and banks are financial and centrally concerned with whether they will achieve the required rate of return from their investment. Hotel management companies, in addition to financial risks, often consider the impact that a particular hotel may have on their brand(s). If, for example, a particular hotel is significantly below standards (for example an old property that has not been refurbished for a number of years), that property may have a negative impact on the brand's image both locally and globally.

HOTELS AS REAL ESTATE

Most of the factors discussed in the preceding section apply to all real estate asset classes. Hotels, however, are typically more complex investments than other real estate assets, such as residential, office or retail assets. The reasons for this are as follows.

First, a hotel will typically have a lower building efficiency (areas that generate revenue) as it requires more back of house areas, such as storage and parking, than other asset classes. In other words, in a typical luxury hotel the revenue-generating areas (hotel rooms, restaurants) often represent less than 60% of the building area. For a comparable residential development this figure is closer to 80%.

Secondly, hotels generally have higher development costs, as they require a higher quality of finishing, requiring more furniture and equipment than is the case for other asset classes. Higher quality often means more luxurious and, equally important, more durable FFE (furniture, fittings and equipment). The utilization of the FFE of a hotel is usually much greater than in other asset classes, which, together with higher-quality requirements, make for greater expense. Furthermore, a hotel has FFE requirements that most buildings in other asset classes do not have – for example hotel room equipment (TVs, radios, bed linen, bathroom linens); kitchen and restaurant equipment (stoves, refrigerators, cooking appliances, serving appliances, plates, glasses, cutlery); housekeeping equipment; conference and banqueting equipment; and much more. Often the FFE cost of a hotel project represents around 10% of the total development cost.

Thirdly, hotels have relatively high(er) operating expenses than other asset classes, often requiring, for example, more staff. The main operating expenses of a hotel include: cost of sales, labour cost and overheads. Cost of sales includes the cost of all materials associated, for example, with food, beverage, flowers, room amenities, and housekeeping material and cleaning supplies amongst others. Labour cost is a very significant cost, particularly for upscale five-star hotels that may employ one member of staff for every hotel room they have. Overheads are also a big cost. These mainly include water, electricity, air conditioning, heating, marketing and administration and maintenance costs. While these costs vary from geographic region to geographic region and from season to season, they are significant. It is not uncommon for a successful five-star hotel to commit approximately 60% of hotel revenues towards operating expenses!

Fourthly, hotels frequently have more complex operating structures than other asset classes, as it may require a hotel management agreement between the owner(s) and the operator (a hotel management company). Owners should consider hotel management agreements and franchise agreements very carefully and before committing to a particular brand ask such questions as: is this the right brand for my hotel? Does the hotel company have enough local expertise to make a difference? What customer markets and segments are they likely to attract? Is their image in line with the building and my vision? Is the length of the agreement in line with my strategic objectives? Are the fees and other conditions being asked by the company in line with the industry norms? Am I better off with a management contract or a franchise agreement?

FACTORS AFFECTING FINANCIAL PERFORMANCE OF HOTEL INVESTMENTS

Despite the complexities of investing in hotels as opposed to other types of asset, the financial returns of a successful hotel are likely to be higher than comparable residential or office developments. However, the financial performance of a hotel investment is affected by many factors, not all within management's control (Raleigh and Roginsky, 1995; Rushmore et al., 1997).

These include, *first*, the impact of location. Location has several dimensions. Proximity to a demand generator is important (for example the business and/or retail district in the case of a city hotel; the beach in the case of a resort) as it can have a direct effect on hotel occupancy and average daily rate. Whether the country/region/city location is a prime destination or an inexpensive destination is important to the business that will be attracted and thus economic performance. Further, a hotel's proximate demand generators are significant as the most successful hotel markets are those that can attract both the leisure and the business traveller. The seasonality of the two market segments has been often complementary: for example business travellers typically use hotels during the week and outside the holiday/summer seasons while leisure travellers, on the other hand, tend to use hotels during the holiday seasons (main holidays) and at weekends (short breaks). This combination is ideal for hotels as it minimizes the slow periods of the year. Such destinations are typically metropolitan cities like Paris, London and New York, but other destinations are heavily impacted by the seasonality of the main market segment. Other factors relating to location that are important include the perceived geopolitical stability of the country/region/city in which a hotel is located as this can affect sources of business: a region/city perceived as unsafe by visitors will impact negatively. National and local government support is also an important consideration, particularly with respect to the provision of infrastructure. Ease of accessibility to an area through rail, road, ports and airports encourages visitors and thus the critical mass which is the basis of success for a local/regional hotel industry. Finally here, and more prosaically, visibility of the location and the hotel from major routes and access points has a positive impact on financial performance, as does the use and condition of the adjacent land plots.

A *second* important factor affecting the financial performance of a hotel investment is the nature and extent of local (and in some cases, global) competition. At the local level there is always the risk that a newer/better hotel will enter the market, or that an existing hotel will offer better service. Another way that hotels compete with each other is through pricing. Often, hotels that are unable to compete with the other local hotels because of inferior product, or inferior location or inferior service, tend to reduce their rates as a way of attracting the more cost-conscious visitors. In all of the above cases the likely result is that increased competition is likely to put pressure on the hotel's occupancy and/or average daily rate and hence revenues/profits. At a global or at least international level, hotel guest loyalty to a particular destination is not guaranteed forever. A family may choose to travel to Florida one year, and Spain the following year, not because they had a bad time in Florida but because modern travellers tend to seek a range of experiences that translates into demand for accommodation in a range of destinations and, concomitantly, increased competition among hotels in those destinations.

Thirdly, the region(s) that the majority of the guests come from (source regions) and the general economic environment in these source regions are important to a hotel's performance. Hotel performance is impacted by economic conditions as both business travellers and holiday makers typically reduce their travel (and hotel stays) during economic downturns. The opposite can, of course, also be true.

Finally here, as previously discussed, hotels are labour-intensive businesses. The availability of a skilled labour force is critical to the success of the hotel. While many destinations around the world rely heavily on expatriate hotel staff, this approach tends to be expensive for a hotel as it increases recruitment costs and can stimulate employee turnover.

CONCLUDING REMARKS

The opening statement of this discussion was that investing in hotels is potentially highly lucrative. While this is the case, it is fair to say that there are many hotel projects that never make it past the planning stage as the owner(s) realize that the likely financial returns of the hotel will be below their expectations. Even worse, plenty of hotels have been developed without the necessary planning and due diligence as a result of which the financial returns to the owner(s) were unacceptable. Despite this, investment in hotels is exciting but needs careful and proper consideration, particularly at the planning stage (Rushmore et al.,

1997). A feasibility study/valuation conducted by an impartial and objective professional is a good starting point. For new developments, the advice of an experienced designer/architect is also critical. The decisions made at this stage will need to be the right ones not only for now but for the next 20–30 years! Similarly, the importance of the right operator and the right brand cannot be emphasized enough. Finally, of course, the right price needs to be paid in order to achieve acceptable financial results. A successful hotel investment needs to be both exciting *and* realistic.

FURTHER READING

Rushmore, S and Baum, E (2001) *Hotels and Motels: Valuations and Market Studies*, Chicago: Appraisal Institute.

REFERENCES

Beals, P and Denton, G (2004) *Hotel Asset Management: Principles and Practices*, East Lansing: EIAHLA.

Raleigh, L E and Roginsky, R J (Eds) (1995) *Hotel Investments: Issues and Perspectives*, 5th edn, East Lansing: EIAHMA.

Rushmore S, Ciraldo, D M and Tarras, J (1997) *Hotel Investments Handbook*, Boston: Warren, Gorham and Lamont.

Constantinos Verginis

Marketing in Hospitality

See also: Consumer behaviour in hospitality; Customer relationship management in hospitality; Hotels, hospitality and sustainability; Hotels and the internet; Information technology in hospitality

An early definition of marketing proposed by the UK-based Chartered Institute of Marketing (1976: 1) was as follows: 'Marketing is the management process responsible for identifying, anticipating and satisfying customer requirements profitably'. The CIM more recently has considered the new developments that the marketing discipline has adopted, including the power of the customer, the influence of technology, fragmentation of markets, new methods of market research, the role of people and ethics. They have proposed a new definition to address these issues as follows: 'Marketing is the strategic business function that creates value by stimulating, facilitating and fulfilling customer demand. It does this by building brands, creating good customer services and communicating benefits' (CIM, 2007: 14).

Marketing in hospitality and tourism involves service marketing, which has different features compared to product marketing. Recently academic commentaries on service marketing have grown together, as have efforts to establish more specific definitions of marketing in a hospitality and tourism context. One example of the latter by the marketing guru Philip Kotler and colleagues is as follows: 'Hospitality marketing is a social and managerial process by which individuals and groups obtain what they need and want through creating and exchanging products and value with others' (Kotler et al., 2006: 31). This definition suggests that marketing is an important social as well as managerial process and focuses on the concept of value, which forms the basis of customer relationship management (CRM).

RECENT EVENTS AND TRENDS IN THE HOSPITALITY AND TOURISM SECTORS

The hospitality and tourism sectors have changed in fundamental ways in recent years. Since the events of 11 September 2001 in the USA there have been other terrorist attacks, often aimed at the tourism sector, for example in major hotel chains such as Marriott, Taj Group and Oberoi. Natural disasters too have had a massive effect on the travel and tourism industry in numerous parts of the globe. In spite of these difficulties, tourism has continued to grow over the last decade. There have also been some fascinating changes: for example the continued growth of new markets such as the outbound market of tourism from China; the increased use of the internet by tourists as an information source and a booking medium with concomitant growth in the numbers of independent travellers; and the use of social networking sites and hand-held technology, which has brought about a rapid period of change for the industry.

These trends and changes, together with the evolving nature of the hospitality consumer's demand, have meant that the hospitality industry has experienced an increasingly competitive environment for high-quality service and customer satisfaction (Parayani et al., 2010). Many changes in consumer demand have developed over the last decade, but as Butler (2009: 348) reminds us, the heart of tourism and hospitality remains centred on simple issues: 'at the core of tourism the basic purpose will remain the same ... namely the pursuit of enjoyment and relaxation in a multitude of forms away from the home for a limited period of time'. An appreciation of how consumers make decisions helps marketers to develop their marketing plans in relation to a number of areas. These include, first, the ability to focus marketing activity at the time when most consumers are making decisions to buy a particular product; secondly, to choose an appropriate marketing medium; and finally, to select appropriate distribution channels (Swarbrooke and Horner, 2007).

One of the key developments in tourism has been what Poon (1993) calls 'new tourists'. These consumers have a very different set of needs and wants, are more quality conscious and require personalized experiences rather than the mass produced services of old. There are three main areas of interest that are related to these 'new tourists'. These are, first, the focus of hospitality customers on the *quality of service*, secondly, the growth of *the green tourist*, and thirdly, the emergence of *the global consumer* (Swarbrooke and Horner, 2007).

Quality of service

In a dynamic environment hospitality consumers are demanding new and different levels of *quality of service*. Since Pine and Gilmore (1999) coined the phrase the 'experience economy', emphasis has been placed on marketing emotional experiences rather than mere products. We have also seen the rise of co-creation, whereby consumers wish to be active rather than passive participants in the creation of these touristic experiences. Ladhari (2000) focused on the customer emotions that were present during service encounters and concluded that it was important for hotel guests to have good opinions of the service–quality relationship and that good experiences lead to emotional satisfaction of guests. Research by Mattila and Enz (2002) also showed that the guests' emotions and moods are significantly associated with their overall perceptions of the hotel and that the development of positive moods in the hotel business is thus important. The development of these emotional experiences has been given a new term in marketing – experiential marketing – which means that organizations that go beyond service excellence and delight customers with innovative experiences of design will lead to the creation of value in the sector (Williams, 2006). One example of a hotel chain that has responded to the desire for emotional experiences is the Starwood group. They recruited Eva Ziegler in 2006 to transform their business, especially in the Le Méridien and W brands, into a lifestyle business that reflected their consumers, whom they perceived as having become well-informed, individualistic, techno-savvy and with a creative mind-set (Starwood, 2010).

The green tourist

The interest in 'green consumerism' has spilt over into the tourism and hospitality agenda in recent years. Green tourists include eco-tourists who are motivated to see the natural history of a destination, alternative tourists who like tourism products that are less packaged, 'intelligent tourists' who want to learn something new from their experiences, and sustainable tourists who are concerned with social justice and economic impact. Ethical tourists are concerned with a broader range of issues, including human resource policies, use of local labour, as well as the economic benefits of tourism development (Swarbrooke, 1999, Swarbrooke and Horner, 2007).

Research has shown that major hotel chains have begun to take corporate social activity very seriously and are beginning to make the most of this in relation to reporting their activity on websites and in other media. This includes work on making hotels 'more green' as well as other activities such as management of diversity amongst their workforce, charitable donations, and work with local communities. Companies such as the French group Accor have been identified as particularly active in this area (Holcomb et al., 2007). The use of local food to provide fresh high-quality products to an increasingly discerning consumer is another opportunity not to be missed, especially by small to medium-size enterprises (Alonso and O'Neill, 2010; Mintel, 2010).

The global consumer

The traditional view of the relationship between consumers and suppliers during marketing has been that the consumer will demand mass produced products at a low price (Ritzer, 1996). The emergence of new types of consumer who demand different types of products and services was predicted to have a major effect on the tourism industry (Sharpley, 1996), and provide opportunities for new types of service ideas. Concern for the environment, the desire for authentic experiences, and an interest in heritage tourism, for example, all demonstrate this new type of tourist behaviour. As well as this desire for more upmarket services we must also remember that the desire for budget experiences has also been a growing sector of the hospitality and tourism sector. Budget airlines have capitalized on this growth as well as hotel chains such as Accor, who have developed their budget brands – Ibis, Etap and F1 (Accor, 2010).

One way that an organization can engage with this increasingly global market is by using Global Distribution Systems (GDS) and Web-based distribution systems (such as Expedia™, Lastminute.com™, Opodo and ebookers.com in the European context for example) have also opened up new opportunities for hospitality companies to target consumers from a variety of cultural backgrounds (Mintel, 2010). Loyalty schemes are also a way in which hospitality and tourism organizations can target consumers from different backgrounds. Perhaps the most exciting marketing development, however, is the increasing use of social media in hotels' marketing communication strategies to enable engagement with consumers across national boundaries (HVS, 2010). The use of social blogging by Bill Marriott of Marriott Hotels and Resorts, for example, has allowed the company to make contact with guests and to reinforce the company's brand image.

CONCLUDING REMARKS

There is a myriad of new trends in the hospitality and tourism sector that organizations have to engage with if they are to be successful in their marketing activity. There are also new technologies that allow the organizations to engage with consumers in a different way. At the heart of the debate, however, the original principles of marketing such as marketing research, market segmentation, positioning and branding within a marketing planning framework still form the backbone of a successful marketing strategy, but organizations that fail to take note of new trends amongst consumers and new methods to communicate with them do so at their peril. It is also important to remember that marketing management requires equal inputs of creativity, serious planning and the ability to communicate both inside and outside the organization.

FURTHER READING

Kotler, P, Bowen, J T and Makens, J C (2006) *Marketing for Hospitality and Tourism*, 4th edn, Upper Saddle River, NJ: Pearson.

Mintel (2011) *The Evolution of Slow Travel – International*, London: Mintel.

REFERENCES

Accor (2010) www.accor.com, last accessed 9 November 2011.

Alonso, A D and O'Neill, M (2010) 'Small hospitality enterprises and local produce: a case study', *British Food Journal*, 112, 11: 1175–89.

Butler, R (2009) 'Tourism in the future: cycles, waves or wheels?', *Futures*, 41, 6: 346–52.

Chartered Institute of Marketing (1976) *Annual Report*, Cookham: The Chartered Institute of Marketing.

Chartered Institute of Marketing (2007) *Tomorrow's Word – Re-evaluating the Role of Marketing*, Cookham: Chartered Institute of Marketing.

Holcomb, J L, Upchurch, R S and Okumus, F (2007) 'Corporate social responsibility: what are top hotel companies reporting?', *International Journal of Contemporary Hospitality Management*, 19, 6: 461–75.

HVS (2010) 'How are hotels embracing social media in 2010?', www.hvs.com/Content/2977.pdf February, last accessed 8 November 2011.

Kotler, P, Bowen, J T and Makens, J C (2006) *Marketing for Hospitality and Tourism*, 4th edn, Upper Saddle River, NJ: Pearson.

Ladhari, R (2000) 'Service quality, emotional satisfaction, and behavioural intentions: a study in the hotel industry', *Managing Service Quality*, 9, 3: 308–31.

Mattila, A and Enz, C (2002) 'The role of emotions in service encounters', *Journal of Service Research*, 4, 4: 268–77.

Mintel (2010) *Hotel Technology – International*, London: Mintel.

Parayani, K, Masoudi, A and Cudney, E (2010) 'QFD application in the hospitality industry – a hotel case study', *Quality Management Journal*, 17, 1: 7–28.

Pine, J and Gilmore, J (1999) *The Experience Economy*, Boston: Harvard Business School Press.

Poon, A (1993) *Tourism, Technology and Competitive Strategies*, Wallingford: CAB International.

Ritzer, G (1996) *The McDonaldization of Society*, rev. edn, Thousand Oaks: Pine Forge Press.

Sharpley, R (1996) 'Tourism and consumer culture in postmodern society', in Robinson, M, Evans, N and Callaghan, P (eds) *Proceedings of the 'Tourism and Culture: Towards the 21st Century Conference*, Centre for Travel and Tourism/Business Education. pp. 203–15.

Swarbrooke, J (1999) *Sustainable Tourism Management*, Wallingford: CAB International .

Swarbrooke, J and Horner, S (2007) *Consumer Behaviour in Tourism*, 2nd edn, Oxford: Butterworth–Heinemann.

Starwood (2010) www.starwoodhotels.com/corporate/profile_detail.html?obj_id=0900c7b980adec5e, last accessed 11 November 2011.

Tsiotsou, R and Ratten, V (2010) 'Future research directions in tourism marketing', *Marketing Intelligence and Planning*, 28, 4: 533–44.

Williams, A (2006) 'Tourism and hospitality marketing: fantasy, feeling and fun', *International Journal of Contemporary Hospitality Management*, 18, 6: 492–5.

marketing in hospitality

Susan Horner and John Swarbrooke

See also: *Food production and service systems; Food, beverage and restaurant management; Gastronomy and haute cuisine*

The term 'meal experience' was coined by UK marketer Graham Campbell-Smith (1967). At the time it was a somewhat revolutionary concept, embracing the idea that foods and beverages were not the only, or necessarily most, important components influencing guests' experiences when dining out. Other tangible and less tangible factors of importance included a restaurant's quality of service, its décor and ambience/atmosphere.

RESEARCH INTO THE MEAL EXPERIENCE

Research into the meal experience is suggestive rather than conclusive. There is uncertainty over the factors *most* important to consumers in evaluating meal experiences. The (UK) National Catering Inquiry (1966: 12) reported that, 'In spite of the trend towards novel décor and a generally more "swinging" atmosphere, people still go to restaurants primarily for a good meal.' Though not the same thing as the meal experience, factors influencing restaurant selection may be regarded as a reasonable indicator of what is important to consumers. In considering five factors influencing restaurant selection (food quality; menu variety; price; atmosphere; and convenience), Lewis (1981) found that food quality was the most important. June and Smith (1987) focused on affluent diners and asked them to indicate the most important factors in selecting a restaurant for each of four occasions (an intimate dinner; a birthday celebration; a business lunch; and a family dinner). They identified liquor and service as the two most important, followed by price, food quality and atmosphere. Auty (1992) found food type, food quality, value for money, image and atmosphere, location, and speed of service to be most important meal experience factors, with price and atmosphere becoming important in making distinctions between restaurants only after food type and quality were considered. Harris and West (1995: 43) examined the expectations of mature restaurant diners (aged 55+) and found a preference among this group for full-service restaurants. A later study of mature diners by Yamanaka et al. (2003) found quality of food, cleanliness and 'reasonable' prices to be the most important criteria in restaurant selection. Clark and Wood (1998) found that the five factors most commonly cited when choosing a restaurant were: range of food; quality of food; price of food; atmosphere; and speed of service. Myung et al. (2008) suggested price was the most important factor in meal choice.

Researchers in fields other than hospitality management have tended to broadly support the concept of the meal experience as defined by Campbell-Smith. Finkelstein (1989: 3–5) notes that the 'physical appearance of the restaurant, its ambience and décor, are as important to the event of dining out as are the comes-tibles'. However, she goes on to argue that in restaurants, people behave in ways in which they believe they are expected to behave and in so doing do not engage in authentic social interaction or experience real enjoyment. Warde and Martens (1999: 128–30) profoundly disagree with Finkelstein from the standpoint of undertaking perhaps the most significant empirical research into the meal experi-ence to date. Far from being unreflective 'dupes' submissive to the imperatives of the restaurants, Warde and Martens' respondents clearly gave considerable thought to the dining out experience and 47% 'agreed strongly' with the proposition that 'I always enjoy myself when I eat out' with a further 35% 'agreeing slightly'. Further, some 82% had 'liked a lot' their last experience of eating out. Dissecting the elements of the meal experience most enjoyed by respondents, Warde and Martens found aspects of sociability (those very aspects of the meal experience that Finkelstein suggests are at best artificial and at worst acted-out without any 'real' enthusiasm) likely to be most pleasing, nearly 97% saying they liked the company and the conversation.

THE 5A MODEL OF THE MEAL EXPERIENCE

In hospitality management, the dominant model for understanding the meal expe-rience over the last decade or so has been inspired by one or other aspect of the so-called five-aspect or 5A model of the meal experience developed by Gustafsson (2004: 11) which reasserts the view that 'meals consist of much more than the food to be eaten' and is proposed as 'a tool for understanding and handling the different aspects involved in producing commercial meals and offering guests the best pos-sible meal experience' (Gustafsson et al., 2006: 90). The model is essentially an encompassing one, comprising five elements (see Edwards and Gustafsson, 2008). In an inner central circle are three core elements – room, meeting and product. The room represents the physical setting of the meal; the meeting constitutes the inter-personal relations between diners and other diners and personnel; the product is the gastronomic blending of food and drink. This circle is encompassed within a second, the area between their boundaries representing the management control system of the business/organization providing the meal. The management control system includes administrative (economic, legal and technical) aspects of delivering the meal experience. In turn, this circle is enclosed within a third, the space between its boundaries and that of the second circle representing 'atmosphere', which is 'radiated' by interaction of the other variables.

Despite generating a considerable number of studies that work with a largely common model of the meal experience, research in the 5A tradition has thus far not significantly advanced our knowledge and understanding of the relative impor-tance of the range of objective and subjective dimensions to the meal experience. Arguably, one reason for this is the unwieldy nature of the 5A model itself, but perhaps more limiting in respect of *all* the research into the (commercial) meal experience is the tendency to view it in isolation from the wider food system(s) of which it is a part (see, for example, Beardsworth and Keil, 1997; Wood, 2004).

A WIDER WORLD OF MEAL EXPERIENCES

The commercial meal experience does not exist in a timeless vacuum but is the product of an individual's history, learning and resources mediated by economic and societal systems and structures. The commercial meal experience is, first, one 'localized' instance of a wider system of network influences (connections to other parts of the food system) that begins in the family and/or home and, second, part of the wider economic and social fabric of which 'dining', in a generalized sense, is part. A flaw in existing research is to underrate these influences, which influence consumers' motivations and expectations, and ultimately help form their judgements of (commercial) meal experiences.

As an example of this, consider the motivation underlying the decision to participate in a commercially provided meal experience. Pavesic (1989: 45, italics in original) notes that:

> Customers will evaluate a restaurant as a place to *eat-out* or as a place to *dine-out*. If a restaurant is considered an *eat-out* operation during the week (a substitute for cooking at home), customers will be more price conscious. If a restaurant is considered a *dine-out* operation, the visit is regarded more as a social occasion or entertainment and price is not as much of a factor.

It requires little investigative imagination to realize that a customer's expectations of an 'eat-out' meal experience as opposed to a 'dine-out' one may potentially differ with equally varying consequences for the evaluation of that experience. Existing approaches to the study of the meal experience tend to ignore or marginalize such considerations, focusing overly on the *in situ* factors affecting diners. Indeed, the meal experience concept resonates with more recently fashionable academic discourse on the so-called 'experience economy' (Pine and Gilmore, 1999) and its applications in the hospitality context. Hemmington (2007: 749) thus states that, in the hospitality industry, 'customers do not buy service delivery, they buy experiences; they do not buy service quality, they buy memories; they do not buy food and drink, they buy meal experiences'. The difficulty with this view is that empirical testing of concepts related to the 'experience economy' is at an early stage and evidence as to Hemmington's assertions is at best tenuous.

CONCLUDING REMARKS

The 'meal experience' remains a fundamental and largely uncritically accepted marketing concept in hospitality. A cynic might argue that this is because it reassures hospitality providers that the quality of food and beverages need not be that great if the non-food and beverage elements within the meal experience can be manipulated to guide customers to positively evaluate that experience. Some years ago, Johns et al. (1996: 23) noted that whilst 'it was impossible to identify clearly the factors which make up the meal experience', some of their evidence supported the view that 'food was the most important element of the majority of meal experiences'. Wood (2000a) concurred, implying that the core elements (i.e. food and drink) in the meal experience retained a central importance, with other factors being, in essence, peripheral, implying that the importance of the non-food and drink aspects of the meal experience have been exaggerated in their importance to consumers. Such views are suggestive, not conclusive. Both intuitively and logically, it would, of course, be unsurprising to find that relatively 'concrete' factors such as the quality and variety of food and drink are regarded as most important by consumers in evaluating meal experiences. However, it will seemingly be some time yet before research of sufficient sophistication is able to shed light on such matters.

FURTHER READING

Wood, R C (2000a) 'How important is the meal experience? Choices, menus and dining environments', in Wood, R (ed.) *Strategic Questions in Food and Beverage Management*, Oxford: Butterworth–Heinemann. pp. 28–47.

REFERENCES

Auty, S (1992) 'Consumer choice and segmentation in the restaurant industry', *The Service Industries Journal*, 12, 3: 324–39.

Beardsworth, A and Keil, T (1997) *Sociology on the Menu: An Invitation to the Study of Food and Society*, London: Routledge.

Campbell-Smith, G (1967) *The Marketing of the Meal Experience*, Guildford: University of Surrey Press.

Clark, M A and Wood, R C (1998) 'Consumer loyalty in the restaurant industry: a preliminary exploration of the issues', *International Journal of Contemporary Hospitality Management*, 10, 4: 139–44.

Edwards, J and Gustafsson, I-B (2008) 'The five aspects meal model', *Journal of Foodservice*, 19, 1: 4–12.

Finkelstein, J (1989) *Dining Out: A Sociology of Modern Manners*, Cambridge: Polity Press.

Gustafsson, I-B (2004) 'Culinary arts and meal science – a new scientific research discipline', *Food Service Technology*, 4, 1: 9–20.

Gustafsson, I-B, Öström, Å, Johansson, J and Mossberg, L (2006) 'The five aspects meal model: a tool for developing meal services in restaurants', *Journal of Foodservice*, 17, 2: 84–93.

Harris, K J and West, J J (1995) 'Senior savvy: mature diners' restaurant service expectations', *Florida International University Hospitality Review*, 13, 2: 35–44.

Hemmington, N (2007) 'From service to experience: understanding and defining the hospitality business', *The Service Industries Journal*, 27, 6: 747–55.

Johns, N, Tyas, P, Ingold, T and Hopkinson, S (1996) 'Investigation of the perceived components of the meal experience using perceptual gap methodology', *Progress in Tourism and Hospitality Research*, 2, 1: 15–26.

June, L and Smith, S L J (1987) 'Service attributes and situational effects on customer preferences for restaurant dining', *Journal of Travel Research*, 26, 2: 20–7.

Lewis, R (1981) 'Restaurant advertising: appeals and consumers' intentions', *Journal of Advertising Research*, 21, 5: 69–74.

Myung, E, McCool, A C and Feinstein, A H (2008) 'Understanding attributes affecting meal choice decisions in a bundling context', *International Journal of Hospitality Management*, 27, 2: 119–25.

National Catering Inquiry (1966) *The British Eating Out*, Glasgow: National Catering Inquiry.

Pavesic, D (1989) 'Psychological aspects of menu pricing', *International Journal of Hospitality Management*, 8, 1: 43–9.

Pine, B J and Gilmore, J H (1999) *The Experience Economy*, Boston: Harvard Business School Press.

Warde, A and Martens, L (1999) 'Eating out: reflections on the experience of consumers in England', in Germov, J and Williams, L (eds) *A Sociology of Food and Nutrition: The Social Appetite*, Oxford: Oxford University Press. pp. 116–34.

Wood, R C (2000a) 'How important is the meal experience? Choices, menus and dining environments', in Wood, R (ed.) *Strategic Questions in Food and Beverage Management*, Oxford: Butterworth–Heinemann. pp. 28–47.

Wood, R (2004) 'Closing a planning gap? The future of food production and service systems theory', *Tourism and Hospitality Planning and Development*, 1, 1: 19–37.

Yamanaka, K, Almanza, B, Nelson, D and De Vaney, S (2003) 'Older Americans' dining out preferences', *Journal of Foodservice Business Research*, 6, 1: 87–103.

Roy C. Wood

Meetings, Incentives, Conferences/conventions and Events/exhibitions (MICE)

See also: Customer relationship management in hospitality; Industry structure and sectors; Service quality in hospitality

MICE is an acronym for four major segments of the group market: meetings, incentives, conventions and exhibitions, all of which have experienced substantial growth fueled by rapid globalization and contribute significantly to the business of the hospitality industry (FutureWatch, 2004). Inconsistent definitions and measurement practices make estimates of the size and significance of the MICE industry uncertain and difficult to compare (Crouch and Ritchie, 1998). According to a study by PriceWaterhouseCoopers (2011a), the economic impact of MICE in the largest market, the USA, is considerable, representing $263 billion in spending and contributing $106 billion to GDP annually. In addition to the primary economic impact of direct spending, the MICE industry creates considerable secondary benefits through indirect spending by convention-related businesses to pay for wages, supplies, equipment and taxes.

MEETINGS

Meetings vary in size from a few people to several thousand and are held to communicate, inform, exchange ideas, teach, train or celebrate. They can be held in many different venues, from hotels to sports stadiums. There are many different types of meeting. The most important tend to be: assemblies (large formal gatherings during which the leadership of an association or corporation addresses its members); conventions/conferences; colloquia (usually where academicians or scientists deliver lectures followed by a question and answer session); symposia (formal presentation of material by a number of experts on a particular subject); and special events (Schlentrich, 2008). A special event is a one-time or infrequently occurring occasion outside the normal programmes or activities of the sponsoring or organizing body (van der Wagen and Carlos, 2005: 4), which range in scale from mega-events such as the Olympics, to community festivals and programmes at parks (Getz, 1989: 125).

INCENTIVES

Corporations use incentive travel to motivate, reward and recognize employees for outstanding performance, service and commitment (Cecil, 2005: 340). The incentive market is composed of two major sub-sectors: group and individual incentive travel. Group incentive travel provides an excellent opportunity to convey a sense of 'belonging' to a corporation, encouraging team spirit and camaraderie (Witt et al., 1992: 277). Individual incentive travel focuses on many of the same objectives as group travel, but is usually attended by fewer people (Meetings Market Report, 2004). Incentive programmes are usually staged at upscale international destinations and include high-quality leisure and entertainment experiences. Spouses are normally invited. The largest share of the incentive market is derived from insurance companies and car dealerships (Astroff and Abbey, 2002: 184). Almost all incentive programmes involve special entertainment, themed food and beverage functions, and either spectator or participative events. It is not uncommon for larger companies to charter a jet or an entire cruise ship for their incentive programme (Schlentrich, 1999). In addition, incentive travel packages normally include exclusive transportation and first class accommodation (Cecil, 2005: 340). The importance of the incentive segment is reflected in the fact that the Society of Incentive and Travel Executives is an international association with 1,800 members in 82 countries (Society of Incentive and Travel Executives, 2006).

CONVENTIONS

A convention is an assembly, often periodic (typically annually), and usually large (ranging from several hundred to tens of thousands) of delegates or representatives of a political, religious, commercial or other organization. Conventions usually have a formal structure, extend for a period of many days and include several functions such as board of director meetings, general assemblies, symposiums and workshops. In Europe the term congress is generally employed to describe an event that in the USA would be called a convention.

A conference is a near-synonym for the term 'convention', usually implying much discussion and participation (Astroff and Abbey, 2002: 9). A conference is an event used by an organization to meet and exchange views, convey a message, open a debate, or give publicity to an area of opinion on a specific subject (Shock, 2005: 424). Conferences can be large or small. A 'summit' is the term used to describe a conference that is attended by heads of government or high-level officials.

EXHIBITIONS

Exhibitions and trade shows are a lucrative and fast-growing segment of the MICE industry (Astroff and Abbey, 2002: 475). Broadly, it is possible to distinguish between (a) exhibitions and expositions and (b) trade shows. The former are events designed to bring together purveyors of products, equipment and services in an environment in which they can display or demonstrate these to audiences that would otherwise be difficult and expensive to reach.

Trade shows or fairs are regularly scheduled and normally independent events held in the same location on an annual basis during which suppliers present their products or services in an exhibit format, such as booths or displays. They are generally not open to the public, though some with a wider appeal (such as travel, food, car and home building) are increasingly open to the general public on specific days. Trade shows are designed to allow companies to meet potential customers face-to-face in a brief period of time inexpensively, and are an important and cost-effective promotional, marketing and sales tool, not least in Europe where around 20% of a company's business marketing communication budget is allocated to trade show participation compared to around 10% for the USA (Sandler, 1994, see also Seringhaus and Rosson, 2001: 878). Visitors to trade shows pay an entrance fee and are given the opportunity to inspect products and receive demonstrations and brochures, as well as verbal information from vendors. Two of the largest and most established international trade fairs are the Frankfurt Book Fair, the world's largest book fair, established in 1949, with more than 7,000 exhibitors from over 100 countries and approximately 285,000 visitors from about 120 countries in 2005 (Frankfurt Book Fair, 2006); and the International Tourism Bourse, the world's largest travel trade show, established in 1994 in Berlin, with more than 10,000 exhibitors from 110 countries and approximately 130,000 visitors from 180 countries in 2003 (International Tourism Bourse, 2006).

MEETING OR EVENT PLANNERS

The meeting or event planner is an intermediary who is responsible for the planning and supervision of an event (Schlentrich, 1999). A meeting planner is either a part- or full-time member of the organization that is sponsoring an event, or is an externally contracted professional. As a result of the recent trend of outsourcing, both corporations and associations are increasingly contracting their meeting and convention planning needs to independent meeting planners (Toh et al., 2005: 431). Tasks that the meeting planner performs are: to meet with the sponsor to determine the objectives of the event; review the history of prior meetings; analyse trends and prices; review the policies of the sponsoring organization; identify the meeting format; and profile the targeted attendee. The top five criteria for meeting planners in their selection of a destination and venue are value for money, overall cost, reputation for hosting successful events, desirable destination image and support services for events (DiPietro et al., 2008: 271).

CONCLUDING REMARKS: TRENDS IN MEETINGS AND CONVENTIONS

The MICE industry is currently experiencing three major trends. The *first* is the continuing growth of China as an economic powerhouse, reflected in the number of international association meetings held in mainland China, which increased from 83 in 2000 to 245 in 2009 (Lowe, 2011). The growth of the Chinese convention and meeting sector can be attributed in large part to the government's investment in airports, railroads and highways as well as state of the art convention and exhibition centers. These government initiatives have been mirrored by investments in upscale hotel properties with extensive meeting facilities by international hotel groups such as InterContinental Hotels, Marriott International, Hilton, Starwood, Hyatt and Accor in mainland China.

A *second* major trend is the growing disillusionment with reliance on impersonal electronic communication such as email and video conferencing in the business world. According to a study by Embassy Suites Hotels (2011), 76% of businessmen believe that spending less face-to-face time with clients had a negative impact on their business relationships. In addition, business travellers estimate that 50% of prospects become customers when an in-person meeting takes place versus only 31% without one (World Travel and Tourism Council, 2011a). Despite growth in the use of communications technologies in business, in-person meetings are still felt to be an indispensable component of developing and maintaining strong business relationships.

A *third* trend is the focus on sustainability. The majority of meeting planners, for example, now enquire about sustainability efforts on their requests for venue proposals and attempt to source locally produced food and beverages for their events (Shapiro, 2009). In addition, the International Tourism Partnership and the World Travel and Tourism Council recently collaborated on an initiative to unite efforts by the leading international hotel chains to reduce the carbon footprint (World Travel and Tourism Council, 2011b).

The MICE sector is increasingly important to the business of hospitality organizations and, notwithstanding difficult economic circumstances, is likely to remain so in the future.

FURTHER READING

Fenich, G G (2011) *Meetings, Expositions, Events and Conventions: An Introduction to the Industry*, 3rd edn, Upper Saddle River: Prentice Hall.

Professional Convention Management (2011) *Professional Management: Comprehensive Strategies for Meetings, Conventions and Events*, 5th edn, Chicago: Professional Convention Educational Association.

REFERENCES

Astroff, M T and Abbey, J R (2002) *Convention Sales and Services*, 6th edn, Las Vegas: Waterbury Press.

Cecil, A K (2005) 'Incentive travel', in Pizam, A (ed.) *International Encyclopedia of Hospitality Management*, Oxford: Butterworth–Heinemann. pp. 339–40.

Crouch, G I and Ritchie, J R B (1998) 'Convention site selection research: a review, conceptual model, and propositional framework', *Journal of Convention and Exhibition Management*, 1, 1: 49–69.

DiPietro, R B, Breiter, D, Rompf, P and Godlewska, M (2008) 'An exploratory study of differences among meeting and exhibition planners in their destination selection criteria', *Journal of Convention and Event Tourism*, 9, 4: 258–76.

Embassy Suites Hotels (2011) *Third Annual Business Travel Survey*, McLean, VA: Hilton Worldwide.

Frankfurt Book Fair (2006) www.frankfurt-book-fair.com, last accessed 14 March 2006.

FutureWatch (2004) *A Comparative Outlook on the Global Business of Meetings*, supplement to *The Meeting Professional* (January), Dallas, TX: Meeting Professionals International and American Express (also found at www.hospitalitynet.org/file/152001272.pdf, last accessed 20 November 2011).

Getz, D (1989) 'Special events: defining the product', *Tourism Management*, 10, 2: 125–37.

International Tourism Bourse (2006) www.itb-berlin.de/en, last accessed 14 March 2006.

Lowe, C M (2011) 'Emerging meetings market: China', *Meetings and Conventions Magazine*, 46, 1: 15.

Meetings Market Report (2004) *Meetings and Conventions Magazine (Supplement)*, 46, 1: 15.

PriceWaterhouseCoopers (2011a) 'The economic significance of meetings to the U.S. economy', http://meetingsmeanbusiness.com/docs/Economic%20Study%20Release.pdf, last accessed 20 November 2011.

Sandler, G (1994) 'Fair dealing', *Journal of European Business*, 4, 1: 46–9.

Schlentrich, U A (1999) 'Conference and convention management', in Verginis, C S and Wood, R C (eds) *Accommodation Management: Perspectives for the International Hotel Industry*, London: Thomson. pp. 150–71.

Schlentrich, U A (2008) 'The MICE industry: meetings, incentives, conventions and exhibitions', in Brotherton, B and Wood, R C (eds) *The Sage Handbook of Hospitality Management*, London: Sage. pp. 400–20.

Seringhaus, F H R and Rosson, P J (2001) 'Firm experience and international trade fairs', *Journal of Marketing Management*, 17, 7–8: 877–901.

Shapiro, M J (2009) 'Still thinking green', *Meetings and Conventions Magazine*, 44, 10: 28.

Shock, P J (2005) 'Meetings', in Pizam, A (ed.) *International Encyclopedia of Hospitality Management*, Oxford: Butterworth–Heinemann. pp. 424–5.

Society of Incentive and Travel Executives (2006) www.site-intl.org, last accessed 14 March 2006.

Toh, R S, DeKay, C F and Yates, B (2005) 'Independent meeting planners: roles, compensation, and potential conflicts', *Cornell Hotel and Restaurant Administration Quarterly*, 46, 4: 431–43.

key concepts in
hospitality management

van der Wagen, L and Carlos, B R (2005) *Event Management for Tourism, Cultural, Business, and Sporting Events*, Upper Saddle River: Prentice Hall.

Witt, S F, Gammon, S and White, J (1992) 'Incentive travel: overview and case study of Canada as a destination for the UK market', *Tourism Management*, 13, 3: 275–87.

World Travel and Tourism Council (2011a) *Business Travel: A Catalyst for Economic Performance*, www.wttc.org/site_media/uploads/downloads/WTTC_Business_Travel_2011.pdf, last accessed 20 November 2011.

World Travel and Tourism Council (2011b) 'Hotel companies demonstrate leadership through new initiative', www.wttc.org/news-media/news-archive/2011/hotel-companies-demonstrate-leadership-through-new-initiative/, last accessed 20 November 2011.

Udo A. Schlentrich

Operations Management in Hospitality

See also: Food production and service systems; Front office management; Hospitality management education; Service quality in hospitality; Revenue management

According to Jones (2008: 2), 'operations management is the study of how goods get manufactured and service gets delivered'. This definition emphasizes the study of operations rather than the practice of operations management and recognizes that operations management is strongly grounded in operations research. Initially it was a branch of mathematical science designed to provide the numeric data required to make complex operational decisions. Over time, however, the discipline of decision science emerged and this later developed into the field of management science, which draws on psychology as well as quantitative analyses to establish management best practice.

Among the more well-known proponents of management science was Frederick Winslow Taylor, whose seminal book *The Principles of Scientific Management*, published in 1911, explained how productivity could be improved by breaking jobs down into simple tasks and training unskilled workers to perform those tasks in a continual sequence. More recently termed 'production lining', Lockwood and Jones (2000) explain this as the breaking down of production activities into steps that can be completed on a production line. Although little has been written on 'Taylorism' in hospitality management, a Tayloristic approach has been a core feature of hospitality management practice for some time. The commercial kitchen 'partie system', where labour is divided into key sectors and sub-sectors each headed by a chef (meaning chief) responsible for the efficient operation of a section within a large commercial kitchen, is one example. Another is the management of food production and service in so-called quick-service restaurants (QSRs), particularly international franchises such as McDonald's, where relatively simple tasks are performed by unskilled workers trained to adhere to guidelines and specifications developed around a series of low-level tasks. Taylor's task-orientated approach also employed time and motion studies to establish the number of times a task could be performed within a specific time period. These studies have been used to set industry benchmarks, not unlike some of those in the hospitality industry today, such as the number of rooms a chambermaid/room attendant should be able to clean during one shift.

Unlike the manufacturing sector where Taylor's work was concentrated, hospitality businesses operate under different conditions, which is why hospitality operators require professional specialist training. These conditions include fluctuating levels of business during a 24 hour operating cycle, perishability of products, labour intensity with a mix of permanent and casual labour, and the need for strong financial management (Sasser et al., 1978; Yu, 1999). Add to this the requirement to develop, implement, monitor and evaluate a series of processes and procedures to control product and service standards at all levels of the operation and the need for a systematic approach to operations management becomes obvious.

Reflecting on hospitality management operations systems, Ball (2008) differentiates between the systems theory and analysis that is used to conduct research in hospitality operations, and the systems that drive the practical operation of hospitality businesses. He asserts that there are two operational systems in hospitality; accommodation (known as lodging in North America) and foodservice operations. However, these two operational areas are supported by a series of sub-systems that include the production system, developed for the kitchen or bar to produce food and beverages; and the service system, which specifies the manner in which products are served to customers. There are also various systems that are employed to influence customer demand, for example sales and reservations systems. Together these interacting systems allow hospitality provision to be presented to guests as a single, unified offering (Cracknell et al., 2000). Management science looks at the inter-relationships between all functional areas of an operation to ensure that each area operates in a manner that is congruent with, and supportive of, the overall organizational concept. This perspective recognizes the distinction between operations in practice and operations management, suggesting that all organizational areas can contribute to, or have an impact on, the overall system or operation.

The organizational structure within the hospitality industry divides the main functional activities into departments. These can differ slightly between accommodation and non-accommodation hospitality businesses. However, the most complex entity – a full-service, luxury hotel – uses an organizational structure that typically comprises five departments. These are: rooms division, food and beverage, sales and marketing, human resources (HR) and financial control (Hayes and Ninemeier, 2007). While only rooms division and the food and beverage department are profit centres that engage in production and service, the other three departments are also strongly connected to these operations and are managed accordingly. Their contribution to operations management is described later.

Rooms division is the name given to the department that is the first point of call when overnight guests arrive at a hotel. This department is responsible for checking guests in and out, allocating charges to guest accounts and handling customer service, including laundry, housekeeping and in-room amenities. As such, the department falls into what Johnston (1993) refers to as a customer processing operation, that is, an operation that does not produce products, provides limited services – such as servicing rooms – but is heavily involved in information processing (reservations, check-in and billing). Rooms division operations are heavily supported by the sales and marketing department, which uses sophisticated operations management tools (for example revenue management) to provide vital information to assist in rooms division operations.

The food and beverage department is the most complex in terms of hospitality operations in that successful operation involves developing and implementing purchasing specifications; selecting suppliers; purchasing large quantities of perishable products; storing and controlling inventory; standardizing dishes and recipes; preparing, cooking and serving meals and drinks; conducting menu engineering or similar techniques; and analysing profit sensitivity (Cross et al., 2009; Lillicrap and Cousins, 2006). The food and beverage department is assisted in many of these tasks by the financial control department, which oversees inventory control, stocktaking, the calculation of food cost, employee costs and operating costs as well as menu pricing.

CHALLENGES FOR HOSPITALITY OPERATORS

One of the most critical challenges for both rooms division and the food and beverage department is the management of capacity. While both departments receive capacity management support from sales and marketing and human resources, there are also a number of capacity management issues that are controlled within the food and beverage department. The majority of these are connected with volume and variety, that is, the amount of food or beverages that needs to be produced (volume) and the number of menu options (variety) available to guests (Lockwood and Jones, 2000). The more options available and/or the level of customization of dishes that guests are allowed to request, the more difficult it becomes to operate efficiently when capacity is high. That is why 'quick-service' restaurants with limited menus can manage large volumes of orders more easily than full-service restaurants. Full-service restaurants can, however, take steps to operate efficiently through intelligent menu design and by selecting menu items that do not place excessive burdens on individual pieces of equipment, for example deep fryers.

Operations management techniques can also be introduced to optimize dining room capacity. Examples include providing additional sittings during dining periods, involving customers in service (for instance, introducing buffet service), utilizing space other than that in the dining room, such as the bar or lounge for pre-dinner drinks or coffee, and introducing a table d'hôte menu to reduce the number of steps in the sequence of service (Sill, 1991).

TRENDS AND ISSUES

Over the last decade the sales and marketing and financial control departments have become more important to hospitality operations management because the information that these departments provide is used to make decisions that can have a dramatic impact on revenue. This department engages in sophisticated statistical techniques such as yield/revenue management to systematically capture and evaluate trend data in order to predict future sales (Cross et al., 2009). The information gained through these processes is then used to influence customer behaviour using promotional strategies when sales are predicted to be low, and price optimization strategies when sales are predicted to be high. The process recognizes that hotel rooms and meal periods are perishable resources and that hospitality operators need to sell their products and services at a price that maximizes yield in order to remain competitive. Revenue management also allows hospitality operators to proactively manage distribution channels so that as many rooms as possible are sold directly to the public at 'rack rates', with fewer being sold via travel agents or internet booking sites, which involves discounting and paying commission.

The human resources department also has a role in hospitality operations management because the hospitality industry is labour-intensive which means that the management of payroll has a significant impact on profit. HR has a direct influence on operations because the recruitment, training and development of employees, as well as the management of overtime, penalty rates, holiday shifts, insurance and employee benefits, are under this department's control. Operations management decisions within HR include determining the optimum number of full- and part-time employees, as well as tactical staff rostering based on sales forecasting.

CONCLUDING REMARKS

Managing large-scale hospitality operations is complex and requires key decision making skills as well as the ability to plan, budget, implement, control, motivate, promote, analyze and use this analysis to continually improve. As new technology is brought to bear on hospitality management practice, there is potential for each of the systems and sub-systems that encompass hospitality operations to become more integrated, strengthened and supported by all functional departments. This will allow more emphasis to be placed on providing exceptional service to guests, thereby exceeding their expectations and promoting the conditions for both guest loyalty and positive word of mouth communication.

FURTHER READING

Ball, S, Jones P, Kirk, D and Lockwood, A (2002) *Hospitality Operations: A Systems Approach*, London: Continuum.

Kirk, D (1995) 'Hard and soft systems: a common paradigm for operations management', *International Journal of Contemporary Hospitality Management*, 7, 5: 13–16.

Lovelock, C (1983) 'Classifying services to gain strategic marketing insights', *Journal of Marketing*, 47, 3: 9–20.

key concepts in hospitality management

REFERENCES

Ball, S (2008) 'Hospitality systems', in Jones, P (ed.) *Handbook of Hospitality Operations and IT*, Oxford: Butterworth–Heinemann. pp. 19–43.

Cracknell, H L, Nobis, G and Kaufman, R J (2000) *Practical Professional Catering*, 2nd edn, London: Thompson.

Cross, R G, Higbie, J A and Cross, D Q (2009) 'Revenue management's renaissance: a rebirth of the art and science of profitable revenue generation', *Cornell Hospitality Quarterly*, 50, 1: 56–81.

Hayes, D and Ninemeier, J (2007) *Hotel Operations Management*, 2nd edn, New York: Pearson.

Johnston, R (1993) 'A framework for developing a quality strategy in a customer processing operation', *International Journal of Quality and Reliability Management*, 4, 4: 37–46.

Jones, P (2008) 'Operations management: theoretical underpinnings', in Jones, P (ed.) *Handbook of Hospitality Operations and IT*, Oxford: Butterworth–Heinemann. pp. 1–19.

Lillicrap, D and Cousins, J (2006) *Food and Beverage Service*, 7th edn, London: Hodder Arnold.

Lockwood, A and Jones, P (2000) 'Managing hospitality operations', in Lashley, C and Morrison, A (eds) *In Search of Hospitality: Theoretical Perspectives and Debates*, Oxford: Butterworth–Heinemann. pp. 157–77.

Sasser, W E, Olsen, R P and Wyckoff, D D (1978) *Management of Service Operations: Text Cases and Readings*, Boston: Allyn and Bacon.

Sill, B (1991) 'Capacity management – making your service delivery more productive', *Cornell Hotel and Restaurant Administration Quarterly*, 31, 4: 77–88.

Taylor, F W (1911) *The Principles of Scientific Management*, New York: Harper Brothers.

Yu, L (1999) *The International Hospitality Business: Management and Operations*, New York: Haworth Press.

G. Barry O'Mahony

Organizational Behaviour in Hospitality

See also: Human resource management in hospitality

Organizational behaviour is the academic study of organizational processes using social science methodology. It studies issues ranging from individual behaviour (for example how tips might or might not motivate a waiter); to group processes (for example why there is friction between the waiters and the chefs in a restaurant); to broader organization-wide structures and culture (for example why there is high turnover of waiting staff in one restaurant but not in another, similar, one).

Organizational behaviour seeks to understand how organizations work and how people work within them; this can give insights into how to operate more effectively within organizations. Whilst many models used in organizational behaviour are relevant across all industry sectors, including the hospitality industry, there are certain issues and themes that are particularly important for students of hospitality management.

Hospitality organizations all provide some combination of food, drink and/or accommodation to those who are away from home. But they range from micro-organizations (someone who takes in guests in their own home) to global hotel companies, such as Hilton or Intercontinental. There are organizations that are rooted in the norms and practices of their local communities, such as a British pub, or an American diner or a French café, but there are also organizations that try to transfer the same brand or concept across the world, like McDonald's and Starbucks. However, what hospitality organizations all have in common is that they involve both service and production operations. Food is prepared in some way as well as being served, rooms are 'made up' as well as sold.

PEOPLE IN HOSPITALITY ORGANIZATIONS

If you are student looking for part-time work, on a gap year looking for some extra income while you are travelling, a migrant looking for your first job in your new country or someone who has just been made redundant and there is not much other work available, you will often apply for work in restaurants, hotels or bars. Few formal skills are needed to get your first job in the sector: indeed you may not even need to speak the local language well for back of house work such as being a room attendant or porter. You can often work flexible hours or on a temporary basis. It can also be fun employment, if it allows you to be paid to spend time in environments where you would have liked to spend your leisure time. But the fact that hospitality work can be available to people who would have difficulty finding other work, can make it seem as if it is *only* for these people: low-skilled and low-paid work that you do out of necessity or convenience rather than out of choice.

There are, of course, jobs in the sector that everyone recognizes as skilled: notably, chefs in high-class restaurants and hotels. Many entry-level roles actually do require quite high levels of skills and knowledge but this is often tacit knowledge, that is, the know-how that the person brings with them to the role and which is often unrecognized and unrewarded (for example room attendants are typically women who have considerable experience cleaning in a domestic environment).

'Emotional labour' and 'aesthetic labour' are two types of tacit skill that are important in front of house, customer service roles. Hochschild (1983) used the term 'emotional labour' to describe the way in which people in customer service roles are paid to manage their emotions for the benefit of the customer: to give 'service with a (genuine) smile' regardless of how they are feeling or being treated by customers. 'Aesthetic labour' (Nickson et al., 2001) refers to another skill that customer service staff are expected to bring to their work: that they are expected to 'look good' and 'sound right' and appropriately embody the image that the organization wants to project. The notion of 'aesthetic labour' can be used to explain why young and middle-class people, such as students, are desirable employees in fashionable bars and restaurants: they already know how to behave and look the part.

Other studies have built on Hochschild's (1983) and Nickson et al.'s (2001) work and drawn attention to some of the negative features of hospitality employment. Guerrier and Adib (2000), for example, investigated the abuse and harassment (including sexual harassment) that hospitality workers are sometimes subjected to by their customers. But it is important not to overstate these negative features. Service staff can be very skilled at, and enjoy, controlling customers in subtle ways (for example by pretending not to have seen customers). But this skill may not always be used to the best advantage of the employer. For instance, when staff are focused on maximizing their tips, they are likely to pay more attention to those customers they expect to be generous tippers. The efforts of employees to maximize their income and to exert control over customers can sometimes go beyond actions that decrease customer satisfaction to become scams or frauds (see Peacock and Kübler, 2001 for some illustrations).

MOTIVATING AND CONTROLLING STAFF

Hospitality managers are, therefore, tasked with managing a workforce with mainly 'transferable skills', whose members can easily move to other organizations, and who may have little commitment to a long-term career in their organization or even in the hospitality industry. They are also managing people who are difficult to control directly, as they may be working out of the sight of supervisors (for example room attendants) or because one is trying to influence not just what they do but also how they feel (to smile *and* to mean it). Further hospitality organizations are, what Korczynski (2002) terms, customer-oriented bureaucracies. This means that managers are subject to the dual pressures of, on the one hand, minimizing costs and processing customers as quickly and easily as possible and, on the other hand, of treating each customer as an individual and giving them exemplary service.

One approach is to make maximum use of technology and to simplify and standardize work so that it is difficult for even the least skilled and committed worker to 'mess up'. Whilst this is a less easy process in an industry such as hospitality than in manufacturing, it can be done, especially in operations aimed at a budget market: for example meals can be pre-prepared in a central operation so they only need 'finishing' locally, obviating the need for skilled chefs (airline food is a good example of this). Self-service check-in machines can be used in hotels to reduce the need for receptionists. Bedrooms can be designed with simple furniture to make them easy and quick to clean. This approach has been criticized by academics and others on the grounds that it creates deskilled jobs that are also de-motivating and unrewarding. One famous critique is from Ritzer (1996), who discusses the spread and broader consequences of this approach, which he terms

'McDonaldization', named after the fast food company. The alternative approach is to try to enrich rather than de-skill jobs and to 'empower' staff to use their initiative to provide better service and find solutions to customers' problems. One of the tensions that managers face is in finding a balance between the requirement to provide a standardized product and service so that customers know what to expect (especially in branded operations) and the need to empower staff to use their initiative where appropriate. Lashley's (2000b) case study on the restaurant chain TGI Fridays provides a good illustration of this.

For empowerment practices to work effectively, an appropriate organizational culture needs to be in place. Culture refers to the beliefs and practices that determine how things actually work and get done rather than the way in which they are supposed to be done. An organization's culture, as understood and enacted by its employees, can sometimes operate in opposition to the practices that managers say should be encouraged: for example managers may say that staff should treat all customers equally well but the organizational culture may encourage staff to believe that, in practice, it is more important to treat regulars well and new customers can be ignored. Cultural beliefs are passed on from more experienced employees to new employees.

There is considerable debate about the extent to which managers can control and change culture. Organizational culture is influenced not just by management actions but also the wider context in which the organization operates. In many parts of the hospitality industry, there is a strong occupational culture: that is, there are shared beliefs about how 'things are done' in a particular job regardless of the organization in which someone is working. For example, Cameron et al. (1999) discuss the competing influences of occupational culture and organizational culture for chefs in hotels. Further, organizational culture is likely to be influenced by the national culture in the country where the organization is operating. Groschl and Doherty (2006) show how performance appraisal is enacted and interpreted differently by French and British managers within the same international hotel company. Ogbonna and Harris (2002) argue that, in practice, many managers take what they term as a 'realist' perspective towards managing and changing organizational culture. They believe that it is not possible to completely control culture through top-down initiatives but it is possible to influence the behaviour and attitudes of 'core staff', that is those who are more committed to the company and likely to stay for a longer period.

CONCLUDING REMARKS

Organizational behaviour is a broad area of study and this essay can only touch upon some of the themes within it that are particularly relevant to the hospitality industry. This is an industry that is heavily dependent for its success on the way in which junior, often poorly paid and transient, employees do their jobs. There is no simple recipe for managing these employees effectively, but the insights that the study of organizational behaviour can provide into why they act as they do can help managers devise ways of improving their performance.

Guerrier, Y (2008) 'Organization studies and hospitality management', in Brotherton, B and Wood, R (eds) *The Sage Handbook of Hospitality Management*, London: Sage. pp. 257–72.

Lashley, C (1997) *Empowering Service Excellence: Beyond the Quick Fix*, London: Cassell.

REFERENCES

Cameron, D, Gore, J, Desombre, T and Riley, M J (1999) 'An examination of the reciprocal affects of occupational culture and organizational culture: the case of chefs in hotels', *International Journal of Hospitality Management* 18, 3: 225–34.

Groschl, S and Doherty, L (2006) 'The complexity of culture: using the appraisal process to compare French and British managers in a UK-based international hotel organization' *International Journal of Hospitality Management*, 25, 2: 313–34.

Guerrier, Y and Adib, A (2000) '"No, we don't provide that service": The harassment of hotel employees by customers', *Work, Employment and Society*, 14, 4: 689–705.

Hochschild, A (1983) *The Managed Heart*, Berkeley: University of California Press.

Korczynski, M (2002) *Human Resource Management in Service Work*, Basingstoke: Palgrave.

Lashley, C (2000b) 'Empowerment through involvement: a case study in TGI Fridays', *Personnel Review*, 29, 6: 333–49.

Nickson, D, Warhurst, C, Witz, A and Cullen, A-M (2001) 'The importance of being aesthetic', in Sturdy, A, Grugulis, I and Wilmott, H (eds) *Customer Service: Empowerment and Entrapment*, Basingstoke: Palgrave.

Ogbonna, E and Harris, L (2002) 'Managing organizational culture: insights from the hospitality industry', *Human Resource Management Journal*, 12, 1: 33–53.

Peacock, M and Kübler, M (2001) 'The failure of "control" in the hospitality industry', *International Journal of Hospitality Management*, 20, 4: 353–65.

Ritzer, G (1996) *The McDonaldization of Society*, rev. edn, Thousand Oaks: Pine Forge Press.

Yvonne Guerrier

Procurement in Hospitality

See also: Accommodation, lodging and facilities management; Beverages and beverage management; Design for hotels; Food, beverage and restaurant management; Housekeeping management; Operations management in hospitality

Procurement can be defined as the acquisition of goods and services for the purpose of consumption or re-sale. Procurement in hospitality requires a sound knowledge of: where and how products may be sourced; factors affecting availability of supply;

the availability of substitute sources of supply; the implications of alternative suppliers with regard to quality; guest expectations of products and services; and the ability to use the hospitality organization's resources effectively to negotiate preferential terms for the business.

In the context of the foodservice and lodging sectors, many purchases require relatively high investment, for example furniture and computer hardware and quotidian wear such as linens, cutlery and guest amenities. Consideration is therefore warranted in terms of the requisite durability of purchases, supplier access, and after-sales support in order to ensure that purchase decisions offer maximum value and minimum risk of loss to the establishment. The profitability of a hospitality operation is dependent upon the ability of the hospitality operator to proactively seek suppliers who can provide required products to a high degree of quality and at a competitive price. In order to deal with these complex issues both the foodservice and lodging sectors have developed strategies to reduce the associated risks and costs.

FOOD AND BEVERAGE PROCUREMENT

Purchases made by the hospitality industry contribute much to the UK economy. Around £41 billion is spent per annum on products and labour across the sector in the UK, of which food and beverage procurement accounts for around £13 billion (*Horizons for Success*, 2008; Oxford Economics, 2010), representing around a 1000% increase in expenditure between 1973 and 2008 (*Horizons for Success*, 2008; Ryan, 1980). Over time, increases in the value of food and beverage procurement have been caused primarily by the democratization of the eating-out market. Whilst fast food emerged with initiatives such as Wimpy Bars, in the 1950s, it was not until the 1970s that there was any significant attempt to popularize consumption outside the home (Ryan, 1980). Lower prices and the introduction of less intimidating service styles (for example counter service) facilitated this change. Early stages of growth were slow but by the 1990s foodservice had significantly diversified in terms of both the nature of the type of food sold, and the increasing diversity of production and service systems.

Between the 1970s and the 1990s the UK observed the spread of fast food, counter service establishments. By the late 1990s the turnover for the burgers sector alone amounted to over £1.4 billion per annum. The industry also saw a significant growth in the pub meal sector, stimulated in part by increasingly stringent drink–drive regulations. By 1995, revenue generated from meals taken in pubs had reached a value of £3.1 billion, amounting to around 1 in 6 of all meals eaten out of the home, many of which were consumed in branded pub-restaurants such as Brewer's Fayre, Weatherspoons and Beefeater (Eastham et al., 2001). In parallel, the sector noticed the rapid expansion and popularity of other key popular dining venues, such as Café Rouge, Nando's, Wagamama, and Frankie and Benny's, offering standardized products and service styles. Such standardization presented challenges in order to ensure consistency of customer experience. Typically located in areas with high rents and business rates, these firms sought ways to maximize spatial and labour efficiency. By outsourcing production and later menu development to catering supply companies, they were able to standardize the product, as well as increase the ratio of meals served per labour and spatial input. In turn, catering supply companies identified small scale manufacturing units who offered the flexibility of quick production line turnabout necessary to this sector.

From market conditions characterized by many businesses competing in both the supply and restaurant sectors, there is now a more concentrated supply sector, with 30% of the supply to foodservice coming from the top three catering supply firms, i.e. Brakes, 3663 and Booker. It is probable that a further 20% is purchased from the six major discount and mainstream grocery retailers (Horizons for Success, 2008; Institute of Grocery Distribution, 2009).

LODGING PROCUREMENT

The goods and services offered by lodging operations are distinct in nature from food and beverage but procurement issues are similar. Specific figures relating to the level of expenditure on products by the lodging sector do not appear to be available, but can be assumed to constitute a significant amount of industry spending. The approach a lodging operation decides to adopt in purchasing its goods and services will depend on its management structure, the level of service being offered and the number of business activities (for example food and beverage, spa services) within the property (Schnitzler, 1982). Where lodging establishments offer specialized and extended service there will be a need for greater investment in purchasing, with potentially larger ranges and volumes of products required of a higher quality and cost. Some of the common items a lodging operation would need to procure would include guest amenities, linens, cleaning chemicals, paper, furniture, fixtures, equipment, uniforms, food and beverage, energy and labour, and indeed the building itself. As with foodservice, there is an increasing focus on cost control, a particularly critical issue in volatile markets, which can see significant price fluctuations.

Increasingly, lodging operations are using technology, particularly the internet, to buy goods and services online. This process of e-procurement is part of a continued shift towards bringing operators together with their chosen distributors and enabling a streamlined and automated flow of the purchasing cycle (Kothari et al., 2005): for example Thistle Lodging Operations has implemented an e-procurement order processing system for its food, beverage and housekeeping supplies enabling staff across all their lodging operations to order from approved suppliers through one dedicated website any time of the day. It is estimated this will result in a saving of more than £150,000 a year (Thomas, 2007).

Lodging operators are also looking for suppliers who can satisfy their product and service needs during expansion. Luxury, boutique and budget lodging operations are the growing segments of the lodging operation market, with each having different procurement requirements. Indeed there is increasing demand from consumers that businesses operate responsible and ethical business practices and request information on how products are sourced before making a purchasing decision. Before procuring, lodging operations will require suppliers' product verification to ensure the product complies with sustainable business practices.

Many lodging organizations operate centralized purchasing or in certain cases cluster their procurement function at a regional level, which results in costs savings as a result of bulk buying. Such is the case of Hilton, which is trying to increase consistency for all brands for televisions, beds and textiles (Higgins, 2005). These businesses can also engage in large buying programmes, which afford them the opportunity to hold prices for a while but provide them with the time to prepare their operations for price changes. Moreover, as a strategy to reduce cost and to be more efficient in operations, many lodging operations have outsourced their procurement functions, to companies such as Avendra, The Parker Company and Purchasing Management International.

Avendra was developed through an initiative initially between Hyatt Hotels Cooperation and Marriot International and was subsequently joined by Club Corps and the Intercontinental Hotel Group in order to increase these organizations' respective leverage from e-procurement (Lawlor and Jayawardena, 2003). The company has now evolved to service not only those companies that form part of the joint venture but a range of hotel groups throughout the USA and is now one of the major players in e-procurement in the hospitality industry. In 2010, the company served 4,800 properties in the USA, with a value of US$3 billion (Hotel and Motel Management, 2010). Its main function is to offer purchasing services plus e-commerce to the North American hospitality industry in order to save time, reduce costs, increase quality, facilitate ordering methods, increase ordering accuracy and enhance customer satisfaction (Lawlor and Jayawardena, 2003). Unlike Avendra, The Parker Group is more international in its focus. This organization acts as the procurement agent for businesses such as such as Fairmont, Shangri-La and Starwoods. Some of the services offered by The Parker Group include global sourcing, line-item budgeting, bidding for products, preparing model rooms, order creation and expedition, freight management, warehousing and vendor payment (Parker International, 2009). The Parker Company caters to 18 international properties with a value of US$315 million (Hotel and Motel Management, 2010).

CONCLUDING REMARKS

In recent decades, many businesses, including hospitality businesses, have looked for ways of adding value and reducing costs as markets have became more competitive. An important development has been the realization that building sourcing process excellence has significant implications for value growth and that in order to compete in a highly competitive market procurement needs to shift from being a passive service function to one that proactively sets goals, establishing strategies in line with both the business environment and overall organizational mission (Anderson and Katz, 1998; Carr and Smeltzer, 1997, 1999).

The hospitality industry has focused on cost-cutting through contracting out (outsourcing) business functions. Outsourcing does present risks for the business when the goods and service have commercial and or operational importance to an organization; supply disruptions can have major implications on profitability. There has been increasing emphasis within certain bodies of literature that collaborative, bilateral relationships may not be always an appropriate way for sourcing strategy (Jackson, 1985). The critical issue for hospitality businesses is to identify the appropriate sourcing strategy in order to maximize profits. This is also dependent upon the level of mutuality of dependency that can be adjusted through time.

FURTHER READING

Eastham, J F, Ball, S and Sharples, L (2001) 'The catering and food retail sectors', in Eastham, J F, Sharples, L and Ball, S (eds) *Food Supply Chain Management: Issues for the Hospitality and Retail Sectors*, Oxford: Butterworth–Heinemann. pp. 3–20.

Feinstein, A H and Stefanelli, J M (2008) *Purchasing, Selection and Procurement for the Hospitality Industry*, 7th edn, Hoboken: Wiley.

REFERENCES

Anderson, M and Katz, P (1998) 'Strategic sourcing', *International Journal of Logistics Management*, 9, 1: 1–13.

Carr, A and Smeltzer, L (1997) 'An empirically based operational definition of strategic purchasing', *European Journal of Purchasing and Supply Management*, 3, 4: 199–207.

Carr, A and Smeltzer, L (1999) 'The relationship of strategic purchasing to supply chain management', *European Journal of Purchasing and Supply Management*, 5, 1: 43–51.

Eastham, J F, Ball, S and Sharples, L (2001) 'The catering and food retail sectors', in Eastham, J F, Sharples, L and Ball, S (eds) *Food Supply Chain Management: Issues for the Hospitality and Retail Sectors*, Oxford: Butterworth–Heinemann. pp. 3–20.

Higgins, M S (2005) 'Procurement becomes full service support systems', *Hotel and Motel Management*, May 16: 16–17.

Horizons for Success (2008) *UK Foodservice Industry in 2008 Report*, London: Horizons for Success (available from www.horizonsforsuccess.com, last accessed 1 February 2010).

Hotel and Motel Management (2010) 'H&MM's 2010 purchasing survey', *Hotel and Motel Management*, July, 22–4.

Institute of Grocery Distribution (2009) *UK Grocery and Foodservice Outlook*, London: Institute of Grocery Distribution.

Jackson, B (1985) 'Build customer relationships that last', *Harvard Business Review*, 63, 6: 120–8.

Kothari, T, Hu, C and Roehl, S R (2005) 'e-Procurement: an emerging tool for the hotel supply chain management', *International Journal of Hospitality Management*, 24, 3: 369–89.

Lawlor, F and Jayawardena, C (2003) 'Purchasing for 4,000 hotels: the case of Avendra', *International Journal of Contemporary Hospitality Management*, 15, 6: 346–8.

Oxford Economics (2010) *Economic Contribution of the Hospitality Industry*, report prepared by Oxford Economics for the British Hospitality Association, Oxford: Oxford Economics.

Parker International (2009) www.parkerinternational.com, last accessed 1 September 2011.

Ryan, C (1980) *An Introduction to Hotel and Catering Economics*, Nottingham: Stanley Thornes.

Schnitzler, H (1982) 'Purchasing for a new hotel', *Cornell Hotel and Restaurant Administration Quarterly*, 23, 2: 83–91.

Thomas, D (2007) 'Thistle implements e-procurement system to save costs', available from www.caterersearch.com/Articles/2007/08/28/315680/thistle-implements-e-procurement-system-to-save-costs.htm, last accessed 22 August 2011.

Jane F. Eastham and Alisha Ali

Revenue Management

See also: Accommodation, lodging and facilities management; Front office management; Hotels and the internet; Information technology in hospitality; Marketing in hospitality

In the late 1980s the term revenue management, or yield management as it was called then, was first introduced in the hospitality industry by Marriott (Kimes, 2003). Revenue management can be defined as 'the art and science of applying disciplined tactics that predict consumer behaviour at the micro market level and that optimize product availability and price to maximize revenue growth' (Cross, 1997: 33). A simpler and more commonly used definition is to sell the right *product*, for the right *price*, to the right *person*, in the right *period* and in the right *place*.

The discipline of revenue management originated in the airline industry which, in the 1970s, started to experiment with heavily discounted fares in order to fill seats that would otherwise fly empty. Together with overbooking (which is the practice whereby airlines sell more seats than they have available to avoid the risk of being left with empty seats due to last minute cancellations or passengers not showing up), flexible pricing was employed to maximize revenues and operate planes as efficiently as possible. With more rates available, price-sensitivity became an important criterion to distinguish different types of passengers or segments. To avoid cannibalization of rates, whereby lower fares are booked by price-insensitive travellers (those who would normally book at a variety of prices), a commonly used restriction was a special early-bird offer, a discounted rate for passengers who booked at least 21 days in advance (McGill and van Ryzin, 1999). Next to attaching restrictions to special fares, airlines would also control the availability of seats on offer for these prices, a process known as capacity management.

Constantly shifting patterns of demand for hotel rooms have led to the need to re-forecast such demand on a continuous basis. The increasing complexity of the distribution landscape has led the hotel industry to develop sophisticated revenue management systems able to deal with a growing amount of data to be analyzed in real time (Littlewood, 2005; Mainzer, 2004). The return on investment in revenue management systems can be considerable. In the US airline industry such strategies initially brought companies such as American Airlines a staggering $1.4 billion in additional revenue over a 3-year period (Smith et al., 1992) and Continental Airlines saw profits increase by $50m to $100m per year (Weatherford and Kimes, 2003). Comparable figures for hotel companies who successfully apply revenue management indicate that a revenue increase of 3–7% is realistic, with 80% of that increase contributing directly to the bottom-line performance of the hotel (Cross, 1997).

REQUIREMENTS FOR REVENUE MANAGEMENT

Many service providers use revenue management as a strategic tool, including restaurants, car rental companies and theatres. These services share certain core characteristics, including perishability; a fixed capacity; high fixed and low variable costs; a different willingness to pay by various groups of consumers; and a tendency to rely on advance booking of the products (Kimes, 1989). To illustrate these requirements, think of a hypothetical hotel chain in the UK, where there is an offer to book a room for as little as £1. The explanation for this to-good-to-be-true offer is that the company is trying to have otherwise unsold rooms booked by people who are price-sensitive and would normally not stay in their hotels. At the same time, booking restrictions are attached to make sure that price-insensitive guests still book at a higher rate. Since the number of rooms available for this special offer are restricted and varied per hotel, per day, any one hotel can only sell those rooms that normally would be empty. The added benefit of this offer for the hotel company is the ability to generate auxiliary revenue in the food and beverage outlets at the same time. Besides the restricted availability, additional restrictions such as the requirement to book a minimum number of days in advance can also be applied as well.

As might be concluded from the previous example, one of the additional objectives of the inclusion of booking restrictions is to relocate demand to more suitable times for a hotel by offering price-sensitive and time-flexible guests an incentive for booking in a less busy period. This enables a hotel to save its limited capacity for the high-paying guests on busy days and thereby optimize the average daily rate (the average room revenue generated by the hotel per sold room). Also, instead of denying potential guests on busy days, hotels try to move time-flexible guests to periods of slow demand and thereby optimize the occupancy (the percentage of the total available rooms that has been sold) (Sahay, 2007).

THE 5PS OF REVENUE MANAGEMENT

As noted earlier, revenue management is best described in terms of price (which rates do you make available to be booked?); product (what is included?); person (for whom do you make this product available?); place (where do you make your prices available to be booked?); and period (how long in advance do you make your products available?).

When hotels are in the process of determining rates for an upcoming period it is imperative they predict demand accurately and have a good understanding of what the market is willing to pay for their products. If a hotel product is overpriced this might lead to unsold inventory and possible last-minute panic measures in trying to fill these otherwise empty rooms. On the other hand, if a hotel is positioned too cheaply in the market, it might end up with a 100% occupancy rate at a considerably lower average daily rate (ADR) owing to people booking below their normal willingness to pay.

The rapid growth of the internet as a distribution channel, and thus the development of widespread opportunities for customers to compare prices before making a reservation, mean that price and place are closely related. With the vast majority of hotels both now and in the past making use of, and becoming dependent on, multiple distribution channels (online intermediaries), they have also relinquished control of pricing their own products. Third party websites charge substantial commissions for selling a hotel's inventory, as well as usually including 'best rate guarantee' and 'last room availability' clauses in contracts, with the consequence that the cost of distribution can take a substantial part of a hotel's profit. One response to this loss of grip on the pricing and distribution of their own products has been the introduction of rate parity, whereby hotels set a consistent rate structure across all distribution channels (Gazzoli et al., 2008). In order to further regain control of pricing, there is also some current discussion of introducing net rate parity, whereby hotels may communicate to their distribution partners how much they want to receive in return for their product and allowing intermediaries to add a mark up.

THE REVENUE MANAGEMENT PROCESS AND PERFORMANCE INDICATORS

For a hotel to make the most of its pricing and revenue optimization process, a result oriented culture is best supported by a structured revenue management process. Since there is no right or wrong in revenue management, nor is there a detailed process that will work in any company alike, the revenue management process essentially comes down to formulating clear objectives that are in line with a hotel's identity and strategic direction. Numerous sources have described the steps companies should take in order to optimize revenue (Cross, 1997; Griffin, 1995; Jauncey et al., 1995; Queenan et al., 2011; Weatherford and Kimes, 2003), all with the following in common: the need to analyze historical information; to forecast demand; to engage in capacity management; and in effective pricing. With the growing importance and availability of electronic distribution systems, distribution is now regarded by many experts as an important and separate step in the revenue management process (Gazzoli et al., 2008; Kimes, 2008; KPMG, 2005).

Many hotel operators look at average daily rate (ADR) and their occupancy percentage as the main performance indicators. Consider the example whereby a hotel has sold one room at the highest published rate (called the rack rate) and all others rooms remain empty. ADR will show as an impressive result on the night audit report. Similarly, if the entire hotel is booked with lowly rated business, the occupancy percentage will be close to 100%, but total revenue and ADR will be lower than they could have been. When looked at individually, these metrics have limited value, but once combined, they produce a very useful indicator: the RevPAR (revenue per available room). RevPAR is the total rooms revenue divided by the number of available rooms for a particular period, or can be calculated by multiplying the occupancy percentage with the ADR for a specific period. The RevPAR can be used to (a) draw conclusions about the room revenue the hotel has achieved in relation to either the forecast or the budget for a specific period; and (b) to compare the hotel's own performance to those of its competitors, regardless of the size of the hotel, as long as they are classified in the same category. But how would one evaluate the performance of a hotel, based on a RevPAR that is 10%

above forecast while competitors have all shown RevPARs for the same period some 20% above target? To take economic and market conditions into account, the revenue generation index (RGI) is introduced, calculated by dividing the hotel's RevPAR by that of its competitive set.

The main disadvantage of both the RevPAR and the RGI is that they fail to take auxiliary revenue into account and therefore give an incomplete picture of a hotel's *overall* performance, based on its limited capacity. Therefore, an even more accurate performance standard for revenue management incorporating the total revenue from all departments per available room, as well as the operating cost, is the GOPPAR: the gross operating profit per available room.

CONCLUDING REMARKS

Revenue management is one of the most rapidly growing disciplines in the hotel industry, increasingly incorporated in strategic decision making (Cross et al., 2009). A study by Kimes (2008) shows the need for hotels to address career path development for revenue managers in the hotel industry. Successful revenue managers understand and master the art of making the right decisions, based on the information that is predominantly procured from scientific data.

FURTHER READING

Kimes, S E (2008) 'Hotel revenue management: today and tomorrow', *Cornell Hospitality Report*, 8, 4.

REFERENCES

Cross, R G (1997) 'Launching the revenue rocket: how revenue management can work for your business', *Cornell Hotel and Restaurant Administration Quarterly*, 38, 2: 32–43.

Cross, R G, Higbie, J A and Cross, D Q (2009) 'Revenue management's renaissance', *Cornell Hospitality Quarterly*, 50, 1: 56–81.

Gazzoli, G, Kim, W G and Palakurthi, R (2008) 'Online distribution strategies and competition: are the global hotel companies getting it right?', *International Journal of Contemporary Hospitality Management*, 20, 4: 375–87.

Griffin, R K (1995) 'A categorization scheme for critical success factors of lodging yield management systems', *International Journal of Hospitality Management*, 14, 3–4: 325–38.

Jauncey, S, Mitchell, I and Slamet, P (1995) 'The meaning and management of yield in hotels', *International Journal of Contemporary Hospitality Management*, 7, 4: 23–6.

Kimes, S E (1989) 'The basics of yield management', *Cornell Hotel and Restaurant Administration Quarterly*, 30, 3: 14–19.

Kimes, S E (2003) 'Revenue management: a retrospective', *Cornell Hotel and Restaurant Administration Quarterly*, 44, 5–6: 131.

Kimes, S E (2008) 'Hotel revenue management: today and tomorrow', *Cornell Hospitality Report*, 8, 4.

KPMG (2005) *Global Hotel Distribution Survey 2005: Managing Pricing across Distribution Channels*, http://kpmgpt.lcc.ch/dbfetch/52616e646f6d495621686df3ccf6c42176ee2edf8aeb53af/g_hotel.pdf, last accessed 14 February 2011.

revenue management

Littlewood, K (2005) 'Forecasting and control of passenger bookings', *Journal of Revenue and Pricing Management*, 4, 2: 111–23.

Mainzer, B W (2004) 'Future of revenue management: fast forward for hospitality revenue management', *Journal of Revenue and Pricing Management*, 3, 3: 285–9.

McGill, J I and van Ryzin, G J (1999) 'Revenue management: research overview and prospects', *Transportation Science*, 33, 2: 233–56.

Queenan, C C, Ferguson, M E and Stratman, J K (2011) 'Revenue management performance drivers: an exploratory analysis within the hotel industry', *Journal of Revenue and Pricing Management*, 10, 2: 172–88.

Sahay, A (2007) 'How to reap higher profits with dynamic pricing', *Sloan Management Review*, 48, 4: 53–60.

Smith, B C, Leimkuhler, J F and Darrow, R M (1992) 'Yield management at American Airlines', *Interfaces*, 22, 1: 8–31.

Weatherford, L R and Kimes, S E (2003) 'A comparison of forecasting methods for hotel revenue management', *International Journal of Forecasting*, 19, 3: 401–15.

Stan Josephi

Service Quality in Hospitality

See also: Customer relationship management in hospitality; Hotels and the internet; Operations management in hospitality

Service quality is defined as the gap between customers' expectations and their perceptions of service performance; that is, what the customer expected or predicted that they would receive in terms of the quality of service during service delivery, compared with what they perceive or believe the quality of service to have been after the service has been received. The notion of a gap or failure to meet the expectations of customers was first introduced by Parasuraman, Zeithaml and Berry (1985) whose SERVQUAL study identified a series of dimensions that make up the service experience. Since then many scholarly studies have sought to advance our understanding of service quality and, although there are a variety of views on the value of the various processes and procedures that have emerged since then, the notion of a gap between expectations and perceptions of service as a means to assess service quality has prevailed. Proponents of the SERVQUAL model assert that meeting or exceeding customer expectations in each of the following five dimensions can result in customer satisfaction.

1   Reliability. The ability to perform the promised service dependably and accurately, which has implications for recruitment, training and the ongoing professional development of service employees.
2   Tangibles. The appearance of physical facilities, equipment, personnel and communications materials. From a hospitality perspective, this includes the design and appearance of hospitality space, employee uniforms, menus and wine lists.
3   Responsiveness. The willingness to help customers and to provide prompt service, which is a product of service culture as well as the disposition of employees in terms of social attributes such as friendliness.
4   Assurance. The knowledge and courtesy of employees and their ability to convey trust and confidence, which includes the ability of employees to demonstrate confidence in product knowledge and competence in service skills.
5   Empathy. The provision of caring, individualized attention to customers, which includes being able to distinguish and prioritize guests' needs.

PROCESSES AND PROCEDURES

Service quality management has its roots in the statistical control systems designed for use in goods manufacturing industries. The fundamental elements of these systems include control measures that are put in place at each stage of the production process in order to ensure that goods are produced with minimal defects. Among the more well-known of these systems is that developed in Japan after World War II. There, the concept of continuous improvement, based on an analysis of each step in the production process, was introduced, and has since inspired a raft of quality control systems (Deming, 1986; Juran, 1988). These include 'Total Quality Management', 'Six Sigma' and a number of variants, some of which are provided under the auspices of accrediting bodies such as the International Standards Organization (see www.ISO.org).

Adapting these processes to the service environment has included developing a service philosophy and a systematic approach to constant improvement in service delivery as well as producing specifications and directions for the recruitment, training and development of employees (Lahap et al., 2010). Because meeting or exceeding guests' expectations is crucial to perceptions of service quality, there are also a number of potential errors or gaps associated with the planning and delivery of services that are identified in SERVQUAL methodology and need to be considered.

The first potential gap – gap one – is known as the *customer expectation–management perception gap* and is about the goals management develop in relation to what they perceive their guests expect. Whether guest expectations are established by market research or through a combination of research and market experience, it is crucial to properly understand their needs and wants otherwise the entire operation will fail to provide service that meets guests' expectations. It is also important to note that guests' expectations are influenced by a number of exogenous factors, including previous service experience and their expectations of the brand as well as independent ratings such as hotel star ratings, all of which provide cues about the levels of service.

The second potential error or gap is the *management perception–service quality specification* gap. This assumes management understand what guests expect (gap one) but have difficulty in translating this into the types of service specifications that can direct employees in service delivery, and in their service interactions with guests. This is also a complex issue because service transactions, also known as moments of truth, are social acts between individual employees and guests (Norman, 1991). Consequently, the service specification gap includes developing an appropriate organizational culture and an overarching service ethos.

The third error or gap is known as the *service quality specification–service delivery* gap and is closely linked with gap two above. This gap occurs when the specifications or guidelines that have been developed to direct employees to perform the service are in place, but service employees are unable to deliver services in accordance with those guidelines. There are a number of reasons why this can occur, including lack of training or skill in service delivery techniques, specifications that are too complex to interpret, or service techniques that are too complicated to deliver within a specified timeframe.

The fourth and final gap is known as the *service delivery–external communications* gap, and bridging this gap involves ensuring that that all communications with potential customers are congruent with the service capabilities of the establishment. Many hospitality businesses fail because their external communications exaggerate the standard of products and service that can be provided. Customers' expectations can be heightened by glowing, commissioned newspaper articles and advertising in elite magazines, which give the impression of deluxe facilities, as well as photos on websites – especially where camera and digital techniques are used to give the impression of increased size and space in hotel rooms and guest facilities. The internet has become a powerful marketing tool for many service businesses. However, gaps between external communications and service abilities are now becoming more easily identified by potential guests through their use of sites like TripAdvisor® to verify claims made on websites. Reviews provided on these sites can quickly alert potential guests to inflated claims leading to loss of business (Wood, 2010).

As well as addressing the five dimensions of service quality outlined earlier, it is critical to ensure that the quality systems and procedures adopted by a hospitality organization address all of these potential gaps to deliver standards of service that meet the expectations of guests. Providing consistent levels of service within hospitality businesses is even more complex because the provision of food, drink and accommodation involves a series of sub-systems that must interconnect to produce and deliver these core products at the same time. As such, a number of fundamental issues that are unique to hospitality operations need to be considered.

The most significant issue for hospitality management is to introduce and manage an effective service system that can produce and reproduce service at a consistent level of quality. One way of doing this is to identify and map the critical factors that make up the functional elements of the service system and to predict the 'moments of truth' that are likely to occur during delivery. Management can then create and employ a service blueprint to present each step in the service delivery process so that guidelines and procedures can be developed to direct employees in the delivery of that service (Bitner et al., 2008). This process can also identify the technological and physical support required to assist in delivering appropriate service standards to guests as well as identifying potential fail points at each step in the service process. In this way, standards can be continually improved.

A critical dimension of hospitality provision, however, is that service quality will inevitably be judged on the behaviour of contact personnel. As noted earlier, service delivery is a social process and the specialist 'soft' skills required to ensure that the social behaviour of employees meets with guests' expectations are sometime absent or beyond management control. Consequently, creating a workplace culture that values employees as well as attracting, developing, motivating and retaining qualified and customer-orientated employees, must be the primary goal of hospitality businesses seeking to deliver high-quality service to guests (Berry and Parasuraman, 1991). This can best be achieved by developing jobs that satisfy employee needs, which will help to build an organization of employees willing to satisfy the needs of guests. This strategy, which is known as 'internal marketing', has the potential to create strong relationships between employees and guests, which, in turn, lead to guest loyalty (Gounaris, 2008).

CHALLENGES FOR HOSPITALITY PROVIDERS

A major challenge for hospitality businesses is that introducing quality control systems requires considerable investment in implementation, maintenance and evaluation. As the systems are designed to improve a firm's competitive advantage over a long period of time, many hospitality businesses, particularly those that are not operated by major corporations, find these systems either too complex or too expensive to employ, especially when a return on investment can take some time to be realized.

Those that do invest in such systems need to understand that the outcome of meeting or exceeding guests' expectations is guest satisfaction. This is an important issue because, in the past, achieving guest satisfaction has been thought to provide both a competitive advantage and to develop customer loyalty. Customer loyalty or the retention of guests has many benefits, such as generating more profit for the organization and stimulating positive word of mouth communication. However, notwithstanding the apparent logic of this argument, customer loyalty has been found to be more complex than just achieving guest satisfaction (Reichheld and Detrick, 2003).

CONCLUDING REMARKS

In the global hospitality environment, achieving consistent levels of service quality is essential in order to remain competitive and to ensure that the standards expected at the level in which the hospitality business is operating can be maintained. Selecting a suitable framework to guide service provision can be complicated; however, the first step in this process is to establish a guest-orientated service culture and to ensure that employees have the appropriate skills, attributes and knowledge to ensure delivery at the standards required to satisfy the expectations of guests.

Breiter, D and Bloomquist, P (1998) 'TQM in American hotels: an analysis of application', *Cornell Hotel and Restaurant Administration Quarterly*, 39, 1: 25–33.

Sophonsiri, S, O'Mahony, B and Sillitoe, J (2010) 'Towards a model of relationship development for hospitality practice', *International Journal of Hospitality and Tourism Systems*, 3, 1: 64–79.

REFERENCES

Berry, L L and Parasuraman, A (1991) *Marketing Services: Competing Through Quality*, New York: The Free Press.

Bitner, M J, Ostrom, A M and Morgan, F (2008) 'Service blueprinting: a practical technique for service innovation', *California Management Review*, 50, 3: 66–94.

Deming, W E (1986) *Out of the Crisis*, Cambridge, MA: MIT Press.

Gounaris, S (2008) 'Antecedents of internal marketing practice: some preliminary empirical evidence', *International Journal of Service Industry Management*, 19, 3: 400–34.

Juran, J M (1988) *Juran's Quality Control Handbook*, New York: McGraw-Hill.

Lahap, J B, Mahony, G B and Sillitoe, J F (2010) 'Developing a service delivery improvement model for the Malaysian hotel sector', *Proceedings of the 3rd Asia Euro Conference: Transformation and Modernisation in Tourism, Hospitality and Gastronomy*.

Norman, R (1991) *Service Management: Strategy and Leadership in Service Business*, 2nd edn, Chichester: Wiley.

Parasuraman, A, Zeithaml, V A and Berry, L L (1985) 'A conceptual model of service quality and its implications for future research', *Journal of Marketing*, 49, 4: 41–50.

Reichheld, F and Detrick, C (2003) 'Loyalty: a prescription for cutting costs', *Marketing Management*, 12, 5: 24–5.

Wood, R C (2010) 'Let's make hotels get "five star" right', *The Hospitality Review*, 12, 4: 35–7.

G. Barry O'Mahony

Service, Service Industries and the Hospitality Sector

See also: Hospitality and hospitality management; Hospitality management education; Human resource management in hospitality

Everybody knows, or thinks they know, that the hospitality industry is a service industry – indeed, in some American academic hospitality writing it is not unusual to refer, in error, to the hospitality industry as '*the* service industry', the definitive article as it were. A service industry is normally defined in contrast to a manufacturing industry, the latter primarily being involved in the production of physical, tangible goods, the former focused upon the provision of some service or services that are not physically tangible. Further, in the period since the 1960s, it has been routinely claimed, and is now regarded as a simple 'truth', that the proportion of global economic output and employment accounted for by services has exceeded that of other sectors such that we live in a 'post-industrial' or 'service' society. As the discussion that follows reveals, all such claims are problematic and require careful scrutiny.

A POST-INDUSTRIAL 'SERVICE' SOCIETY?

Fuchs (1968) was one of the first writers to systematically seek to understand the role of services in the economy (see Hughes, 1982 for a still relevant and exemplary summary of many of the, in particular, economic dimensions to the service sector) but it was Daniel Bell (1973) and subsequent similar claimants who predicted the coming of 'post-industrial society', the three most important features of which were: (a) a change from a goods-producing to a service economy; (b) the growth in pre-eminence of white-collar workers within the occupational structure, and within this category the growth in importance of what would today be called 'knowledge workers'; and (c) increasing mastery and use of technology, and the incorporation of technology into increasing aspects of life.

Many writers were sceptical of Bell's thesis. Kumar (1978) argued that so-called post-industrial society characteristics could be traced back to the nineteenth century, with service employment being a normal feature of early industrialization in most economies. In this respect, economies such as those of the UK were anomalous in having, albeit only for a short period in history, the majority of its workforce engaged in manufacturing. Jonathan Gershuny (1978, see also Gershuny, 1979) objected to the ways in which writers like Bell (1973) apparently confused definitions of services based on service 'products' and those based on service employment. For Gershuny, many services are consumable at the instant of production, being always consumed 'once and for all'. Goods, in contrast, are material things that maintain an existence after the production process. From an analysis of UK household expenditure from 1954 to 1974, Gershuny found no increase in the percentage of household expenditure on services but did find evidence of patterns of substitution. Thus, needs previously met externally to the household were now met by the purchase of capital goods: for example entertainment needs previously met by cinemas or theatres were replaced by television; domestic help in the form of human labour was replaced by domestic appliances; the need for public transport was superseded by the acquisition of a private means of transport. In each case, a good was substituted for a service. Further, over the same period, the price of services rose rapidly relative to goods, such that *real* consumption of the former declined dramatically. It is on the basis of this evidence that Gershuny expresses scepticism about the idea that goods production has given place, in terms of economic dominance, to the production of services. Instead, capital investment no longer takes place exclusively in industry but occurs in households via the purchase of capital goods that facilitate the satisfaction of needs previously met by services normally external to the household.

Similarly, Gershuny suggests that definitions of service employment should be constrained to describing employment in industries whose final product is a service in the 'once and for all' sense, as noted in the preceding paragraph. The apparent growth in services employment noted by proponents of post-industrial society theories is, Gershuny suggests, a problem of misclassification. He notes that a large proportion of service workers are closely connected with the production of goods in the widest sense (e.g. distribution). The majority of financial services are also associated with the production or purchase of goods. Therefore, though service workers may 'officially' constitute a majority of the workforce, this does not imply that the production of services predominates over that of goods.

Gershuny's contribution to the debate over post-industrial society theory was paralleled in one strand of largely unrelated academic Marxism. At a time when 'service industries' were still largely ignored by academic social scientists, Harry Braverman (1974: 360) argued that: 'When the worker does not offer his labour directly to the user of its effects, but instead sells it to a capitalist, who re-sells it on the commodity market, then we have the capitalist form of production in the field of services' (Braverman, 1974: 360). Like Gershuny, Braverman argues that much 'service' work is in fact more like manufacturing work and he uses the example of chefs and cooks preparing a meal to illustrate his point, reinforcing this by considering chambermaids who, though classed as service employees, in their work, produce a tangible good (a clean room for sale).

The 'goods versus services' debate has not progressed with the same vigour that marked its early appearance. It has been somewhat 'squeezed' by the rise of more fashionable ideas, not least those concerning 'postmodernism' (Kumar, 2004). As noted earlier, there appears to be a broad acceptance – irrespective of its 'factual' legitimacy – that we live in an economic world now dominated by services. This is despite the warnings of those such as Unvala and Donaldson (1988: 468), who distinguished between emerging 'economic' and 'marketing' traditions in discussions of the nature of services, concluding that: 'new employment and continued employment in services cannot be safely predicted without a detailed analysis of (a) criteria for characterising services ... [.]. This needs (c) detailed research on the similarities and differences between services at company, industry and unit level.'

In so far as these writers' recommendations have been followed, debate has been perhaps most vigorous within the discipline of marketing (e.g. Gronroos, 2007; Palmer, 2007) with the consequence that wider economic issues play less of a role in such discussions, and the issues raised by writers such as Gershuny and Braverman remain largely unresolved. This said, other writers, for example Greenfield (2002: 21), continue to follow an economically 'purist' path in arguing that demand for services is subordinate to demand for goods – that is, 'no services can be produced without a prior investment in capital goods having been made'.

IMPLICATIONS FOR THE HOSPITALITY INDUSTRY

At a common sense level, it seems fairly obvious that hospitality falls into the service industry category. Yet if we follow Gershuny's (1978) prescription, then only those hospitality services consumed 'once and for all' and delivered personally may be considered 'true' services, tacit support for which comes from Braverman (1974) in his example of chefs and chambermaids. It is fairly straightforward to accept the chef as a producer of manufactured goods rather than a service worker but do we regard the outcome of a chambermaid's efforts – a clean room – as a product or a service? In Gershuny's terms, a service is consumed once and for all: a hotel bedroom is not consumed once and for all, it endures.

These questions – like those relating more generally to the goods–services dichotomy – have, in the case of the hospitality industry, been largely sidelined rather than resolved, either letting the matter rest with the uncontroversial view that the sector combines both production and service elements or, as has become somewhat commonplace in many nominally 'service' industries, referring to 'service products' as if in some way this removes questions relating to the conceptualization of services. Somewhat ironically, such a position is consistent with the neo-Marxist views of Braverman (1974), who suggests that the goods–services dichotomy is of interest only to academics, the capitalist being concerned only with the creation of profit.

Yet, the presence of relatively distinct goods and (personal) services within the hospitality sector does arguably have consequences for understanding certain features of the industry. Two examples may serve to illustrate this. *First*, advances in science and technology have allowed development of food production and service systems that permit the separation of production from service/consumption thus furnishing operators with a wider range of choices as to the models of hospitality and hospitality management that can be developed in contrast to the traditional model of same-site production, service and consumption. This has implications not only for the type, cost of production and service, and the nature of the consumer experience but also for the quantity and skill-levels of the employees required to operate particular production and service configurations. Chefs and service personnel employed in such contexts enjoy significantly different experiences of work compared to those, say, working in a fine dining restaurant, in terms of skill requirements, the discretion and autonomy allowed in practising their trades, and degree of customer interaction. Put more simply, the modern hospitality industry is arguably much more production and 'goods' driven than it is 'service' driven, not least in its food-service sectors.

Secondly, service industries in general and hospitality in particular are often associated with low-skilled, poorly paid jobs and generally poor conditions of employment. However, this caricature disguises both the character and diversity of work in the hospitality industry, not least in the contrast between relatively skilled and relatively well-paid jobs on the one hand (manager, hotel engineer, senior chefs and cooks), medium-skilled and paid work (most supervisors in whatever department) and low-skill and low-paid (but focused on customer delivery) jobs on the other (for example foodservice, routine front desk positions and cleaning jobs).

CONCLUDING REMARKS

The obviousness of the 'fact' that hospitality is a service industry has become ingrained despite the objection that the blanketing of all hospitality processes, products, services and forms of employment under the 'service' heading is not actually very obvious at all. Awareness of the nature of the relationship between goods and services, and the concept of a service industry, are not simply interesting topics for academic debate but also influence how we conceive of aspects of the hospitality industry and the characteristics it exhibits, and how we relate to our customers and respond to their needs and expectations. In this respect such distinctions demand continuing study and reflection.

FURTHER READING

Miles, S (2001) *Social Theory in the Real World*, London: Sage.

REFERENCES

Bell, D (1973) *The Coming of Post-Industrial Society*, London: Heinemann.
Braverman, H (1974) *Labor and Monopoly Capital*, New York: Monthly Review Press.
Fuchs, V (1968) *The Service Economy*, New York: National Bureau of Economic Research.
Gershuny, J (1978) *After Industrial Society: The Emerging Self-Service Economy*, London: Macmillan.
Gershuny, J (1979) 'The informal economy: its role in post-industrial society', *Futures*, 11: 3–15.
Greenfield, H I (2002) 'A note on the goods/services dichotomy', *The Service Industries Journal*, 22, 4: 19–21.
Gronroos, C (2007) *Service Management and Marketing: Customer Management in Service*, 3rd edn, Chichester: Wiley.
Hughes, H L (1982) 'The service economy, de-industrialisation and the hospitality industry', *International Journal of Hospitality Management*, 1, 3: 145–50.
Kumar, K (1978) *Prophecy and Progress*, Harmondsworth: Penguin.
Kumar, K (2004) *From Post-industrial to Post-modern Society: New Theories of the Contemporary World*, London: Wiley Blackwell.
Palmer, A (2007) *Principles of Services Marketing*, 5th edn, London: McGraw-Hill.
Unvala, C and Donaldson, J (1988) 'The service sector: some unresolved issues', *The Service Industries Journal*, 8, 4: 459–46.

Roy C. Wood

Strategy and Strategic Management in Hospitality

See also: Marketing in hospitality; Operations management in hospitality

Strategy can be simultaneously one of the most fascinating and confusing concepts in business studies. The word 'strategy' derives from the ancient Greek *strategos* which in turn is a synthesis of two other words, *stratos* which means 'army' and *egoume* which means 'to lead' (Cummings, 1993). Thus strategy, in a directional sense, is about allocating resources, establishing policies, managing procedures and assigning responsibilities to ensure organizational change and success (Knowles, 1996). Furthermore, in terms of implementation, a strategy is supported and defined by the process of strategic management. The multidimensional and cross-sectoral applicability of this term (it can be, and is, applied to a variety of activities, including military tactics, politics, management theories and other aspects of human interaction), has created a blurry understanding of what strategy and strategic management is all about, confining its perceived usability mostly to large international corporations.

Hospitality and hotel businesses are by definition the most global industries within the services sector (Litteljohn, 1997; Mace, 1995; Whitla et al., 2007). Interestingly enough, the industry is heavily represented, in market share terms, by large hotel chain-owned properties. However, considering absolute numbers, the international hospitality market is dominated by small and medium-sized enterprises (SMEs), often owner-managed and/or family owned. This aspect of the industry, together with the increased concentration of distribution channel providers (through mergers and acquisitions), force SMEs to compete over *availability* of affordable distribution networks in order to make their services and products accessible, in what is for them a vast market. Furthermore, constantly shifting tourist consumer preferences and the availability of a wide range of offerings has largely created a price-sensitive global market. In difficult and challenging economic times, such as the crisis of 2008, forecasting becomes a nightmare for many businesses (Song et al., 2011) and organizing around effective strategies becomes increasingly important in an industry that remains dynamic but at the same time proves to be exceptionally susceptible to external pressures.

The hospitality industry has enjoyed substantial growth in recent decades, with the resultant creation of an ideal battlefield for competitive forces. Managers employ various strategies to increase performance levels, hoping that this will lead to the development of a competitive advantage (Pereira-Moliner et al., 2010). In this respect, strategies are deployed at three different levels (adopted from Enz, 2010): corporate level, business level and functional or operational level. Most firms competing in hospitality use a combination of strategies at different levels, depending on the nature of services provided and the geographic location where they are offered.

CORPORATE LEVEL STRATEGY

Corporate level strategy defines the scope of the industries that organizations wish to compete in. Major corporate strategies are concerned with concentration; related and unrelated diversification; vertical and horizontal integration; mergers and acquisitions; and restructuring.

Concentration occurs when organizations choose to focus on one industry, aiming to become the market leaders in that industry, or in a particular segment of that industry. Even though concentration strategies may prove to be quite profitable there is always the risk that the organization ends up operating in a mature market with little room to grow and with high exit costs. Nevertheless, this strategy has great success stories, such as Domino's Pizza, which has been operating since the late 1960s and now has more than 9,000 stores worldwide.

Diversification is a strategy in which firms decide to reduce the risk of operating in single markets by venturing into other markets that may be more attractive in terms of growth. This can be done through expansion or reallocation of resources. Diversification can take place within the broader spectrum of a firm's current activities thus reaching markets with similar products, services or resource-conversion processes of different parts of the organization (Enz, 2010). This popular strategic option is called *related diversification* and a very successful example would be the case of Yum! Brands, which is the world's largest restaurant company in terms of system restaurants. Yum! Brands own nearly 38,000 restaurants in more than 110 countries and territories, and more than 1 million associates own brands such as KFC, Pizza Hut and Taco Bell. Alternatively, diversification could be in totally new (for the firm) markets with the hope to identify more lucrative areas to operate in or in order to reduce the danger of operating in a single market. This is termed *unrelated diversification* and an excellent example would be the Indian Tobacco Group (ITC) in India. The group has a very strong presence in a wide range of markets, such as cigarettes, specialty papers, stationery, agri-business, packaged foods, personal care and, of course, hotels, with ITC Hotels owning 100 luxury hotels in more than 90 destinations.

Integration strategies are similar to the process of diversification: both approaches aim to reduce the risk of deploying in a single or generally too few markets. The real difference is that with integration strategies firms aim to affect their production by getting involved in different stages of the supply chain with ownership and control (Enz, 2010). *Vertical integration* means that firms own part of their suppliers at different levels of the supply chain, upstream or downstream. A good example would be Goody's, a well-known fast food brand in Greece who managed to counter competition from McDonald's, establishing a lead position in the market. They ventured into Goody's Catering, providing burgers to the chain but also bread to the retail consumer market through companies such as SELECT A.E. with great success. *Horizontal integration* is a strategy that focuses on expanding at one level of the value chain. Successful examples would include easyJet buying out its main rival Go for £374m, or Avis Budget Group, which offers car rentals through Avis, Budget and Budget Trucks at more than 10,000 rental points internationally.

Most strategies aim to ensure survival and growth. Some firms choose new venturing whereas others choose to invest in other established firms, hoping to gain in knowledge, market position and resources. This is why *mergers and acquisitions* are a common phenomenon in contemporary business, including the hotel industry (Park and Jang, 2011). It can be considerably faster and more cost-efficient to buy an existing hotel or hotels rather than build one, new build construction projects often being constrained by such factors as land costs and environmental constraint. A *merger* describes a situation where two or more firms are merged into one with common processes and resources. *Acquisition* on the other hand refers to a partial or full buy-out of a firm. An interesting example is Bentley Forbes, a commercial real estate investment and operations company, who decided to enter the hotel industry by acquiring properties such as Four Seasons Resort and Club Dallas at Las Colinas in 2006 under Bentley Forbes Hospitality Group, LLC (www.bentleyforbes.com).

Restructuring usually refers to strategies such as downsizing (which is very common, especially as a reactive strategy and means selling underperforming assets); 'downscoping', which usually means reducing the range of markets that a firm competes in; and organizational restructuring, which entails significant changes in organizational structures, or redesign of processes to increase performance.

BUSINESS LEVEL STRATEGY

Business level strategy defines how organizations establish and attempt to maintain their competitive position against rivals in market(s) that they have selected. Enz (2010) suggests that at the level of an individual business the generic strategies identified by Porter (1980) – overall cost leadership; differentiation; best value; and focus – which refer mainly to the creation of conditions that will enable businesses to gain a competitive advantage in any given marketplace, are, with some adaptations (see Enz, 2005), relevant to the hospitality industry.

Overall cost leadership is a strategy where a firm aims to produce its goods and services at a lower cost than its competitors, thus increasing flexibility and (potentially) profitability and/or lower pricing if required. This strategy is extremely important in the hotel business, where the market has high price elasticity, which means that a change in pricing would result to an equally significant change to demand. This strategy entails strict and efficient cost control and, often, substantial economies of scale. A good example in the aviation industry would be low cost airlines like AirAsia or Ryanair, or in the hotel industry such concepts as easyHotel. Nevertheless, we should bear in mind that cost leadership practices and strategies may also be embedded in luxury property management without necessarily being detected by the consumer.

Differentiation relies on competing by creating in the minds of consumers a perception of uniqueness (or at least a high level of distinctiveness) in products and/or services offered such that they are differentiated from the immediate competition. Lately global tourism and hospitality products have tended to increase conformity but there remain interesting examples of differentiation such as boutique hotels and themed restaurants. *Best value strategies* are those strategies which focus on retaining and enhancing the elements that customers value more and reducing cost where it is least noted. The hospitality industry comprises both tangible and intangible services, products and surroundings and a complex cost structure with numerous cost drivers. It can therefore make sense to find acceptable quality compromises that play to those elements highly valued by customers. Such a strategy, carefully formulated and implemented, can constitute a balanced position between cost leadership and differentiation. *Focus strategies*, as the term suggests, involve focusing on a specific target market or markets, on a particular product or service line, or even a geographic region. This strategy can be combined with all the above.

FUNCTIONAL OR OPERATIONAL LEVEL STRATEGY

Functional or operational level strategies are important to modern strategic management and entail managing day-to-day operations in divisions and departments within organizations. At one level, this involves alignment of organizational resources and departments such as finance, marketing and human resources with business and corporate level strategies (Mintzberg et al., 1998). These divisions/ departments are responsible for implementing and co-ordinating business and corporate level strategies, striving to ensure that the organization's strategic choices are realized. They also provide input for overall strategy formulation and revision.

CONCLUDING REMARKS

The process of strategic management is a dynamic one requiring commitment in planning, implementation and the ability to understand markets and forces of competition. In essence, companies of any market position and size cannot survive into the long term if they do not grasp the necessity of having a strategic outlook to the future. Strategy is not an exact science but requires realism in formulation, co-ordination in application and clear measures for the assessment of the success of strategic intent.

FURTHER READING

Campbell, D, Stonehouse, G and Houston, B (1999) *Business Strategy*, Oxford: Butterworth–Heinemann.

REFERENCES

Cummings, S (1993) 'Brief case: "The First Strategist"', *Long Range Planning*, 26, 3: 133–5, in Wit, B and Meyer, R (2010) *Strategy: Process, Content, Context, An International Perspective*, London: Cengage Learning. pp. 25–6.

Enz, C (2005) *Hospitality Strategic Management: Concepts and Cases*, Hoboken: Wiley.

Enz, C (2010) *Hospitality Strategic Management: Concepts and Cases*, 2nd edn, Hoboken: Wiley.

Knowles, T (1996) *Corporate Strategy for Hospitality*, Harlow: Longman Group Limited.

Litteljohn, D (1997) 'Internationalization in hotels: current aspects and development', *International Journal of Contemporary Hospitality Management*, 9, 5/6: 187–98, cited in Whitla et al., 2007.

Mace, E (1995) 'International trends in the hotel industry or, survival in the global economy', *Hotel and Motel Management*, 210, 10: 11–13, cited in Whitla et al., 2007.

Mintzberg, H, Ahlstrand, B and Lampel, J (1998) *Strategy Safari: A Guided Tour Through the Wilds of Strategic Management*, New York: Free Press.

Park, K and Jang, S (2011) 'Mergers and acquisitions and firm growth: investigating restaurant firms', *International Journal of Hospitality Management*, 30, 1: 141–9.

Pereira-Moliner, J, Claver-Cortés, E and Molina-Azorín, J (2010) 'Strategy and performance in the Spanish hotel industry', *Cornell Hospitality Quarterly*, 51, 4: 513–28.

Porter, M (1980) *Competitive Strategy: Techniques for Analyzing Industries and Competitors*, New York: Free Press.

Song, H, Lin, S, Witt, S and Zhang, X (2011) 'Impact of financial/economic crisis on demand for hotel rooms in Hong Kong', *Tourism Management*, 32, 1: 172–86.

Whitla, P, Walters, P and Davies, H (2007) 'Global strategies in the international hotel industry', *International Journal of Hospitality Management*, 26, 4: 777–92.

Theodore Benetatos

Women, Gender and Hospitality Employment

See also: Human resource management in hospitality; Service, service industries and the hospitality sector

157

It's a girl! From the time a child is born, gender impacts every aspect of life – gender always matters. Regardless of any intentions to provide children with a gender-neutral upbringing, the world is full of gendered messages (Arliss, 1991). While little girls dress in lace-trimmed skirts smile and whisper, boys race their cars and tackle each other on the playground. As girls become women and enter the workplace, gender stereotypes and expectations follow.

The 1970s saw a significant increase in women occupying middle management positions, and there was increasing optimism that by the turn of the twenty-first century women would be equal to men in the business world in both numbers and wages. Such is not the case. While attention to women's career development has increased substantially, much more remains to be accomplished before women enjoy the benefits, senior positions and privileges of their male colleagues. In many circumstances, not least the hospitality environment, women continue to be viewed as less motivated, capable and reliable than their male counterparts. In what follows, the current position of women seeking leadership roles in the hospitality industry is examined. Several of the challenges these women confront as they work to develop their management careers are identified, and suggestions are made as to the ways in which women themselves, their male colleagues and the organizations for which they work can co-operate to create an environment that facilitates women's career development.

WOMEN IN HOSPITALITY MANAGEMENT

While women are entering the hospitality workforce at an accelerating rate – and are projected to constitute an even higher percentage of employees in the decades ahead – the vast majority of those positions continue to be part-time, low-status and low-paid (Martin, 2000). Women who advance in management often find that their careers eventually stall, with upper-level management remaining predominantly white and male. For instance, Catalyst (2001) studied women's roles in the industry's 100 largest restaurant chains and found that while the majority of employees were female, women held only 8% of the board seats and 4% of the highest management titles. The study suggested that, at the present rate, it would take nearly 40 years for women to occupy half of the corporate office positions.

While women are entering academic programmes in hospitality management at higher rates than ever before, they are also leaving the industry in greater numbers than their male counterparts. The characteristics of hospitality organizations make this environment among the most challenging for women who seek senior-level management positions (Blomme et al., 2010; Brownell, 1994). This is because senior managers have generally worked their way up the career ladder in positions that require long and irregular work hours. It is not unusual for hospitality employees at all levels to have holiday and weekend schedules, making it difficult or impossible to achieve a satisfying work/family balance. Many women feel their only option is to choose between a fulfilling personal life and a successful career (Brownell, 1998). Promotions often require relocation, another complication for those with a growing family. In addition, the nature of work in hospitality is likely to take women into settings traditionally associated with gender-linked behaviour – late nights in bars and lounges can be uncomfortable for many women.

CHALLENGES FOR WOMEN IN HOSPITALITY MANAGEMENT

A number of obstacles make it difficult for women to compete on an equal footing with men in the hospitality workforce (Archer, 2003). Two challenges repeatedly emerge as problematic for women who seek upper-level positions: 'old boy networks', and the lack of mentoring opportunities.

Networks are informal social relationships depending upon friendship and camaraderie. They play a powerful role in determining opinion leaders (those who have significant influence within the organization) and members support the agendas of others in the network and benefit from their organization-specific experiences and insights. Networks are particularly active in hospitality organizations where opportunities for informal conversation abound. Too frequently, however, women feel they are excluded from these interactions – they are not invited to happy hour after work or to the golf course at the weekend. As a consequence, women do not learn about what is going on, or build the informal relationships that could help them advance in their careers. The term 'old boy network' is often employed to refer to the fact of male-only information-sharing of a type that serves as a barrier to women's growth and career development (Linehan, 2001; Oakley, 2000). It seems that women in the twenty-first century readily secure middle-level management positions, but that senior roles are reserved for those who 'fit' the existing culture and who feel comfortable with other top executives, i.e. men.

Mentoring is a form of coaching, with the goal of helping an employee, or protégé, to be successful in his or her career. Women who are new to hospitality organizations find that being mentored is a significant advantage, as a senior coach can help them navigate organizational politics and establish priorities. A mentor can also introduce them to colleagues who can orientate them to the organization's norms and culture. Knowing who in the organization has influence, choosing what company events to attend, or recognizing the importance of specific routines can be invaluable to a new or junior manager. When the time comes, mentors can help prepare their protégés for moving up the career ladder by making introductions to key organizational members and providing the types of experiences that will prepare the individual for her next job.

Three main obstacles have hindered women's ability to find suitable mentors and therefore their ability to move into upper-level management positions. First, men often feel uncomfortable with a female protégé because mentoring often requires spending considerable time together. Because they feel more comfortable meeting with another man than a young woman, they tend to select their male colleagues to champion. Secondly, since the number of women in senior management positions is relatively small, they are less available to serve as mentors to their female colleagues. Finally, mentoring as an activity is seldom tied to an organization's reward system, thus making it difficult to find qualified individuals willing to spend time helping young hospitality professionals to succeed (Ragins and Scandura, 1994).

WHAT MEN CAN DO

Women are not the only ones to experience work and family conflicts. Balance is not just a woman's concern: men who speak out about the importance of quality family time and the stress resulting from a lack of balance help organizations recognize that this is a significant issue. Single parents of both genders find themselves particularly affected by lack of family-friendly policies in hospitality organizations. While men recognize some of the challenges confronting women, they view these issues as less significant than their female colleagues, thus hindering change. Men can help women in hospitality management by taking the issues they identify seriously and working to promote practices – both formal and informal – that are non-discriminatory. When men offer to orient and mentor female colleagues, invite women to join in casual conversations, or make sure that events that were once male-only are appropriate for the growing number of women managers looking to move up the career ladder, they facilitate positive change.

WHAT ORGANIZATIONS CAN DO

Progressive hospitality organizations are reaffirming their commitment to develop and retain women managers (Woods and Viehland, 2000). Some best practices in human resource management include providing such benefits as flexible work hours, an active mentoring programme and onsite day care facilities. Still other companies have implemented job sharing, family leave and a compressed work week.

Women also need to know that they are being treated fairly and compensated equally for work accomplished. Companies that are transparent in communicating their promotion criteria and assess performance through clearly articulated standards encourage women to seek career advancement. Women moving into hospitality management will also be looking for organizational cultures that support women's professional development. They will want to see role models, women who have moved up through the company and who are well respected by their colleagues.

VALUING WOMEN IN MANAGEMENT

Dowling's *The Cinderella Complex*, published in 1981, drew attention to gender stereotyping in the workplace and the difficulties women had with gaining visibility and promotions. One of the most significant findings, however, was that women most often looked to the organization to treat them fairly and recognize the good work they were doing (Dowling, 1981). Men, on the other hand, had clearer career goals and put deliberate strategies in place not only to reach their objectives but to gain recognition as well. This served as a powerful lesson. To succeed in management, women must identify a career path and cultivate skills that facilitate their career development and draw attention to their contributions.

Confidence and assertiveness are crucial to professional advancement (Dickerson and Taylor, 2000). Traditionally, women have short-changed the extent of their contribution to the organization. Today's successful women recognize the value they add, are assertive, and take the initiative in asking for what they need, whether resources or raises. To achieve their career goals, they may need to request a mentor, join their male colleagues in the lounge after work and deliberately increase the frequency of casual, informal conversations with all colleagues. Women who do not speak up go largely unrecognized, regardless of their talents.

Women bring a set of competences to their management positions that successful hospitality organizations require. Numerous studies confirm that there are management style differences between men and women (Kolb, 1999; Pounder and Coleman, 2002). Typical of a feminine style are competences such as building consensus, effective listening, teambuilding, inclusive communication and valuing diversity. Women are less directive and more empowering. They value relationships, fostering collaborative decision making and creative problem solving. Women also tend to provide more feedback to employees than do their male counterparts (Burke and Collins, 2001; Oshagbemi and Gill, 2002).

CONCLUDING REMARKS

Women have come a long way in the workforce but much remains to be accomplished. A renewed commitment is needed in order that hospitality companies might fully benefit from the talents and energy women are ready to invest in their careers. In the diverse, global hospitality industry, women are well positioned to provide the leadership needed to build the inclusive and agile organizations of the future.

FURTHER READING

Brownell, J and Walsh, K (2008) 'Women in hospitality', in Brotherton, B and Wood, R C (eds) *The Sage Handbook of Hospitality Management*, London: Sage. pp. 107–28.

REFERENCES

Archer, J (2003) 'Survey studies barriers to women leaders', *Education Week*, 22, 25: 1–3.

Arliss, L (1991) *Gender Communication*, Englewood Cliffs: Prentice Hall.

Blomme, R J, van Rheede, A and Tromp, D M (2010) 'The use of the psychological contract to explain turnover intentions in the hospitality industry: A research study on the impact of age categories and gender on turnover intentions of highly educated employees', *International Journal of Human Resource Management*, 21, 1: 144–62.

Brownell, J (1994) 'Women in hospitality management: general managers' perceptions of factors related to career development', *International Journal of Hospitality Management*, 13, 2: 101–17.

Brownell, J (1998) 'Striking a balance: the future of work and family issues in the hospitality industry', in Kwansa, F and Cummings, P (eds) *Family Studies*, New York: Haworth Press. pp. 109–23.

Burke, S and Collins, K (2001) 'Gender differences in leadership styles and management skills', *Women in Management Review*, 16, 5: 244–56.

Catalyst (2001) *Cracking the Glass Ceiling: Catalyst's Research on Women in Corporate Management, 1995–2000*, New York: Catalyst.

women, gender and hospitality employment

161

Dickerson, A and Taylor, M A (2000) 'Self-limiting behaviour in women: self-esteem and self-efficacy as predictors', *Group and Organization Management*, 25, 2: 191–209.

Dowling, C (1981) *The Cinderella Complex*, New York: Summit Books.

Kolb, J A (1999) 'The effect of gender role, attitude toward leadership and self confidence on leader emergence: implications for leadership development', *Human Resource Development Quarterly*, 10, 4: 305–20.

Linehan, M (2001) 'Networking for female managers' career development: empirical evidence', *Journal of Management Development*, 20, 9: 823–9.

Martin, R (2000) 'New study quantifies gender disparity in senior positions', *Nation's Restaurant News*, 34, 12: 58.

Oakley, J G (2000) 'Gender-based barriers to senior management positions: understanding the scarcity of female CEOs', *Journal of Business Ethics*, 27, 4: 321–34.

Oshagbemi, T and Gill, R (2002) 'Gender differences and similarities in the leadership styles and behaviour of UK managers', *Women in Management Review*, 18, 6: 288–98.

Pounder, J S and Coleman, M (2002) 'Women – better leaders than men? In general and educational management it still "all depends"', *Leadership and Organization Development Journal*, 23, 3: 122–33.

Ragins, B and Scandura, T (1994) 'Gender differences in expected outcomes of mentoring relationships', *Academy of Management Journal*, 37, 4: 957–71.

Woods, R and Viehland, D (2000) 'Women in hotel management', *Cornell Hotel and Restaurant Administration Quarterly*, 41, 5: 51–4.

Judi Brownell

consolidated bibliography

Accor (2010) www.accor.com, last accessed 9 November 2011.

Accor (2011) *Accor Company Profile*, www.accor.com/en/group/accor-company-profile.html, last accessed 17 February 2012.

Adrià, F (1998) *Los secretos de El Bulli: Recetas, técnicas y reflexiones*, Barcelona: Altaya.

Adrià, F, Blumenthal, H, Keller, T and McGee, H (2006) 'Statement on the "new cookery"', *The Observer*, www.guardian.co.uk/uk/2006/dec/10/foodanddrink.obsfoodmonthly, last accessed 18 January 2012.

Alba, J W and Hutchinson, J W (1987) 'Dimensions of consumer expertise', *Journal of Consumer Research*, 13, 4: 411–54.

Aliouche, E H and Schlentrich, U A (2009a) 'Does franchising create value? An analysis of the financial performance of US public restaurant firms', *International Journal of Hospitality and Tourism Administration*, 10, 2: 93–108.

Aliouche, E H and Schlentrich, U A (2009b) 'International franchise assessment model: entry and expansion in the European Union', *Entrepreneurial Business Law Journal*, 3, 2: 517–37.

Alonso, A D and O'Neill, M (2010) 'Small hospitality enterprises and local produce: a case study', *British Food Journal*, 112, 11: 1175–89.

Anderson, J (1995) *Local Heroes*, Glasgow: Scottish Enterprise.

Anderson, M and Katz, P (1998) 'Strategic sourcing', *International Journal of Logistics Management*, 9, 1: 1–13.

Archer, J (2003) 'Survey studies barriers to women leaders', *Education Week*, 22, 25: 1–3.

Arliss, L (1991) *Gender Communication*, Englewood Cliffs: Prentice Hall.

Ashley, B, Hollows, J, Jones, S and Taylor, B (2004) *Food and Cultural Studies*, London: Sage.

Astroff, M T and Abbey, J R (2002) *Convention Sales and Services*, 6th edn, Las Vegas: Waterbury Press.

Auty, S (1992) 'Consumer choice and segmentation in the restaurant industry', *The Service Industries Journal*, 12, 3: 324–39.

Bader, E E (2005) 'Sustainable hotel business practices', *Journal of Retail and Leisure Property*, 5, 1: 70–7.

Ball, A, and Roberts, L (2003) 'Restaurants', in Brotherton, B (ed.) *The International Hospitality Industry*, Oxford: Butterworth–Heinemann. pp. 30–58.

Ball, S (2005) *The Importance of Entrepreneurship to Hospitality, Leisure, Sport and Tourism*, Hospitality, Leisure, Sport and Tourism Network, May (see www.heacademy.ac.uk/assets/hlst/documents/projects/Entrepreneurship/ball.pdf).

Ball, S (2008) 'Hospitality systems', in Jones, P (ed.) *Handbook of Hospitality Operations and IT*, Oxford: Butterworth–Heinemann. pp. 19–43.

Ball, S, Jones P, Kirk, D and Lockwood, A (2003) *Hospitality Operations: A Systems Approach*, London: Continuum.

Bardi, J A (2010) *Hotel Front Office Management*, 5th edn, New York: Wiley.

Barrows, C and Powers, T (2008a) *Introduction to the Hospitality Industry*, 7th edn, New York: Wiley.

Barrows, C and Powers, T (2008b) *Introduction to Management in the Hospitality Industry*, 9th edn, New York: Wiley.

Barrows, C W (1999) 'Introduction to hospitality education', in Barrows, C W and Bosselman, R H (eds) *Hospitality Management Education*, New York: Haworth Press. pp. 1–20.

Barrows, C W and Johan, N (2008) 'Hospitality management education', in Brotherton, B and Wood, R C (eds) *The Sage Handbook of Hospitality Management*, London: Sage. pp. 146–62.

Batt, R (2000) 'Strategic segmentation in front-line services: matching customers, employees and human resource systems', *International Journal of Human Resource Management*, 11, 3: 540–61.

Baum, T (2006) *Human Resource Management for Tourism, Hospitality and Leisure*, London: Thomson.

Beals, P and Denton, G (2004) *Hotel Asset Management: Principles and Practices*, East Lansing: EIAHLA.

Beardsworth, A and Keil, T (1997) *Sociology on the Menu: An Invitation to the Study of Food and Society*, London: Routledge.

Becker, H (1978) 'Arts and crafts', *American Journal of Sociology*, 83, 4: 862–88.

Beldona, S and Cobanoglu, C (2007) 'Importance-performance analysis of guest technologies in the lodging industry', *Cornell Hotel and Restaurant Administration Quarterly*, 48, 3: 299–312.

Bell, D (1973) *The Coming of Post-Industrial Society*, London: Heinemann.

Bell, D (2009) 'Tourism and hospitality', in Jamal, T and Robinson, M (eds) *The Sage Handbook of Tourism Studies*, London: Sage. pp. 19–34.

Bell, D, Deighton, J, Reinartz, W J, Rust, R T and Swartz, G (2002) 'Seven barriers to customer equity management', *Journal of Service Research*, 5, 1: 77–85.

Bendapudi, N and Berry, L L (1997) 'Customers' motivations for maintaining relationships with service providers', *Journal of Retailing*, 73, 1: 15–37.

Berry, L (1995) 'Relationship marketing of services – growing interest, emerging perspectives', *Journal of the Academy of Marketing Science*, 23, 4: 236–45.

Berry, L L and Parasuraman, A (1991) *Marketing Services: Competing Through Quality*, New York: The Free Press.

Bitner, M J, Ostrom, A M and Morgan, F (2008) 'Service blueprinting: a practical technique for service innovation', *California Management Review*, 50, 3: 66–94.

Blanck, J (2007) 'Molecular gastronomy: overview of a controversial food science discipline', *Journal of Agricultural and Food Information*, 8, 3: 77–85.

Blomme, R J, van Rheede, A and Tromp, D M (2010) 'The use of the psychological contract to explain turnover intentions in the hospitality industry: a research study on the impact of age categories and gender on turnover intentions of highly educated employees', *International Journal of Human Resource Management*, 21, 1: 144–62.

Boden, M (1990) *The Creative Mind*, London: Weidenfeld & Nicolson.

Bohdanowicz, P (2005) 'European hoteliers' environmental attitudes: greening the business', *Cornell Hotel and Restaurant Administration Quarterly*, 46, 2: 188–204.

Bohdanowicz, P, Simanic, B and Martinac, I (2005) 'Environmental training and measures at Scandic Hotels, Sweden', *Tourism Review International*, 9, 1: 7–19.

Bolton, B and Thompson, J (2004) *Entrepreneurs: Talent, Temperament and Technique*, 2nd edn, Oxford: Butterworth–Heinemann.

Bosman, N and Levie, J (2009) *Global Entrepreneurship Monitor: 2009 Global Report*, www.gemconsortium.org/docs/265/gem-2009-global-report, last accessed 17 February 2012.

Braverman, H (1974) *Labor and Monopoly Capital*, New York: Monthly Review Press.

Brealey, R A, Myers, S C and Marcus, A J (2009) *Fundamentals of Corporate Finance*, 6th edn, New York: McGraw-Hill.

Breiter, D and Bloomquist, P (1998) 'TQM in American hotels: an analysis of application', *Cornell Hotel and Restaurant Administration Quarterly*, 39, 1: 25–33.

Brotherton, B (1999) 'Towards a definitive view of the nature of hospitality and hospitality management', *International Journal of Contemporary Hospitality Management*, 11, 4:165–73.

Brotherton, B (2000) *Introduction to the UK Hospitality Industry: A Comparative Approach*, Oxford: Butterworth–Heinemann.

Brotherton, B (2003) *The International Hospitality Industry: Structures, Characteristics, and Issues*, Oxford: Butterworth–Heinemann.

Brotherton, B (2005) 'The nature of hospitality: customer perceptions and implications', *Tourism and Hospitality Planning and Development*, 2, 3: 139–53.

Brotherton, B and Wood, R C (2000) 'Defining hospitality and hospitality management', in Lashley, C and Morrison, A (eds) *In Search of Hospitality – Theoretical Perspectives and Debates*, Oxford: Butterworth–Heinemann. pp. 134–56.

Brotherton, B and Wood, R C (2008) *The Sage Handbook of Hospitality Management*, London: Sage.

Brotherton, B and Wood, R C (2008a) 'Editorial introduction', in Brotherton, B and Wood, R C (eds) *The Sage Handbook of Hospitality Management*, London: Sage. pp. 1–34.

Brotherton, R and Wood, R C (2008b) 'The nature and meanings of hospitality', in Brotherton, B and Wood, R C (eds) *The Sage Handbook of Hospitality Management*, London: Sage. pp. 37–61.

Brown, T (2009) *Change by Design. How Design Thinking Transforms Organizations and Inspires Innovation*, New York: HarperCollins.

Brownell, J (1994) 'Women in hospitality management: general managers' perceptions of factors related to career development', *International Journal of Hospitality Management*, 13, 2: 101–17.

Brownell, J (1998) 'Striking a balance: the future of work and family issues in the hospitality industry', in Kwansa, F and Cummings, P (eds) *Family Studies*, New York: Haworth Press. pp. 109–23.

Brownell, J and Walsh, K (2008) 'Women in hospitality', in Brotherton, B and Wood, R C (eds) *The Sage Handbook of Hospitality Management*, London: Sage. pp. 107–28.

Buhalis, D and O'Connor, P (2006) 'Information and communications technology – revolutionising tourism', in Buhalis, D and Costa, C (eds) *Tourism Management Dynamics – Trends, Management and Tools*, Burlington: Elsevier. pp. 196–210.

Burke, S and Collins, K (2001) 'Gender differences in leadership styles and management skills', *Women in Management Review*, 16, 5: 244–56.

Butcher, J (2008) 'Ecotourism as life politics', *Journal of Sustainable Tourism*, 16, 3: 315–26.

Butler, J (2008) 'The compelling "hard case" for "green" hotel development', *Cornell Hospitality Quarterly*, 49, 3: 234–44.

Butler, R (2009) 'Tourism in the future: cycles, waves or wheels?', *Futures*, 41, 6: 346–52.

Cahill, D J (2006) *Lifestyle Market Segmentation*, New York: Haworth Press.

Cameron, D, Gore, J, Desombre, T and Riley, M J (1999) 'An examination of the reciprocal affects of occupational culture and organizational culture: the case of chefs in hotels', *International Journal of Hospitality Management* 18, 3: 225–34.

Campbell, D, Stonehouse, G and Houston, B (1999) *Business Strategy*, Oxford: Butterworth–Heinemann.

Campbell-Smith, G (1967) *The Marketing of the Meal Experience*, Guildford: University of Surrey Press.

Carr, A and Smeltzer, L (1997) 'An empirically based operational definition of strategic purchasing', *European Journal of Purchasing and Supply Management*, 3, 4: 199–207.

Carr, A and Smeltzer, L (1999) 'The relationship of strategic purchasing to supply chain management', *European Journal of Purchasing and Supply Management*, 5, 1: 43–51.

Carroll, B and Siguaw, J (2003) 'The evolution of electronic distribution: effects on hotels and intermediaries', *Cornell Hotel and Restaurant Administration Quarterly*, 44, 4: 38–50.

Catalyst (2001) *Cracking the Glass Ceiling: Catalyst's Research on Women in Corporate Management, 1995–2000*, New York: Catalyst.

Cecil, A K (2005) 'Incentive travel', in Pizam, A (ed.) *International Encyclopedia of Hospitality Management*, Oxford: Butterworth–Heinemann. pp. 339–40.

Chartered Institute of Marketing (1976) *Annual Report*, Cookham: Chartered Institute of Marketing.

Chartered Institute of Marketing (2007) *Tomorrow's Word – Re-evaluating the Role of Marketing*, Cookham: Chartered Institute of Marketing.

Chen, C (2006) 'Identifying significant factors influencing consumer trust in an online travel site', *Information Technology and Tourism*, 8, 2: 197–214.

Chen, J, Sloan, P and Legrand, W (2009) *Sustainability in the Hospitality Industry: Principles of Sustainable Operations*, Oxford: Butterworth–Heinemann.

consolidated bibliography

Chessbrough, H (2006) *Open Innovation: The New Imperative for Creating and Profiting from Technology*, Boston: Harvard Business School Press.

Cho, W and Olsen, M (1998) 'A case study approach to understanding the impact of information technology on competitive advantage in the lodging industry', *Journal of Hospitality and Tourism Research*, 22, 4: 376–94.

Chung, L H and Parker, L D (2010) 'Managing social and environmental action and accountability in the hospitality industry: a Singapore perspective', *Accounting Forum*, 34, 1: 46–53.

Clark, M A and Wood, R C (1998) 'Consumer loyalty in the restaurant industry: a preliminary exploration of the issues', *International Journal of Contemporary Hospitality Management*, 10, 4: 139–44.

Clarke, A and Chen, W (2007) *International Hospitality Management: Concepts and Cases*, Oxford: Butterworth–Heinemann.

Cousins, J, O'Gorman, K and Stierand, M (2010) 'Molecular gastronomy: basis for a new culinary movement or modern day alchemy?', *International Journal of Contemporary Hospitality Management*, 22, 3: 399–415.

Cracknell, H L, Nobis, G and Kaufman, R J (2000) *Practical Professional Catering*, 2nd edn, London: Thompson.

Cross, R G (1997) 'Launching the revenue rocket: how revenue management can work for your business', *Cornell Hotel and Restaurant Administration Quarterly*, 38, 2: 32–43.

Cross, R G, Higbie, J A and Cross, D Q (2009) 'Revenue management's renaissance: a rebirth of the art and science of profitable revenue generation', *Cornell Hospitality Quarterly*, 50, 1: 56–81.

Crouch, G I and Ritchie, J R B (1998) 'Convention site selection research: a review, conceptual model, and propositional framework', *Journal of Convention and Exhibition Management*, 1, 1: 49–69.

Csíkszentmihályi, M (1997) *Creativity: Flow and the Psychology of Discovery and Invention*, New York: HarperCollins.

Cummings, S (1993) 'Brief case: "The First Strategist"', *Long Range Planning*, 26, 3: 133–5, in Wit, B and Meyer, R (2010) *Strategy: Process, Content, Context, An International Perspective*, London: Cengage Learning. pp. 25–6.

Czepiel, J (1990) 'Service encounters and service relationships: implications for research', *Journal of Business Research*, 20, 1: 13–21.

Davis, B, Lockwood, A and Stone, S (2008) *Food and Beverage Management*, Oxford: Butterworth–Heinemann.

Deakins, D and Freel, M (2003) *Entrepreneurship and Small Firms*, 3rd edn, London: McGraw-Hill.

Dean, T J and McMullen, J S (2007) 'Toward a theory of sustainable entrepreneurship: reducing environmental degradation through entrepreneurial action', *Journal of Business Venturing*, 22, 1: 50–76.

Deming, W E (1986) *Out of the Crisis*, Cambridge, MA: MIT Press.

Department of Trade and Industry (1998) *Our Competitive Future: Building the Knowledge Driven Economy: Analysis and Background*, Cm 4176, London: The Stationery Office, available from http://webarchive.nationalarchives.gov.uk/+/http://www.dti.gov.uk/comp/competitive/wh_ch2_1.htm.

Dickerson, A and Taylor, M A (2000) 'Self-limiting behaviour in women: self-esteem and self-efficacy as predictors', *Group and Organization Management*, 25, 2: 191–209.

DiPietro, R B, Breiter, D, Rompf, P and Godlewska, M (2008) 'An exploratory study of differences among meeting and exhibition planners in their destination selection criteria', *Journal of Convention and Event Tourism*, 9, 4: 258–76.

Dowling, C (1981) *The Cinderella Complex*, New York: Summit Books.

Dwyer, F R, Schurr, P H and Oh, S (1987) 'Developing buyer–seller relationships', *Journal of Marketing*, 51, 2: 11–27.

Dyché, J (2004) *The CRM Handbook*, Boston: Addison-Wesley.

Eastham, J F, Ball, S and Sharples, L (2001) 'The catering and food retail sectors', in Eastham, J F, Sharples, L and Ball, S (eds) *Food Supply Chain Management: Issues for the Hospitality and Retail Sectors*, Oxford: Butterworth–Heinemann. pp. 3–20.

Edwards, G and Edwards, S (2007) *The Dictionary of Drink: A Guide to Every Type of Beverage*, Phoenix Mill: Sutton Publishing.

Edwards, J and Gustafsson, I-B (2008) 'The five aspects meal model', *Journal of Foodservice*, 19, 1: 4–12.

Elkington, J (1997) *Cannibals with Forks: The Triple Bottom Line of 21st Century Business*, Oxford: Capstone.

Ellis, R C and Stipanuk, D M (1999) *Security and Loss Prevention Management*, 2nd edn, East Lansing: EIAHMA.

Embassy Suites Hotels (2011) *Third Annual Business Travel Survey*, McLean, VA: Hilton Worldwide.

Enz, C (2001) 'What keeps you up at night? Key issues of concern for lodging managers', *Cornell Hotel and Restaurant Administration Quarterly*, 42, 2: 38–45.

Enz, C (2004) 'Issues of concern for restaurant owners and managers', *Cornell Hotel and Restaurant Administration Quarterly*, 45, 4: 315–32.

Enz, C (2005) *Hospitality Strategic Management: Concepts and Cases*, Hoboken: Wiley.

Enz, C (2010) *Hospitality Strategic Management: Concepts and Cases*, 2nd edn, Hoboken: Wiley.

Enz, C A and Siguaw, J A (1999) 'Best hotel environmental practices', *Cornell Hotel and Restaurant Administration Quarterly*, 40, 5: 72–7.

Estis-Green, C (2008a) *Sales and Marketing in a Web 2.0 World*, New York: HSMAI Foundation.

Estis-Green, C (2008b) *Demystifying Distribution 2.0*, New York: HSMAI Foundation.

Fattorini, J (1997) *Managing Wine and Beverage Sales*, London: Thomson.

Fattorini, J E (2000) 'Is there such a thing as beverage management? Drink and the food and beverage consumer', in Wood R C (ed.) *Strategic Questions in Food and Beverage Management*, Oxford: Butterworth–Heinemann. pp. 172–86.

Fayol, H (1930) *Industrial and General Administration*, London: Pitman.

Federal Trade Commission (2007) 'FTC issues updated franchise rule', Bureau of Consumer Protection, Washington, DC, www.ftc.gov/opa/2007/01/franchiserule.shtm, last accessed 24 January 2012.

Feinstein, A H and Stefanelli, J M (2008) *Purchasing, Selection and Procurement for the Hospitality Industry*, 7th edn, Hoboken: Wiley.

Fenich, G G (2011) *Meetings, Expositions, Events and Conventions: An Introduction to the Industry*, 3rd edn, Upper Saddle River: Prentice Hall.

Ferguson, P (1998) 'A cultural field in the making: gastronomy in 19th century France', *American Journal of Sociology*, 104, 3: 597–641.

Finkelstein, J (1989) *Dining Out: A Sociology of Modern Manners*, Cambridge: Polity Press.

Fischler, C (1989) 'La cuisine selon Michelin', in Piault, F (ed.) *Nourritures: Plaisirs et angoisses de la fourchette*, Paris: Autrement. pp. 42–51.

Fischler, C (1993) *L'Homnivore*, 2nd edn, Paris: Odile.

Frankfurt Book Fair (2006) www.frankfurt-book-fair.com, last accessed 14 March 2006.

Frapin-Beaugé, A J M, Verginis, C S and Wood, R C (2008) 'Accommodation and facilities management', in Brotherton, B and Wood, R C (eds) *The Sage Handbook of Hospitality Management*, London: Sage. pp. 383–99.

Fuchs, V (1968) *The Service Economy*, New York: National Bureau of Economic Research.

FutureWatch (2004) *A Comparative Outlook on the Global Business of Meetings*, supplement to *The Meeting Professional* (January), Dallas, TX: Meeting Professionals International and American Express (also found at www.hospitalitynet.org/file/152001272.pdf, last accessed 20 November 2011).

Gazzoli, G, Kim, W G and Palakurthi, R (2008) 'Online distribution strategies and competition: are the global hotel companies getting it right?', *International Journal of Contemporary Hospitality Management*, 20, 4: 375–87.

Gee, D A (1999) 'Facilities management and design', in Verginis, C S and Wood, R C (eds) *Accommodation Management: Perspectives for the International Hotel Industry*, London: Thomson. pp. 172–82.

Gee, D A C (1994) 'The Scottish Hotel School – the first fifty years', in Seaton, A V, Jenkins, C L, Wood, R C, Dieke, P U C, Bennett, M M, MacLellan, L R and Smith, R (eds) *Tourism: the State of the Art*, Chichester: Wiley. pp. xvi–xxiii.

Gershuny, J (1978) *After Industrial Society: The Emerging Self-Service Economy*, London: Macmillan.

Gershuny, J (1979) 'The informal economy: its role in post-industrial society', *Futures*, 11: 3–15.

Getz, D (1989) 'Special events: defining the product', *Tourism Management*, 10, 2: 125–37.

Geyer, R and Jackson, T (2004) 'Supply loops and their constraints: the industrial ecology of recycling and reuse', *California Management Review*, 46, 2: 55–73.

Gill, M, Moon, C, Seamna, P and Turbin, V (2002) 'Security management and crime in hotels', *International Journal of Contemporary Hospitality Management*, 14, 2: 58–64.

Goldstein, N J, Cialdini, R B and Griskevicius, V (2008) 'A room with a viewpoint: using social norms to motivate environmental conservation in hotels', *Journal of Consumer Research*, 35, 3: 472–82.

Goodman, A (2000) 'Implementing sustainability in service operations at Scandic Hotels', *Interfaces*, 30, 3: 202–14.

Gounaris, S (2008) 'Antecedents of internal marketing practice: some preliminary empirical evidence', *International Journal of Service Industry Management*, 19, 3: 400–34.

Graham, T L and Roberts, D J (2000) 'Qualitative overview of some important factors affecting the egress of people in hotel fires', *International Journal of Hospitality Management*, 19, 1: 79–87.

Greenfield, H I (2002) 'A note on the goods/services dichotomy', *The Service Industries Journal*, 22, 4: 19–21.

Gremler, D D and Gwinner, K P (2000) 'Customer–employee rapport in service relationships', *Journal of Service Research*, 3, 1: 82–104.

Griffin, R K (1995) 'A categorization scheme for critical success factors of lodging yield management systems', *International Journal of Hospitality Management*, 14, 3–4: 325–38.

Groenenboom, K and Jones, P (2003) 'Issues of security in hotels', *International Journal of Contemporary Hospitality Management*, 15, 1: 14–19.

Gronroos, C (1995) 'Relationship marketing: the strategy continuum', *Journal of the Academy of Marketing Science*, 23, 4: 252–4.

Gronroos, C (2007) *Service Management and Marketing: Customer Management in Service*, 3rd edn, Chichester: Wiley.

Groschl, S and Doherty, L (2006) 'The complexity of culture: using the appraisal process to compare French and British managers in a UK-based international hotel organization' *International Journal of Hospitality Management*, 25, 2: 313–34.

Guerrier, Y (2008) 'Organization studies and hospitality management', in Brotherton, B and Wood, R (eds) *The Sage Handbook of Hospitality Management*, London: Sage. pp. 257–72.

Guerrier, Y and Adib, A (2000) '"No, we don't provide that service": the harassment of hotel employees by customers', *Work, Employment and Society*, 14: 4, 689–705.

Gummesson, E (1994) 'Making relationship marketing operational', *International Journal of Service Industry Management*, 5, 5: 5–20.

Gupta, S and Wood, R C (2008) 'Human resource challenges in the Indian hotel sector', *Asian Journal of Tourism and Hospitality Research*, 2, 2: 87–96.

Gustafsson, I-B (2004) 'Culinary arts and meal science – a new scientific research discipline', *Food Service Technology*, 4, 1: 9–20.

Gustafsson, I-B, Öström, Å, Johansson, J and Mossberg, L (2006) 'The five aspects meal model: a tool for developing meal services in restaurants', *Journal of Foodservice*, 17, 2: 84–93.

Gutek, B A, Bhappu, A D, Liao-Troth, M A and Cherry, B (1999) 'Distinguishing between service relationships and encounters', *Journal of Applied Psychology*, 84, 2: 218–33.

Hales, C and Klidas, A (1998) 'Empowerment in five-star hotels: choice, voice or rhetoric?', *International Journal of Contemporary Hospitality Management*, 10, 3: 88–95.

Hales, J A (2010) *Accounting and Financial Analysis in the Hospitality Industry*, Harlow: Prentice Hall.

Harris, K J and West, J J (1995) 'Senior savvy: mature diners' restaurant service expectations', *Florida International University Hospitality Review*, 13, 2: 35–44.

Harris, P and Mongiello, M (2006) *Accounting and Financial Management: Developments in the International Hospitality Industry*, Oxford: Butterworth–Heinemann.

Harris, P B and Sachau, D (2005) 'Is cleanliness next to godliness? The role of housekeeping in impression formation', *Environment and Behaviour*, 37, 1: 81–101.

Hayes, D and Huffman, L (1985) 'Menu analysis, a better way', *Cornell Hotel and Restaurant Administration Quarterly*, 25, 4: 64–70.

Hayes, D and Ninemeier, J (2007) *Hotel Operations Management*, 2nd edn, New York: Pearson.

Hemmington, N (2007) 'From service to experience: understanding and defining the hospitality business', *The Service Industries Journal*, 27, 6: 747–55.

Henderson, S C and Snyder, C A (1999) 'Personal information privacy: implications for MIS managers', *Information and Management*, 36, 4: 213–20.

Hennig-Thurau, T and Klee, A (1997) 'The impact of customer satisfaction and relationship quality on customer retention: a critical reassessment and model development', *Psychology and Marketing*, 14, 8: 737–64.

Hermans, O and Melissen, F (2008) 'Introducing the CRM-7-18 model: analysing the need for and introducing a framework for phased design and implementation of guest relationship programs', *Proceedings of the 26th EuroChrie Conference, Dubai, 11–14 October*.

Hermans, O and Mount, D (2010) *Customer Relationship Management in Hospitality: A Theoretical Introduction and Guidelines for Applying the CRM-7-18 Model*, Breda: University of Applied Science.

Hermans, O and Van Ravesteijn, C (2011) 'Informational empowerment: customer dialogue technology and service employees', *Proceedings of the 12th International Research Symposium on Service Excellence in Management (QUIS12), Ithaca, NY, 2–5 June*.

Higgins, M S (2005) 'Procurement becomes full service support systems', *Hotel and Motel Management*, May 16: 16–17.

Hochschild, A (1983) *The Managed Heart*, Berkeley: University of California Press.

Holcomb, J L, Upchurch, R S and Okumus, F (2007) 'Corporate social responsibility: what are top hotel companies reporting?', *International Journal of Contemporary Hospitality Management*, 19, 6: 461–75.

Hoque, K (1999) 'New approaches to HRM in the UK hospitality industry', *Human Resource Management Journal*, 9, 2: 64–76.

Horizons for Success (2008) *UK Foodservice Industry in 2008 Report*, London: Horizons for Success (available from www.horizonsforsuccess.com, last accessed 1 February 2010).

Hospitalitynet.org (2004) Interview with James F. Anhut, Senior Vice President, Brand Development InterContinental Hotels Group (discussing the New Lifestyle Brand from IHG: Hotel Indigo), www.hospitalitynet.org/news/4019492.html, last accessed 10 October 2011.

Hotel and Motel Management (2010) 'H&MM's 2010 purchasing survey', *Hotel and Motel Management*, July, 22–4.

Hotel Association of New York City (2006) *Uniform System of Accounts for the Lodging Industry*, 10th edn, East Lansing, EIAHLA.

Huelin, A and Jones, P (1990) 'Thinking about catering systems', *International Journal of Operations and Production Management*, 10, 8: 42–52.

Hughes, H L (1982) 'The service economy, de-industrialisation and the hospitality industry', *International Journal of Hospitality Management*, 1, 3: 145–50.

Hughes, J C (2002) 'HRM and universalism: is there one best way?', *International Journal of Contemporary Hospitality Management*, 14, 5: 221–8.

HVS (2010) 'How are hotels embracing social media in 2010?', www.hvs.com/Content/2977.pdf February, last accessed 8 November 2011.

Institute of Grocery Distribution (2009) *UK Grocery and Foodservice Outlook*, London: Institute of Grocery Distribution.

Institute of Hospitality (2010) 'Is security ever compromised by investment decisions?', *Hospitality*, Issue 20: 12.

InterContinental Hotels Group (2010) *Annual Report*, www.ihgplc.com/files/reports/ar2010/docs/IHG%20Review_Lo.pdf, last accessed 24 January 2012.

International Franchise Association (2011) 'Frequently asked questions about franchising', www.franchise.org/faq.aspx, last accessed 24 January 2012.

International Tourism Bourse (2006) www.itb-berlin.de/en/, last accessed 14 March 2006.

Jackson, B (1985) 'Build customer relationships that last', *Harvard Business Review*, 63, 6: 120–8.

Jarratt, D (2004) 'Conceptualizing a relationship management capability', *Marketing Theory*, 4, 4: 287–309.

Jauncey, S, Mitchell, I and Slamet, P (1995) 'The meaning and management of yield in hotels', *International Journal of Contemporary Hospitality Management*, 7, 4: 23–6.

Jobber, D (2001) *Principles and Practice of Marketing*, 3rd edn, North Ryde: McGraw-Hill Irwin.

Johansson, F (2006) *The Medici Effect. What Elephants and Epidemics Can Teach Us About Innovation*, Boston: Harvard Business School Press.

Johns, N and Jones, P (1999a) 'Systems and management: mind over matter', *The Hospitality Review*, July: 43–8.

Johns, N and Jones, P (1999b) 'Systems and management: the principles of performance', *The Hospitality Review*, October: 40–4.

Johns, N and Jones, P (2000) 'Systems and management: understanding the real world', *The Hospitality Review*, January: 47–52.

Johns, N, Tyas, P, Ingold, T and Hopkinson, S (1996) 'Investigation of the perceived components of the meal experience using perceptual gap methodology', *Progress in Tourism and Hospitality Research*, 2, 1: 15–26.

Johnson, M D and Selnes, F (2004) 'Customer portfolio management: toward a dynamic theory of exchange relationships', *Journal of Marketing*, 68, 2: 1–17.

Johnston, R (1993) 'A framework for developing a quality strategy in a customer processing operation', *International Journal of Quality and Reliability Management*, 4, 4: 37–46.

Jones, C (2002) 'Facilities management in medium-sized UK hotels', *International Journal of Contemporary Hospitality Management*, 14, 2: 72–80.

Jones, P (1993) 'A taxonomy of foodservice operations', Paper presented at the 2nd Annual CHME Research Conference, Manchester, April.

Jones, P (1994a) 'Foodservice operations', in Jones, P and Merricks, P (eds) *The Management of Foodservice Operations*, London: Cassell. pp. 3–17.

Jones, P (1994b) 'Catering systems', in Davis, B and Lockwood, A (eds) *Food and Beverage Management: A Selection of Readings*, Oxford: Butterworth–Heinemann. pp. 131–44.

Jones, P (2008) 'Operations management: theoretical underpinnings', in Jones, P (ed.) *Handbook of Hospitality Operations and IT*, Oxford: Butterworth–Heinemann. pp. 1–19.

Jones, P and Lockwood, A (2008) 'Researching hospitality management: it's OK to use the "m" word', *The Hospitality Review*, 10, 3: 26–30.

June, L and Smith, S L J (1987) 'Service attributes and situational effects on customer preferences for restaurant dining', *Journal of Travel Research*, 26, 2: 20–7.

Juran, J M (1988) *Juran's Quality Control Handbook*, New York: McGraw-Hill.

Justis, R T and Judd, R J (2008) *Franchising*, 4th edn, Cincinnati: Dame–Thomson Learning.

Kasavana, M L and Brooks, R M (2009) *Managing Front Office Operations*, East Lansing: EIAHLA.

Kasavana, M L and Smith, D I (1982) *Menu Engineering*, East Lansing: Hospitality Publications.

Katsigris, C and Thomas, C (2011) *The Bar and Beverage Book*, Hoboken: Wiley.

Keller, K L, Apéria, T and Georgson, M (2008) *Strategic Brand Management: A European Perspective*, Harlow: Pearson Education.

Kimes, S E (1989) 'The basics of yield management', *Cornell Hotel and Restaurant Administration Quarterly*, 30, 3: 14–19.

Kimes, S E (2003) 'Revenue management: a retrospective', *Cornell Hotel and Restaurant Administration Quarterly*, 44, 5–6: 131.

Kimes, S E (2008) 'Hotel revenue management: today and tomorrow', *Cornell Hospitality Report*, 8, 4.

Kirk, D (1995) 'Hard and soft systems: a common paradigm for operations management', *International Journal of Contemporary Hospitality Management*, 7, 5: 13–16.

Kirk, D (2000) 'The value of systems in hospitality management', *The Hospitality Review*, April: 55–6.

Knowles, T (1996) *Corporate Strategy for Hospitality*, Harlow: Longman Group Limited.

Kolb, J A (1999) 'The effect of gender role, attitude toward leadership and self confidence on leader emergence: implications for leadership development', *Human Resource Development Quarterly*, 10, 4: 305–20.

Korczynski, M (2002) *Human Resource Management in Service Work*, Basingstoke: Palgrave.

Kothari, T, Hu, C and Roehl, S R (2005) 'e-Procurement: an emerging tool for the hotel supply chain management', *International Journal of Hospitality Management*, 24, 3: 369–89.

Kotler, P, Bowen, J T and Makens, J C (2006) *Marketing for Hospitality and Tourism*, 4th edn, Upper Saddle River: Pearson.

KPMG (2005) *Global Hotel Distribution Survey 2005: Managing Pricing across Distribution Channels*, http://kpmgpt.lcc.ch/dbfetch/52616e646f6d495621686df3ccf6c42176ee2edf8aeb 53af/g_hotel.pdf, last accessed 14 February 2011.

Kumar, K (1978) *Prophecy and Progress*, Harmondsworth: Penguin.

Kumar, K (2004) *From Post-industrial to Post-modern Society: New Theories of the Contemporary World*, London: Wiley Blackwell.

Kumar, V and Shah, D (2004) 'Building and sustaining customer loyalty for the 21st century', *Journal of Retailing*, 80, 4: 317–29.

Kurti, N and Kurti, G (1988) *But the Crackling Is Superb: An Anthology on Food and Drink by Fellows and Foreign Members of the Royal Society*, Oxford: Institute of Physics Publishing.

Kusluvan, S, Kusluvan, Z, Ilhan, I and Buyruk, L (2010) 'The human dimension', *Cornell Hospitality Quarterly*, 51, 2: 171.

Ladhari, R (2000) 'Service quality, emotional satisfaction, and behavioural intentions: a study in the hotel industry', *Managing Service Quality*, 9, 3: 308–31.

Lahap, J B, Mahony, G B and Sillitoe, J F (2010) 'Developing a service delivery improvement model for the Malaysian hotel sector', *Proceedings of the 3rd Asia Euro Conference: Transformation and Modernisation in Tourism, Hospitality and Gastronomy*.

Lamminmaki, D (2007) 'Outsourcing in Australian hotels: a transaction cost economics perspective', *Journal of Hospitality and Tourism Research*, 31, 1: 73–110.

Lashley, C (1997) *Empowering Service Excellence: Beyond the Quick Fix*, London: Cassell.

Lashley, C (2000a) 'Towards a theoretical understanding', in Lashley, C and Morrison, A (eds) *In Search of Hospitality: Theoretical Perspectives and Debates*, Oxford: Butterworth–Heinemann. pp. 1–17.

Lashley, C (2000b) 'Empowerment through involvement: a case study in TGI Fridays', *Personnel Review*, 29, 6: 333–49.

Lashley, C (2001) *Empowerment: HR Strategies for Service Excellence*, Oxford: Butterworth–Heinemann.

Lawlor, F and Jayawardena, C (2003) 'Purchasing for 4,000 hotels: the case of Avendra', *International Journal of Contemporary Hospitality Management*, 15, 6: 346–8.

Lee-Ross, D and Lashley, C (2009) *Entrepreneurship and Small Business Management in the Hospitality Industry*, Oxford: Butterworth–Heinemann.

Levie, M (2010) 'Innovation in hospitality', Keynote speech presented at EuroCHRIE Conference, Amsterdam, October 25–28.

Lewis, R (1981) 'Restaurant advertising: appeals and consumers' intentions', *Journal of Advertising Research*, 21, 5: 69–74.

Liladrie, S (2010). 'Do not disturb/please clean room': hotel housekeepers in Greater Toronto', *Race and Class*, 52, 1: 57–69.

Lillicrap, D and Cousins, J (2006) *Food and Beverage Service*, 7th edn, London: Hodder Arnold.

Linehan, M (2001) 'Networking for female managers' career development: empirical evidence', *Journal of Management Development*, 20, 9: 823–9.

Litteljohn, D (1997) 'Internationalization in hotels: current aspects and development', *International Journal of Contemporary Hospitality Management*, 9, 5/6: 187–98, cited in Whitla et al., 2007.

Littlewood, K (2005) 'Forecasting and control of passenger bookings', *Journal of Revenue and Pricing Management*, 4, 2: 111–23.

Lockwood, A and Jones, P (2000) 'Managing hospitality operations', in Lashley, C and Morrison, A (eds) *In Search of Hospitality: Theoretical Perspectives and Debates*, Oxford: Butterworth–Heinemann. pp. 157–77.

Lominé, L L (2003) 'Hospitality, leisure, sport and tourism in higher education in France', *Journal of Hospitality, Leisure, Sport and Tourism Education*, 2, 1: 105–12.

Longart, P (2010) 'What drives word-of-mouth in restaurants?', *International Journal of Contemporary Hospitality Management*, 22, 1: 121–8.

Lovelock, C (1983) 'Classifying services to gain strategic marketing insights', *Journal of Marketing*, 47, 3: 9–20.

Lowe, C M (2011) 'Emerging meetings market: China', *Meetings and Conventions Magazine*, 46, 1: 15.

Lowe, R and Marriott, S (2006) *Enterprise: Entrepreneurship and Innovation*, Oxford: Butterworth–Heinemann.

Lucas, R (2002) 'Fragments of HRM in hospitality? Evidence from the 1998 workplace employee relations survey', *International Journal of Contemporary Hospitality Management*, 14, 5: 207–12.

Lucas, R and Deery, M (2004) 'Significant developments and emerging issues in human resource management', *International Journal of Hospitality Management*, 23, 5: 459–72.

Lugosi, P (2008) 'Hospitality spaces, hospitable moments: consumer encounters and affective experiences in commercial settings', *Journal of Foodservice*, 19, 2: 139–49.

Mace, E (1995) 'International trends in the hotel industry or, survival in the global economy', *Hotel and Motel Management*, 210, 10: 11–13, cited in Whitla et al., 2007.

Mainzer, B W (2004) 'Future of revenue management: fast forward for hospitality revenue management', *Journal of Revenue and Pricing Management*, 3, 3: 285–9.

Mangold, W G, Miller, F and Brockway, G R (1999) 'Word-of-mouth communication in the service marketplace', *Journal of Services Marketing*, 13, 1: 73–89.

Martin, R (2000) 'New study quantifies gender disparity in senior positions', *Nation's Restaurant News*, 34, 12: 58.

Maslow, A H (1946) 'A theory of human motivation', in Harriman, P L (ed.) *Twentieth Century Psychology: Recent Developments in Psychology*, New York: Philosophical Library. pp. 22–48.

Mason, D D M, Tideswell, C and Roberts, E (2006) 'Guest perceptions of hotel loyalty', *Journal of Hospitality and Tourism Research*, 30, 2: 191–206.

Mattel, B and The Culinary Institute of America (2008) *Catering: A Guide to Managing a Successful Business Operation*, Hoboken: Wiley.

Mattila, A and Enz, C (2002) 'The role of emotions in service encounters', *Journal of Service Research*, 4, 4: 268–77.

Mattila, A S (2006) 'How affective commitment boosts guest loyalty (and promotes frequent-guest programs)', *Cornell Hotel and Restaurant Administration Quarterly*, 47, 2: 174–81.

McCall, M, Voorhees, C and Calantone, R (2010) 'Building customer loyalty: ten principles for designing an effective customer reward program', *Cornell Hospitality Report* 10, 9.

McClelland, E, Swail, J, Bell, J and Ibbotson, P (2005) 'Following the pathway of female entrepreneurs: a six-country investigation', *International Journal of Entrepreneurial Behaviour and Research*, 11, 2: 84–107.

McDonald's (2010) *McDonald's 2010 Annual Report*, www.aboutmcdonaldscom/content/dam/AboutMcDonalds/Investors/investors-2010-annual-report.pdf, last accessed 24 January 2012.

McDonald's (2011) www.aboutmcdonalds.com/mcd/our_company.html, last accessed 3 October 2011.

McGill, J I and van Ryzin, G J (1999) 'Revenue management: research overview and prospects', *Transportation Science*, 33, 2: 233–56.

Meetings Market Report (2004) *Meetings and Conventions Magazine (Supplement)*, 46, 1: 15.

Meisner Rosen, C (2001) 'Environmental strategy and competitive advantage: an introduction', *California Management Review*, 43, 3: 8–15.

Mendelsohn, M (2004) *The Guide to Franchising*, 7th edn, London: Cengage.

Mennell, S (1985) *All Manners of Food: Eating and Taste in England and France from the Middle Ages to the Present*, Oxford: Blackwell.

Miles, S (2001) *Social Theory in the Real World*, London: Sage.

Miller, J (1980) *Menu Pricing and Strategy*, Boston: CBI.

Minghetti, V (2003) 'Building customer value in the hospitality industry: towards the definition of a customer-centric information system', *Information Technology and Tourism*, 6: 141–52.

Minniti, M (2006) 'The size and scope of entrepreneurial activity: evidence from a large cross-country dataset', paper prepared for *Exploring Rural Entrepreneurship: Imperatives and Opportunities for Research*, October 26–27, Washington, DC.

Mintel (2010) *Hotel Technology – International*, London: Mintel.

Mintzberg, H, Ahlstrand, B and Lampel, J (1998) *Strategy Safari: A Guided Tour Through the Wilds of Strategic Management*, New York: Free Press.

Mitussis, D, O'Malley, L and Patterson, M (2006) 'Mapping the re-engagement of CRM with relationship marketing', *European Journal of Marketing*, 40, 5–6: 572–89.

Mooney, S (1994) 'Planning and designing the menu', in Jones, P and Merricks, P (eds) *The Management of Foodservice Operations*, London: Cassell. pp. 45–58.

Morrison, A, Rimmington, M and Williams, C (1999) *Entrepreneurship in the Hospitality, Tourism and Leisure Industries*, Oxford: Butterworth–Heinemann.

Mowen J and Minor M (1998) *Consumer Behaviour: A Framework*, 5th edn, Harlow: Prentice Hall.

Myung, E, McCool, A C and Feinstein, A H (2008) 'Understanding attributes affecting meal choice decisions in a bundling context', *International Journal of Hospitality Management*, 27, 2: 119–25.

Namasivasyam, K, Sigaw, J and Enz, C (2000) 'How wired are we?', *Cornell Hotel and Restaurant Administration Quarterly*, 40, 5: 31–43.

Narayana, C L and Markin, R J (1975) 'Consumer behaviour and product performance: an alternative conceptualization', *Journal of Marketing*, 39, 4: 1–6.

National Catering Inquiry (1966) *The British Eating Out*, Glasgow: National Catering Inquiry.

National Restaurant Association (1996) *Uniform System of Accounts for Restaurants*, 7th edn, Washington, DC: NRA.

Neal, C M (2004) *Consumer Behaviour*, North Ryde: McGraw-Hill Irwin.

Nickson, D (2007) *Human Resource Management for the Hospitality and Tourism Industries*, Oxford: Butterworth–Heinemann.

Nickson, D, Warhurst, C, Witz, A and Cullen, A-M (2001) 'The importance of being aesthetic', in Sturdy, A, Grugulis, I and Wilmott, H (eds) *Customer Service: Empowerment and Entrapment*, Basingstoke: Palgrave.

Ninemeier, J D (2010) *Management of Food and Beverage Operations*, East Lansing: EIAHLA.

Nitschke, A A and Frye, W D (2008) *Managing Housekeeping Operations*, East Lansing: EIAHLA (see especially Chapter 1, pp. 3–36.)

Norman, R (1991) *Service Management: Strategy and Leadership in Service Business*, 2nd edn, Chichester: Wiley.

O'Connor, P (1999) *Electronic Information Distribution in Hospitality and Tourism*, London: CAB International.

O'Connor, P (2004) *Using Computers in Hospitality*, 3rd edn, London: Thomson.

O'Connor, P (2007) 'An analysis of hotel trademark abuse in pay-per-click search advertising', in Sigala, M, Mich, L and Murphy, J (eds) *Information and Communications Technology in Tourism 2007*, New York: Springer. pp. 435–46.

O'Connor, P (2008a) 'E-mail marketing by international hotel chains', *Cornell Hospitality Quarterly*, 49, 1: 42–52.

O'Connor, P (2008b) 'Managing hospitality information technology in Europe: issues, challenges and priorities', *Journal of Hospitality and Leisure Marketing*, 17, 1–2: 59–77.

O'Connor, P (2011) 'A benchmark of social media adoption by international hotel companies', *Proceedings of the e-CASE and e-Tech 2011 Conference, Tokyo, International Business Academics Consortium, January.*

O'Connor, P and Piccoli, G (2003) 'Marketing hotels using global distribution systems revisited', *Cornell Hotel and Restaurant Administration Quarterly*, 44, 3: 105–14.

Oakley, J G (2000) 'Gender-based barriers to senior management positions: understanding the scarcity of female CEOs', *Journal of Business Ethics*, 27, 4: 321–34.

OECD (1997) *Proposed Guidelines for Collecting and Interpreting Technological Innovation Data (The Oslo Manual)*, 2nd edn, Paris: Organization for Economic Co-operation and Development.

Ogbonna, E and Harris, L (2002) 'Managing organizational culture: insights from the hospitality industry', *Human Resource Management Journal*, 12, 1: 33–53.

Ojugo, C (2009) *Practical Food and Beverage Cost Control*, New York: Delmar.

O'Mahony, B (2009) 'University kitchen nightmares enter a new ERA', *The Hospitality Review*, 11, 4: 5–7.

Oshagbemi, T and Gill, R (2002) 'Gender differences and similarities in the leadership styles and behaviour of UK managers', *Women in Management Review*, 18, 6: 288–98.

Oxford Economics (2010) *Economic Contribution of the Hospitality Industry*, report prepared by Oxford Economics for the British Hospitality Association, Oxford: Oxford Economics.

Ozler, L (2004) 'Hotel Indigo unveils novel design concept', www.dexigner.com/news/1762, last accessed 10 October 2011.

Palmer, A (2007) *Principles of Services Marketing*, 5th edn, London: McGraw-Hill.

Paraskevas, A (2010) 'Mind games and security tactics: six steps to tackle the terrorist threat to hotels', *Hospitality*, Issue 19, 36–9.

Parasuraman, A, Zeithaml, V A and Berry, L L (1985) 'A conceptual model of service quality and its implications for future research', *Journal of Marketing*, 49, 4: 41–50.

Parayani, K, Masoudi, A and Cudney, E (2010) 'QFD application in the hospitality industry – a hotel case study', *Quality Management Journal*, 17, 1: 7–28.

Park, K and Jang, S (2011) 'Mergers and acquisitions and firm growth: investigating restaurant firms', *International Journal of Hospitality Management*, 30, 1: 141–9.

Parker International (2009) www.parkerinternational.com, last accessed 1 September 2011.

Pavesic, D (1989) 'Psychological aspects of menu pricing', *International Journal of Hospitality Management*, 8, 1: 43–9.

Pavesic, D V (1983) 'Cost/margin analysis: a third approach to menu pricing and design', *International Journal of Hospitality Management*, 2, 3: 127–34.

Payne, A (2005) *Handbook of CRM: Achieving Excellence through Customer Management*, Oxford: Butterworth–Heinemann.

Payne, A and Frow, P (2005) 'A strategic framework for customer relationship management', *Journal of Marketing*, 69, 4: 167–78.

Peacock, M and Kübler, M (2001) 'The failure of "control" in the hospitality industry', *International Journal of Hospitality Management*, 20, 4: 353–65.

Peredo, A M and McLean, M (2006) 'Social entrepreneurship: a critical review of the concept', *Journal of World Business*, 41, 1: 56–65.

Pereira-Moliner, J, Claver-Cortés, E and Molina-Azorín, J (2010) 'Strategy and performance in the Spanish hotel industry', *Cornell Hospitality Quarterly*, 51, 4: 513–28.

Perlmutter, H (1969) 'The tortuous evolution of the multinational corporation', *Columbia Journal of World Business*, 4, 2: 9–18.

Pew Internet and American Life Project (2010) *Online Product Research* www.pewinternet.org/Reports/2010/Online-Product-Research.aspx, last accessed 4 July 2011.

PhoCusWright (2010) 'US online travel penetration stalls as corporate market leads recovery', http://phocuswright.us/library/pressrelease/1484, last accessed 18 February 2012.

PhoCusWright (2011) 'One third of world's travel sales to be booked online by 2012', http://phocuswright.us/library/pressrelease/1603, last accessed 7 March 2012.

Pickworth, J R (1988) 'Service delivery systems in the foodservice industry', *International Journal of Hospitality Management*, 7, 1: 43–62.

Pine, B J and Gilmore, J H (1999) *The Experience Economy*, Boston: Harvard Business School Press.

Pizam, A (2010) 'Hotels as tempting targets for terrorism attacks [Editorial]', *International Journal of Hospitality Management*, 29, 1: 1.

Pizam, A and Shani, A (2009) 'The nature of the hospitality industry: present and future managers' perspectives', *Anatolia*, 20, 1: 134–50.

Plotkin, R (2011) *Successful Beverage Management*, Tucson: Barmedia.

Poiesz, Th B C (1999) *Gedragsmanagement: Waarom Mensen zich (niet) Gedragen*, Wormer: Immerc.

Poon, A (1993) *Tourism, Technology and Competitive Strategies*, Wallingford: CAB International.

Porter, M (1980) *Competitive Strategy: Techniques for Analyzing Industries and Competitors*, New York: Free Press.

Pounder, J S and Coleman, M (2002) 'Women – better leaders than men? In general and educational management it still "all depends"', *Leadership and Organization Development Journal*, 23, 3: 122–33.

Powell, P H and Watson, D (2006) 'Service unseen: The hotel room attendant at work', *International Journal of Hospitality Management*, 25, 2: 297–312.

Pratten, J D (2003) 'The importance of waiting staff in restaurant service', *British Food Journal*, 5, 11: 826–34.

PriceWaterhouseCoopers (2004) *The Economic Impact of Franchised Businesses, Vol. I*, Washington, DC: The International Franchise Association.

PriceWaterhouseCoopers (2007) *The Economic Impact of Franchised Businesses, Vol. III*, Washington, DC: The International Franchise Association.

PriceWaterhouseCoopers (2011a) 'The economic significance of meetings to the U.S. economy', http://meetingsmeanbusiness.com/docs/Economic%20Study%20Release.pdf, last accessed 20 November 2011.

PriceWaterhouseCoopers (2011b) *UK Hotels Forecast 2011 and 2012: How big a party for hotels in 2012?* www.pwc.co.uk/en_UK/uk/assets/pdf/uk-hotels-forecast-2011-2012.pdf, last accessed 10 March 2012.

Professional Convention Management (2011) *Professional Management: Comprehensive Strategies for Meetings, Conventions and Events*, 5th edn, Chicago: Professional Convention Educational Association.

Queenan, C C, Ferguson, M E and Stratman, J K (2011) 'Revenue management performance drivers: an exploratory analysis within the hotel industry', *Journal of Revenue and Pricing Management*, 10, 2: 172–88.

Raghubalan, G and Raghubalan, S (2007) *Hotel Housekeeping Operations and Management*, New Delhi: Oxford University Press.

Ragins, B and Scandura, T (1994) 'Gender differences in expected outcomes of mentoring relationships', *Academy of Management Journal*, 37, 4: 957–71.

Raleigh, L E and Roginsky, R J (Eds) (1995) *Hotel Investments: Issues and Perspectives*, 5th edn, East Lansing: EIAHMA.

Ram, M, Barrett, G and Jones, T (2000) 'Ethnicity and enterprise', in Carter, S and Jones-Evans, D (eds) *Enterprise and Small Business: Principles, Practice and Policy*, 2nd edn, Harlow: Pearson. pp.192–207.

Ransley, J and Ingram, H (2004) *Developing Hospitality Properties and Facilities*, 2nd edn, Oxford: Butterworth–Heinemann.

Rao, H (2009) *Market Rebels: How Activists Make or Break Radical Innovations*, Princeton, NJ: Princeton University Press.

Rao, H, Monin, P and Durand, R (2003) 'Institutional change in Toque Ville: nouvelle cuisine as an identity movement in French gastronomy', *American Journal of Sociology*, 108, 4: 795–843.

Rawstron, C G (1999) 'Housekeeping management in the contemporary hotel industry', in Verginis, C S and Wood, R C (eds) *Accommodation Management: Perspectives for the International Hotel Industry*, London: Thomson. pp. 114–27.

Reichheld, F and Detrick, C (2003) 'Loyalty: a prescription for cutting costs', *Marketing Management*, 12, 5: 24–5.

Richards, G (2002) 'Gastronomy: an essential ingredient in tourism production and consumption', in A-M Hjalager and G Richards (eds), *Tourism and Gastronomy*, London: Routledge. pp. 3–20.

Riewoldt, O (2002) *New Hotel Design*, New York: Watson-Guptill Publications.

Riley, M (2005) 'Food and beverage management: a review of change', *International Journal of Contemporary Hospitality Management*, 17, 1: 88–93.

Ritzer, G (1996) *The McDonaldization of Society*, rev. edn, Thousand Oaks: Pine Forge Press.

Roberts, D and Chan, D H-W (2000) 'Fires in hotel rooms and scenario predictions', *International Journal of Contemporary Hospitality Management*, 12, 1: 37–44.

Robson, S and Ortmans, L (2008) 'First findings from the UK Innovation Survey 2007', *Economic and Labour Market Review*, 2, 4: 47–53.

Rodgers, S (2005) 'Selecting a food service system: a review', *International Journal of Contemporary Hospitality Management*, 17, 2: 157–69.

Rogers, E (1962/2003) *Diffusion of Innovations*, 5th edn, New York: Free Press.

Rosenberg, W and Keener, J B (2001) *Time to Make the Donuts*, New York: Lebhar–Friedman Books.

Rushmore S, Ciraldo, D M and Tarras, J (1997) *Hotel Investments Handbook*, Boston: Warren, Gorham and Lamont.

Rushmore, S and Baum, E (2001) *Hotels and Motels: Valuations and Market Studies*, Chicago: Appraisal Institute.

Rutes, W A, Penner, R H and Adams, L (2001) *Hotel Design, Planning, and Development*, New York: Norton.

Ryan, C (1980) *An Introduction to Hotel and Catering Economics*, Nottingham: Stanley Thornes.

Ryan, C and Stewart, M (2009) 'Eco-tourism and luxury – the case of Al Maha, Dubai', *Journal of Sustainable Tourism*, 17, 3: 287–301.

Saco, R M and Goncalves, A P (2008) 'Service design: an appraisal', *Design Management Review*, 19, 1: 10–19.

Sahay, A (2007) 'How to reap higher profits with dynamic pricing', *Sloan Management Review*, 48, 4: 53–60.

Sandler, G (1994) 'Fair dealing', *Journal of European Business*, 4, 1: 46–9.

Sasser, W E, Olsen, R P and Wyckoff, D D (1978) *Management of Service Operations: Text Cases and Readings*, Boston: Allyn and Bacon.

Scanlon, N L (2007) 'An analysis and assessment of environmental operating practices in hotel and resort properties', *International Journal of Hospitality Management*, 26, 3: 711–23.

Schlentrich, U A (1999) 'Conference and convention management', in Verginis, C S and Wood, R C (eds) *Accommodation Management: Perspectives for the International Hotel Industry*, London: Thomson. pp. 150–71.

Schlentrich, U A (2008) 'The MICE industry: meetings, incentives, conventions and exhibitions', in Brotherton, B and Wood, R C (eds) *The Sage Handbook of Hospitality Management*, London: Sage. pp. 400–20.

Schmidgall, R S (2011) *Hospitality Industry Managerial Accounting*, East Lansing: EIAHLA.

Schneider, M, Tucker, G and Scoviak, M (1998) *The Professional Housekeeper*, 4th edn, New York: Wiley.

Schnitzler, H (1982) 'Purchasing for a new hotel', *Cornell Hotel and Restaurant Administration Quarterly*, 23, 2: 83–91.

Schumpeter, J (1911) *The Theory of Economic Development*, Boston: Harvard University Press.

Segal, D (2009) 'Pillow fights at the Four Seasons', www.nytimes.com/2009/06/28/business/global/28four.html, last accessed 10 March 2012.

Seringhaus, F H R and Rosson, P J (2001) 'Firm experience and international trade fairs', *Journal of Marketing Management*, 17, 7–8: 877–901.

Seven & i Holdings Co Ltd (2011) *Annual Report*, www.7andi.com/en/ir/pdf/annual/2011_all.pdf, last accessed 24 January 2012.

Shamir, B (1981) 'The workplace as a community: the case of British hotels', *Industrial Relations Journal*, 12, 6: 45–56.

Shanks, G and Tay, E (2001) 'The role of knowledge management in moving to a customer-focused organization', *Proceedings of the 9th European Conference on Information Systems, Bled, Slovenia, June 27–29*.

Shapiro, M J (2009) 'Still thinking green', *Meetings and Conventions Magazine*, 44, 10: 28.

Sharpley, R (1996) 'Tourism and consumer culture in postmodern society', in Robinson, M, Evans, N and Callaghan, P (eds) *Proceedings of the 'Tourism and Culture: Towards the 21st Century Conference*, Centre for Travel and Tourism/Business Education. pp. 203–15.

Shock, P J (2005) 'Meetings', in Pizam, A (ed.) *International Encyclopedia of Hospitality Management*, Oxford: Butterworth–Heinemann. pp. 424–5.

Shoemaker, S and Lewis, R C (1999) 'Customer loyalty: the future of hospitality marketing', *International Journal of Hospitality Management*, 18, 4: 345–70.

Siguaw, J and Enz, C (1999) 'Best practices in information technology', *Cornell Hotel and Restaurant Administration Quarterly*, 40, 9: 58–71.

Sill, B (1991) 'Capacity management – making your service delivery more productive', *Cornell Hotel and Restaurant Administration Quarterly*, 31, 4: 77–88.

Slattery, P (2002) 'Finding the hospitality industry', *Journal of Hospitality, Leisure, Sport and Tourism Education*, 1, 1, 19–28.

Smith, B C, Leimkuhler, J F and Darrow, R M (1992) 'Yield management at American Airlines', *Interfaces*, 22, 1: 8–31.

Smith, M, MacLeod, N and Hart Robinson, M (2010) *Key Concepts in Tourist Studies*, London: Sage.

Society of Incentive and Travel Executives (2006) www.site-intl.org, last accessed 14 March 2006.

Solomon, M R, Bamossy, G, Askegaard S and Hogg, M K (2006) *Consumer Behaviour: A European Perspective*, 3rd edn, Harlow: Prentice Hall.

Song, H, Lin, S, Witt, S and Zhang, X (2011) 'Impact of financial/economic crisis on demand for hotel rooms in Hong Kong', *Tourism Management*, 32, 1: 172–86.

Sophonsiri, S, O'Mahony, B and Sillitoe, J (2010) 'Towards a model of relationship development for hospitality practice', *International Journal of Hospitality and Tourism Systems*, 3, 1: 64–79.

Soyer, A B (1857) *Soyer's Culinary Campaign*, London: Routledge.

consolidated bibliography

177

Starwood (2010) www.starwoodhotels.com/corporate/profile_detail.html?obj_id=0900c7b980 adec5e, last accessed 11 November 2011.

Stipanuk, D M (2006) *Hospitality Facilities Management and Design*, East Lansing: EIAHLA.

Stokes, D and Wilson, N (2006) *Small Business Management and Entrepreneurship*, 5th edn, London: Thomson.

Storbacka, K, Strandvik, T and Gronroos, C (1994) 'Managing customer relationships for profit: the dynamics of relationship quality', *International Journal of Service Industry Management*, 5, 5: 21–38.

Storey, J (1992) *Developments in the Management of Human Resources*, Oxford: Blackwell.

Story, L (2007) 'Blackstone to buy Hilton Hotels for $26 billion', www.nytimes.com/2007/07/04/business/04deal.html (accessed 28 August 2012).

Surowiecki, J (2004) *The Wisdom of Crowds: Why the Many Are Smarter Than the Few and How Collective Wisdom Shapes Business, Economies, Societies and Nations*, New York: Doubleday.

Swarbrooke, J (1999) *Sustainable Tourism Management*, Wallingford: CAB International .

Swarbrooke, J and Horner, S (2007) *Consumer Behaviour in Tourism*, 2nd edn, Oxford: Butterworth–Heinemann.

Taylor, F W (1911) *The Principles of Scientific Management*, New York: Harper Brothers.

Taylor, J, Reynolds, D and Brown, D M (2009) 'Multi-factor menu analysis using data envelopment analysis', *International Journal of Contemporary Hospitality Management*, 21, 2: 213–25.

This, H (2006a) 'Food for tomorrow?', *European Molecular Biology Organization Reports*, 7, 11: 1062–6.

This, H (2006b) *Molecular Gastronomy: Exploring the Science of Flavour*, New York: Columbia University Press.

Thomas, D (2007) 'Thistle implements e-procurement system to save costs', available from www.caterersearch.com/Articles/2007/08/28/315680/thistle-implements-e-procurement-system-to-save-costs.htm, last accessed 22 August 2011.

Tikoo, S (1996) 'Assessing the franchise option', *Business Horizons*, May–June: 78–82.

Timmons, J (1994) *New Venture Creation*, Boston: Irwin.

Toh, R S, DeKay, C F and Yates, B (2005) 'Independent meeting planners: roles, compensation, and potential conflicts', *Cornell Hotel and Restaurant Administration Quarterly*, 46, 4: 431–43.

Trettl, R (2011) www.rolandtrettl.com/oben.htm, last accessed 22 October 2011.

Tsiotsou, R and Ratten, V (2010) 'Future research directions in tourism marketing', *Marketing Intelligence and Planning*, 28, 4: 533–44.

Tzschentke, N A, Kirk, D and Lynch, P A (2008) 'Going green: decisional factors in small hospitality operations', *International Journal of Hospitality Management*, 27, 1: 126–33.

UK Statistics Authority – Office for National Statistics [Online], News Release: Input-Output Analyses, August 2006, www.statistics.gov.uk/pdfdir/ioa0806.pdf, last accessed 30 January 2011.

UNWCED (United Nations' World Commission on Environment and Development) (1987) *Our Common Future*, New York: United Nations.

UNESCO (2010) The gastronomic meal of the French (Decision 5.COM 6.14), www.unesco.org/culture/ich/en/RL/00437, last accessed 24 August 2011.

Unvala, C and Donaldson, J (1988) 'The service sector: some unresolved issues', *The Service Industries Journal*, 8, 4: 459–46.

Vallen, G K and Vallen, J J (2009) *Check-In Check-Out: Managing Hotel Operations*, Upper Saddle River: Pearson Prentice Hall.

van der Wagen, L and Carlos, B R (2005) *Event Management for Tourism, Cultural, Business, and Sporting Events*, Upper Saddle River: Prentice Hall.

Verginis, C (1999) 'Front office management', in Verginis, C S and Wood, R C (eds) *Accommodation Management: Perspectives for the International Hotel Industry*, London: Thomson. pp. 97–113.

Verginis, C (1999) 'Front office management', in Verginis, C S and Wood, R C (eds) *Accommodation Management: Perspectives for the International Hotel Industry*, London: Thomson. pp. 97–113.

Verginis, C S and Wood, R C (eds) (1999) *Accommodation Management: Perspectives for the International Hotel Industry*, London: Thomson.

von Krogh, G, Ichijo, K and Nonaka, I (2000) *Enabling Knowledge Creation: How to Unlock the Mystery of Tacit Knowledge and Release the Power of Innovation*, New York: Oxford University Press.

Walker, B (2012) 'The Institute's new President', *Hospitality*, Issue 25, Spring.

Walker, J R (2010) *Introduction to Hospitality Management*, Upper Saddle River: Pearson Prentice Hall.

Waller, K (1996) *Improving Food and Beverage Performance*, Oxford: Butterworth–Heinemann.

Walley, N and Whitehead, B (1994) 'It's not easy being green', *Harvard Business Review*, 72, 3: 46–52.

Wang, Y and Qualls, W (2007) 'Towards a theoretical model of technology adoption in hospitality organizations', *International Journal of Hospitality Management*, 26, 3: 560–73.

Warde, A and Martens, L (1999) 'Eating out: reflections on the experience of consumers in England', in Germov, J and Williams, L (eds) *A Sociology of Food and Nutrition: The Social Appetite*, Oxford: Oxford University Press. pp. 116–34.

Weatherford, L R and Kimes, S E (2003) 'A comparison of forecasting methods for hotel revenue management', *International Journal of Forecasting*, 19, 3: 401–15.

Welsch, H (1998) 'America: North', in Morrison, A (ed.) *Entrepreneurship: An International Perspective*, Oxford: Butterworth–Heinemann. pp. 115–36.

West, A and Purvis, E (1992) 'Hotel design: the need to develop a strategic approach', *International Journal of Contemporary Hospitality Management*, 4, 1: 15–22.

Weston, S (2010) 'Sparkling sales soar at Highland Spring', www.foodbev.com/news/sparkling-sales-soar-at-highland-spring, last accessed 15 January 2011.

Whitla, P, Walters, P and Davies, H (2007) 'Global strategies in the international hotel industry', *International Journal of Hospitality Management*, 26, 4: 777–92.

Wickham, P A (2004) *Strategic Entrepreneurship*, 3rd edn, Harlow: Pearson.

Williams, A (2006) 'Tourism and hospitality marketing: fantasy, feeling and fun', *International Journal of Contemporary Hospitality Management*, 18, 6: 492–5.

Witt, S F, Gammon, S and White, J (1992) 'Incentive travel: overview and case study of Canada as a destination for the UK market', *Tourism Management*, 13, 3: 275–87.

Wood, R C (1991) 'The shock of the new: a sociology of nouvelle cuisine', *Journal of Consumer Studies and Home Economics*, 15, 4: 327–38.

Wood, R C (1997) *Working in Hotels and Catering*, 2nd edn, London: Thomson.

Wood, R C (2000a) 'How important is the meal experience? Choices, menus and dining environments', in Wood, R C (ed.) *Strategic Questions in Food and Beverage Management*, Oxford: Butterworth–Heinemann. pp. 28–47.

Wood, R C (2000b) 'Is food an art form? Pretentiousness and pomposity in cookery', in Wood, R C (ed.) *Strategic Questions in Food and Beverage Management*, Oxford: Butterworth–Heinemann. pp. 153–71.

Wood, R C (2004) 'Closing a planning gap? The future of food production and service systems theory', *Tourism and Hospitality Planning and Development*, 1, 1: 19–37.

Wood, R C (2008) 'Food production and service systems', in Brotherton, B and Wood, R C (eds) *The Sage Handbook of Hospitality Management*, London: Sage. pp. 443–59.

Wood, R C (2010) 'Let's make hotels get "five star" right', *The Hospitality Review*, 12, 4: 35–7.

Woods, R and Viehland, D (2000) 'Women in hotel management', *Cornell Hotel and Restaurant Administration Quarterly*, 41, 5: 51–4.

World Travel and Tourism Council (2011a) *Business Travel: A Catalyst for Economic Performance*, www.wttc.org/site_media/uploads/downloads/WTTC_Business_Travel_2011.pdf, last accessed 20 November 2011.

World Travel and Tourism Council (2011b) 'Hotel companies demonstrate leadership through new initiative', www.wttc.org/news-media/news-archive/2011/hotel-companies-demonstrate-leadership-through-new-initiative/, last accessed 20 November 2011.

consolidated bibliography

Wyckoff, D and Sasser, E (1978) *The Chain Restaurant Industry*, Lexington: Lexington Books.

Xie, G (2000) 'Comparison of textural changes of dry peas in sous vide cook–chill and traditional cook–chill systems', *Journal of Food Engineering*, 43, 3: 141–6.

Yamanaka, K, Almanza, B, Nelson, D and De Vaney, S (2003) 'Older Americans' dining out preferences', *Journal of Foodservice Business Research*, 6, 1: 87–103.

Yu, L (1999) *The International Hospitality Business: Management and Operations*, New York: Haworth Press.

Yu, L (2008) 'The structure and nature of the international hospitality industry', in Brotherton, B and Wood, R C (eds) *The Sage Handbook of Hospitality Management*, London: Sage. pp. 62–89.

Zablah, A (2004) 'An evaluation of divergent perspectives on customer relationship management: towards a common understanding of an emerging phenomenon', *Industrial Marketing Management*, 33, 6: 475–89.